Steve Barrett

DEL QUENTIN WILBER is an award-winning reporter for
The Washington Post. He has spent most of his career covering law enforcement and sensitive security issues, and his
work has been a finalist for the Pulitzer Prize. He lives in
Washington, D.C., with his wife and two sons.

Additional Praise for *Rawhide Down*

"A meticulous reconstruction of the day President Ronald Reagan was shot in 1981 . . . Compelling." —*The Lincoln Journal Star*

"This intensely researched account yields an almost moment-by-moment account of the crisis." —New York *Daily News*

"Mr. Wilber, a *Washington Post* crime reporter who writes clear, crisp prose, fleshes out his gripping narrative with a number of well-told side stories, among them the Chinese fire drill at the White House as Al Haig and Caspar Weinberger butted heads. But in the end, the leading man owns his story, just as he will come to own his audience." —*The Washington Times*

"*Rawhide Down* is a stunning work. Del Quentin Wilber, with the world-class reporting skills he honed on the police beat and a fine sense of narrative, has taken a story we thought we knew and rendered it wholly fresh, vibrant, and revealing." —David Maraniss, winner of the Pulitzer Prize for national reporting

"Del Quentin Wilber has written a compelling and multilayered examination of the near assassination of President Ronald Reagan on March 30, 1981. As a biographer of Reagan who was at the Washington Hilton Hotel that fateful day, I was fascinated by Wilber's meticulous reconstruction. He properly credits the valor and judgment of the Secret Service agents who saved Reagan's life but also analyzes the security deficiencies that made the assassination attempt possible." —Lou Cannon, author of *President Reagan: The Role of a Lifetime*

"A riveting minute-by-minute account of the shooting . . . reveals that Reagan came closer to death than the public knew." —*New York Post*

"A fast-paced read that draws well-crafted characters and gives a vivid sense of the history that brought the story's heroes and Hinckley together that day." —*The Washingtonian*

"The ninety-six months of Ronald Reagan's presidency changed the nation and the world. Del Quentin Wilber's gripping account of the 'near assassination' of the fortieth president shows how close the country—and the world—came to missing more than ninety-three of those months." —George F. Will

"A page-turner from beginning to end . . . You will learn a lot about an event that came razor-close to changing America forever." —Bill O'Reilly, author of *Killing Lincoln: The Assassination That Changed America Forever*

RAWHIDE

★ DOWN ★

THE NEAR ASSASSINATION OF
RONALD REAGAN

DEL QUENTIN WILBER

Picador

Henry Holt and Company
New York

www.picadorusa.com
www.twitter.com/picadorusa • www.facebook.com/picadorusa

Picador® is a U.S. registered trademark and is used by Henry Holt and Company, LLC, under license from Pan Books Limited.

For book club information, please visit www.facebook.com/picadorbookclub or e-mail marketing@picadorusa.com.

Photograph on page 184 courtesy of U.S. Attorney's Office for the District of Columbia

Designed by Meryl Sussman Levavi

The Library of Congress has cataloged the Henry Holt edition as follows:

Wilber, Del Quentin.
    Rawhide down : the near assassination of Ronald Reagan / Del Quentin Wilber. — 1st ed.
        p. cm.
    Includes bibliographical references and index.
    ISBN 978-0-8050-9346-9
 1. Reagan, Ronald—Assassination attempt, 1981.   I. Title.
    E877.3.W55 2011
    973.927092—dc22   2010049808

Picador ISBN 978-1-250-00254-9

First published in the United States by Henry Holt and Company

First Picador Edition: April 2012

10 9 8 7 6 5 4 3 2 1

To Laura

CONTENTS

RAWHIDE
★ DOWN ★

PROLOGUE

A DAY BEFORE THE COURSE OF HIS PRESIDENCY WAS FOREVER changed, Ronald Reagan walked to church with his wife, Nancy. Sunday, March 29, 1981, was bright and warm, and as the Reagans strolled through the White House gates and across Pennsylvania Avenue, the president held the first lady's hand. Trailed by Secret Service agents and a few journalists, the couple waved at onlookers and smiled for camera-toting tourists. As they walked through Lafayette Square, a woman pushed her young child through the security perimeter. Grinning, the president bent over to say hello.

Lately Reagan had not been able to attend church as often as he would have liked. During the previous year's campaign it had been hard enough; since the inauguration, it had been almost impossible. For obvious reasons, security requirements for any trip outside the White House were cumbersome. He also didn't want to impose on parishioners, who had to be screened by Secret Service agents and were often distracted by the presence of the president and his wife.

But that spring morning, the Reagans had chosen to attend the eleven o'clock service at St. John's Church, a place of worship as intimately connected to American history as any in the nation. The Episcopal church, just off the north side of Lafayette Square, was designed by the same architect who rebuilt the White House and the Capitol after they were damaged in the War of 1812. Its half-ton steeple bell had been cast by Paul Revere's son; a piece of stained glass donated by President Chester A. Arthur in memory of his wife hung in its south transept. Nicknamed the Church of the Presidents, St. John's now welcomed the nation's fortieth president, a man who revered both God and country.

The rector, the Reverend John C. Harper, had preached to every president since Lyndon B. Johnson. On this Sunday, the Reverend Harper delivered a sermon about faith and about finding God's handiwork in ordinary things. He told a story about a sculptor who hammered and chiseled a large block of marble into a statue of Christ. When the sculptor was done, a young boy who had watched him at work asked, "Sir, tell me, how did you know there was a man in the marble?"

Harper then made the message of his parable plain. "People have often asked that question of Christians who have seen God in Jesus Christ, in a stone statue, in a stained-glass window, in some human life," he said. "'How did you know He was there?'"

The answer, Harper said, was faith.

Before and after Harper's sermon, the Naval Academy choir sang several hymns, which the president found inspiring. Later, writing in his diary, Reagan commented that the midshipmen "looked & sounded so right that you have to feel good about our country."

Just before noon, the Reagans returned to the White House, this time traveling in an armored limousine. They ate lunch, spent a bit of time rearranging the furniture in the Oval Office, and then retired to the residence.

Only two months into his tenure, Reagan—like every president—had an ambitious political and legislative agenda. But the next day, according to his schedule, would not be especially arduous. The only event of note was a trip to a downtown hotel for a twenty-minute speech to a trade union.

※　※　※

THE BROAD OUTLINES of what happened the following day are well known. The president had just finished giving his speech when he was shot by a deranged gunman. He was rushed to a hospital and underwent surgery; by that evening, it was almost certain that he would live. In the hours and days after the shooting, Reagan's aides worked assiduously to assure the country that the president's life was never in real danger and that he would soon recover. Indeed, Reagan returned to the White House just twelve days after the assassination attempt and gave a stirring speech to Congress less than a month after leaving the hospital.

But much of what happened on March 30, 1981, was not revealed; most especially, the White House kept secret the fact that the president came very close to dying. Over the years, a number of details about that terrifying day have emerged, but only now—after many new interviews with participants and an extensive review of unreleased reports, closely held tape recordings, and private diaries—can the full story be told.

What is also clearer in retrospect is how crucial this moment was to Reagan's ultimate success. Before that day in 1981, the country had suffered through two difficult decades. No president since Eisenhower had served two full terms: Kennedy was slain; Johnson declined to seek a second full term after the debacle in Vietnam; Nixon was forced to resign in the wake of Watergate; Carter served just four years after becoming identified with the country's malaise. During the 1980 election, the nation was haunted by the Iranian hostage crisis, which spoke to deep-seated fears that the United States might be ungovernable or perhaps in irrecoverable decline. Partly out of frustration with politics as usual, voters turned to a former movie star who seemed to promise a fresh approach, even if he was sixty-nine years old when he took the oath of office.

Reagan had not gotten off to a strong start. In the two months following his inauguration, he was relentlessly criticized by Democrats for not caring about the poor, for proposing steep cuts in federal programs, and for sending military advisors to El Salvador, which, some felt, might become another Vietnam. By mid-March, he had the lowest approval rating of any modern president at a similar point in his term: during what should have been his postinauguration honeymoon, only 59 percent of Americans thought he was doing a good job. His commanding victory the previous November seemed all but forgotten, and White House officials and pollsters were preparing for more difficult days ahead.

All that changed on March 30. The news of the shooting stunned the country: teachers wheeled televisions into classrooms, praying citizens filled churches and synagogues, lawmakers darted into back rooms for updates on the president's condition. Only eighteen years after the assassination of President Kennedy, the United States once again teetered on the brink of tragedy. Instead, the nation witnessed triumph. A team of Secret Service agents saved Reagan's life at the scene of the shooting; in the hours that followed, a team of surgeons and nurses saved the president's life a second time.

The real hero of the day, though, was Reagan himself. In the most unscripted moment of his eight highly choreographed years in office, he gave the American people an indelible image of his character. In severe pain, he insisted on walking into the hospital under his own power. Throughout the medical ordeal that followed, he never lost his courage or his humor. The attempt on his life occurred just seventy days into his term, but more than any other incident during his years in the White House, it revealed Reagan's superb temperament, his extraordinary ability to project the qualities of a true leader, and his remarkable grace under pressure.

As THE PRESIDENTIAL limousine raced to the hospital on that terrible Monday in March, the Secret Service agents attending Reagan remained calm and methodical. Even in all the chaos, they never broke protocol by using the president's name when speaking over their radios. Instead, they referred to him by his code name, Rawhide. They used other code names as well: the limousine was Stagecoach; the command post at the White House was Horsepower; Nancy Reagan was Rainbow. At a time when radio traffic wasn't scrambled and anyone with a police scanner could eavesdrop on the movements of the president, the codes were an essential precaution.

Every modern president has been given a code name by the Secret Service. Some code names have been apt; some have not. John F. Kennedy was Lancer, which would later evoke Camelot, the legend often associated with Kennedy. Reagan's predecessor, Jimmy Carter, was Deacon, an appropriate code name for a former Sunday school teacher and devout Christian. But neither Timberwolf (George H. W. Bush) nor Eagle (Bill Clinton) had any particular resonance.

Reagan's code name fit him well. It was first given to him in 1976, when the former California governor was assigned Secret Service protection during his unsuccessful attempt to win the Republican nomination. Because the military—which manages communications for the White House—is responsible for drawing up a list of potential code names, a U.S. Army master sergeant was charged with the task of reviewing an inventory of available military call signs that could be used for Reagan. He thought Rawhide was suitable because the former actor had appeared in several westerns and was known to be a rancher. The sergeant chose a few other potential names and passed the list to the Secret Service, which made the final selection.

By all accounts, Reagan adored the moniker. For one thing, he saw himself as an outdoorsman; he spent much of his free time riding horses, cutting brush, and chopping wood on his picturesque California ranch. For another, he loved westerns. To his regret, he had rarely been given an opportunity to carry a six-shooter in a motion picture; years later, describing his conversations with the powerful head of the Warner Bros. studio, Reagan wrote, "I did wish Jack Warner would think of me on the back of a horse wearing a cowboy hat. . . . But when I'd ask Jack to put me in a western, he'd cast me in another movie in which I'd wear a gray-flannel suit."

Over time, Reagan's code name seemed to become ever more appropriate. As conjured by Hollywood—and there can be no discussion of Reagan's presidency without reference to the movies—the ideal cowboy is a tough but good-hearted loner who fights only when he has to and always for the right reasons. More than two decades after his time in office, Reagan fits that description remarkably well. Exuding rugged individualism, he helped spark the modern conservative movement with his passionate belief that the role of government in American life should be diminished. In the eyes of many, he was the nation's resolute warrior, a leader who waged a sometimes lonely battle against the Soviet Union because he knew his cause was right. But he was never overly impressed with himself; he was kind to ordinary citizens and surprisingly modest about his accomplishments. At the same time, he could seem strikingly distant, even from friends and family. He loved being president, but as the years went on he yearned more and more for his beloved ranch, where he could ride horses and spend time with his wife.

During his eight years in office, Reagan viewed the presidency as a great role to play, and from the start that role was well scripted. His advisors gave him a briefing book every night that mapped out the next day's schedule and outlined what he was expected to say. They carefully crafted speeches and orchestrated photo opportunities calibrated to convey an image of Reagan—the oldest man ever to hold the office of president—as a strong and vibrant leader. They released countless pictures of him on his ranch and even arranged to have him ride a horse during a visit with Queen Elizabeth, thus producing a convincing image of an American icon.

But Reagan never played his role with greater authority than on the day of his near assassination. For that singular moment, Americans perceived a president's character as something separate from his politics. In the months and years that followed, Reagan's courage and grace on that day helped shield him from the effects of mishaps and scandals that would have crippled other administrations. After March 30, he was no longer simply a staunch conservative who advocated an aggressive and controversial agenda. He was Rawhide—the good kind of cowboy and the brave face of America.

When campaigning and after becoming president, Reagan often quoted Thomas Paine, the Englishman who inspired the citizens of the thirteen colonies to fight for their freedom during the American Revolution. Paine once wrote, "I love the man that can smile in trouble, that can gather strength from distress, and grow brave by reflection." That man was the Ronald Reagan who survived an attempt on his life and so made possible his historic presidency.

CHAPTER 1

RENDEZVOUS WITH DESTINY

WHEN PRESIDENT RONALD REAGAN AWOKE AT SEVEN A.M. ON March 30, 1981, the world outside the White House was gray and dreary. Clouds stretched to the horizon, and a wispy mist filtered through the tips of magnolia trees framed by his second-floor window. The president slipped from his bed and strode across the plush beige carpet to the master bathroom, where he showered and shaved. After selecting his day's attire from the modest wardrobe in his walk-through closet, he donned a monogrammed white shirt and a classic blue tie. He dotted his shirt sleeves with a pair of golden bear cuff links, mementos from his days as governor of California. He slipped into a new dark blue pin-striped suit—made by his personal tailor in Beverly Hills and given to him by his wife—and added a black leather belt with a Gucci buckle, a white handkerchief folded symmetrically into his jacket's breast pocket, and his nicest watch on his left wrist. Extremely near-sighted, he wore contact lenses in his blue eyes. After massaging Brylcreem into his thick chestnut-brown hair, he parted it with a swoosh to the left.

Reagan's clothes draped without a wrinkle. Six foot one, lean and muscular, he kept fit by riding horses, cutting wood, and exercising regularly with a wheel that he rolled out and back from his body while kneeling on the floor. The president was proud of his physique and was known, from time to time, to pose for photographs in a way that jokingly showed off his biceps. His handsome face had deep creases that spread from his eyes when he smiled—which was often—and his cheeks were ruddy. Though only seventy days into his presidency, the former movie star appeared distinguished, confident, and entirely comfortable in his new role as the most powerful man in the world.

But his confidence wasn't simply a pose: Ronald Reagan, unlike so many politicians, was remarkably at ease with himself. Long before his arrival in Washington, he had achieved far more than anyone could ever have expected. Born in 1911 and raised in Dixon, Illinois, he grew up the son of an alcoholic shoe salesman. After high school, he attended nearby Eureka College on a scholarship, whereas most of his friends went to work in factories and on farms. As a boy, he had fallen in love with the movies and acted in high school and college plays; by the time he graduated from Eureka with a degree in economics in 1932 he yearned to make a name for himself on the silver screen.

But getting to Hollywood wasn't easy, especially during the Great Depression. He started in radio, convincing a station manager in Davenport, Iowa, to let him announce college football games; soon he was a radio personality in Des Moines. By the spring of 1937, he had managed to work his way to Hollywood, where he landed a seven-year contract. Over the next three decades, Reagan would appear in fifty-three movies, which ran the gamut from romances to dramas. His career, like that of many others, was interrupted by World War II. Because he was not allowed to serve in combat—his eyesight was too poor—the army assigned him to make training films. At war's end, he declined a promotion to major, telling friends that he thought being a captain sounded more dashing.

Originally a Democrat and an ardent admirer of Franklin Delano Roosevelt, Reagan evolved into a staunch Republican. He launched his political career in 1964 by delivering a stirring nationally televised address in support of the ultra-conservative Republican presidential candidate, Barry Goldwater. Two years later, despite widespread skepticism that an actor could win public office, he was elected governor of California. In 1976, he challenged President Gerald Ford for the Republican nomination; when he lost, he was written off as too old to try again. Still ambitious, he refused to ride off into the sunset. In 1980, the year he turned sixty-nine, he won his party's nomination and defeated the Democratic incumbent, Jimmy Carter, in a landslide.

Reagan was arguably the best politician of his era, a performer who wielded his acting skills and charisma to sell his program of lower taxes, less government, and a strengthened military. He deflected concerns about his age and memory with one-liners and jokes. He held his own in debates. But he was much more than an actor turned politician: after serving for eight years as governor of the nation's most populous state and writing by hand hundreds of radio commentaries that dealt extensively with domestic and foreign policy, Reagan had a fully formed political consciousness. He also understood the simple but profound truth that he could achieve much more if he allowed others to underestimate him. Supremely self-confident, he was not bothered by criticism that he was lazy or that he followed a script crafted by political advisors. A plaque on his desk read, "There is no limit to what a man can do or where he can go if he doesn't mind who gets the credit." And he meant it.

THE PETITE FIFTY-NINE-YEAR-OLD woman who joined the president for breakfast that Monday morning in March deserved a great deal of credit for his success. A former movie actress, Nancy Reagan understood the importance of public perception, and for almost thirty years she had worked hard to shape and protect her husband's image. Tough and demanding, she had played a key role during his run for the presidency, and she was not afraid to upbraid staffers who overworked her husband or gave him poor advice. Where Reagan was trusting, his wife was skeptical, and she often counseled him on sensitive political matters. Together, they made a formidable political team, but their marriage went well beyond politics. In the eyes of those who knew them well, they were living an almost fantastical American love story.

Earlier that month, on March 4, the couple had celebrated their twenty-ninth wedding anniversary with a night on the town. As they emerged from a restaurant, Mrs. Reagan was asked by reporters what she thought of her marriage. "It seems like twenty-nine minutes," she replied. They had been too busy to exchange gifts, but Reagan had taken the time to write his wife a love letter. "As Pres. of the U.S., it is my honor & privilege to cite you for service above & beyond the call of duty in that you have made one man (me) the most happy man in *the world* for 29 years. . . . He still can't find the words to tell her how lost he would be without her."

A much more elaborate celebration had occurred less than three weeks after the inauguration, when Mrs. Reagan orchestrated a surprise party for her husband's seventieth birthday. It is difficult to keep a secret in Washington, especially when trying to sneak more than one hundred guests into the White House. Nancy Reagan accomplished the feat by telling her husband that they were going to enjoy an intimate birthday dinner with friends in the residence, and then secretly inviting scores of his closest friends and associates. The impending party immediately began generating news stories, so Mrs. Reagan had to intercept the papers before they reached her news-hungry husband. One morning, Tom Brokaw of NBC's *Today* show mentioned how large the president's birthday party was expected to be; Mrs. Reagan turned to Mr. Reagan and said, "My, that Tom Brokaw certainly exaggerates."

At eight p.m. on February 6, Reagan, wearing a tuxedo, walked into the East Room and was shocked to hear guests shouting "Surprise!" and singing "Happy birthday, dear Ronald!" The spacious, high-ceilinged room, more often used for formal state affairs, was decked out like a flower-filled fairyland, bursting with hyacinths, daffodils, tulips, lilies, and ficus trees. At the center of each table was a cake, and each cake was topped by a leaping horse. Dozens of friends, family members, wealthy backers, and lawmakers attended the party. The former Hollywood stars Jimmy Stewart, Irene Dunne, and George Murphy flew in to celebrate the "thirty-first anniversary of my thirty-ninth birthday," as Reagan jokingly referred to it.

For the occasion, Nancy Reagan wore a sleek white beaded dress, one of her husband's favorites. The couple danced to romantic music played by the Army Strolling Strings, which honored the first lady with the tune "Nancy with the Laughing Face." When Mrs. Reagan took a turn around the dance floor with Frank Sinatra, the president made a show of cutting in. The first couple reveled late into the evening and did not retire until after midnight.

Now, a little more than seven weeks later, the Reagans finished their breakfast at about 8:30 a.m. The president gave his wife an affectionate kiss and headed for the elevator to make the short trip to his office. As always, the day ahead of him had been scheduled in detail. At 9:15 a.m., he was due to speak by phone with West Germany's chancellor about the growing crisis in Poland; he would then attend his daily national security briefing. Later that morning, he would meet with Hispanic supporters in the Cabinet Room. The day's biggest event was a speech to a trade union at a downtown hotel. Afterward, he would return to the White House, where he was to meet business executives. The script noted that in the afternoon he had ample "staff time"—a euphemism for relaxation, which sometimes meant a nap—and his official day was scheduled to end at 5:30 p.m. with a haircut. Then, after the Reagans hosted a dinner in the residence for the secretary of health and human services and his wife, the president would have a quiet hour or two before going to bed.

REAGAN'S FIRST TASK that morning was to shake hands and deliver a pep talk. At 8:34 a.m., he emerged from the elevator on the first floor and was met by his so-called body man, David Fischer, and one of his rotating military aides, army lieutenant colonel Jose Muratti. Fischer, a boyish-looking thirty-two-year-old with a thick mustache, carried the documents Reagan would require in the next few hours and attended to the president's needs as they arose, from fetching Reagan's suit jacket to taking notes about a promised favor. Muratti, wearing a crisp green uniform and polished black shoes, shadowed the president and held the "football," the satchel that contained the country's nuclear war plans. Reagan carried the other tool necessary for launching a nuclear attack—an authentication card—in his jacket pocket.

Reagan, Fischer, and Muratti walked down the hall to the Blue Room, a handsome oval room with white walls, blue window sashes, and a beautiful view of the South Lawn. Presidents typically received guests here, and Reagan quickly took his place at the head of a receiving line and began to say hello to a stream of political appointees, all of whom he would be addressing in a few minutes. He shook a hand and smiled; a White House photographer's camera clicked. He shook another hand, smiled, and a camera clicked again. Some politicians look stiff in such settings; others fake it, pouring on bogus charm. But Reagan always seemed to decant just the right mix of poise and charisma to make strangers feel, if only for a few seconds, as if they were his friends.

Reagan shook hands with more than sixty people in eleven minutes, and then everyone filed into the East Room. Gone were the flower arrangements and tables stacked with cakes that had greeted the president on his birthday; this morning, three rows of wooden chairs with white cushions had been placed in a semicircle around a small stage. Reagan took the podium to loud applause, which echoed off the room's bare white walls. The men and women present that day were all fervent supporters; a number of them had worked on the 1976 and 1980 campaigns. Now they were administration officials charged with carrying out the president's agenda.

"Sit down," Reagan began. "You're at work."

The group laughed.

"Well," Reagan said, "I just wanted to tell you that every day won't start this way while you are here. I've long taken seriously the lesson, you know what they say, 'If you get up earlier in the morning, get to work earlier than everyone else, you work harder than everyone else, you stay longer in the day, you'll leave a lot more money to your kids.'"

Everyone chuckled.

"And you leave it a lot sooner," the president said. "So judge yourself accordingly and pace yourself accordingly."

Reagan, as he so often did, was making fun of himself. He was an incorrigible comedian who started many meetings with a joke and could instantly eliminate tension in a room with a clever quip. In his desk in the White House residence, he kept a stack of index cards filled with one-liners and funny stories. His prodigious memory, fortified by memorizing scores of screenplays, allowed him to recall complicated jokes and yarns he had not heard or repeated in years. A master at exploiting his comedic skills for political advantage, he was adept at turning the humor on himself. Even his most fervent admirers admitted he was not the hardest worker in the world: whereas Presidents Johnson, Nixon, and Carter were known to work sixteen-hour days, Reagan made it clear that the Oval Office clock must be set to his internal nine-to-five schedule. And if he wanted to take an afternoon off to go horseback riding—he liked to tell aides, "There is nothing better for the inside of a man than the backside of a horse"—he didn't hesitate to do it. The previous Wednesday, in fact, he and several staff members had hopped on the presidential helicopter to go riding on the wooded trails around the U.S. Marine Corps base at Quantico.

By making fun of his own work ethic, even in settings such as this one, Reagan effectively defused a political weapon wielded by his opponents, who had often tried to remind voters of his relatively advanced age. The jokes also endeared him to his audiences, who admired his humility and knew that only a secure man could laugh at himself in this way.

"It may sound like a tired cliché, talking about a team," Reagan continued. "We are a team, and our goal is a strong prosperous nation at peace, and team play is the only way I know how to do it." This was no exaggeration: Reagan had been a passionate believer in teamwork ever since his days as a guard on his high school football team and later on the Eureka College squad.

"Right now," the president told his audience, "the country is in trouble, and you can be a major part in changing this situation." He exhorted the officials to work hard so that in their lifetimes no one could write a book called *The Rise and Fall of the United States of America.*

Continuing, the president said: "Maybe some of you were subjected to me a couple of times here and there during the campaign—I took pleasure in quoting some words of Thomas Paine, words that he said to his fellow Americans back when this nation was trying to be born. And he said, 'We have it in our power to begin the world over again.' So let our prayer be that we can live up to this opportunity that God has given us and we can build the world over again."

It was a minor speech to a relatively small circle of advisors, and it lasted just three minutes and fifteen seconds. Yet it revealed something important about Reagan and his beliefs. On the one hand, the president was acknowledging that the country confronted serious problems. In March 1981, after all, the nation's economy was anemic and the Soviet Union seemed ascendant. But Reagan, a perpetual optimist, did not believe he was witnessing the end of the American century, and his deep faith was fundamental to that conviction. As a boy, he had often heard his mother, a devout member of the Disciples of Christ, explain that God had a purpose for everyone. She instilled in her son the belief that even life's most disheartening setbacks and seemingly random twists of fate were all part of God's plan. In particular, Reagan had long believed that God had something special in store for the United States, that his fellow citizens were capable of prevailing because they were destined for greatness. As he had put it decades earlier, in a commencement address, "I, in my own mind, have thought of America as a place in the divine scheme of things that was set aside as the promised land. . . . I believe that God in shedding his grace on this country has always in the divine scheme of things kept an eye on our land and guided it as a promised land."

The previous year, in his speech accepting the Republican nomination for president, Reagan had made a similar point by quoting Franklin Roosevelt and speaking of America's "rendezvous with destiny." He had also once again invoked his faith: at the end of the rousing address, he asked the delegates if they could begin their "crusade joined together in a moment of silent prayer." The riotous hall went instantly still and remained so until Reagan brought on a huge wave of cheering when he closed with "God bless America!"

The president's audience this morning was more restrained but no less enthusiastic, and they responded to his brief remarks with energetic applause. At 8:50, shadowed by his body man and his military aide, Reagan left the East Room and walked to the Oval Office. As he strode along the West Colonnade, he was joined by two additional men. Their eyes were intently scanning the South Lawn, and even a casual observer would have concluded that they were not there to carry the president's papers or serve his needs. They were Secret Service agents, and their job was to look for trouble, even within the White House gates.

EARLIER THAT MORNING, Agent Jerry Parr of the Secret Service had waved to the uniformed officer at the guardhouse and driven his government sedan through the open northwest gate of the White House. He parked along a driveway near the West Wing and headed into his office in the Old Executive Office Building. As he entered Room 10 at about 7:00 a.m., Parr lifted up the sole of each of his black shoes so a deputy could inspect them for chicken manure. The unusual ritual dated from the day Parr had inadvertently tracked chicken droppings from his backyard throughout Secret Service headquarters—an embarrassing gaffe that could not be repeated in the White House, especially by the agent in charge of the presidential protective detail.

Parr had begun the morning, as he did most workdays, with a pre-dawn jog. He was a husky man and it wasn't a challenging run, but it got his blood and mind churning. Huffing from his two-story white colonial in a distant Maryland suburb, Parr spent about twenty minutes running a two-mile circuit through the tree-lined streets of his neighborhood. After a quick breakfast and a shower, he put on a white shirt and a plain blue-gray suit: his work uniform. Its purpose was to make him invisible on the street and in the corridors of power.

Parr's many years fixing power lines in the blazing Florida sun had left him grizzled; his skin was perpetually tanned and his forehead and cheeks were creased with deep lines. Dark bags rimmed his brown eyes, but those eyes were bright and constantly moving—scanning left and right, up and down, lingering on anything that seemed suspicious. Even at home or when at rest, he noticed things that were out of place: a half-open window; a rustling shade; a delivery man wearing the wrong kind of shoes; the one scowl in a sea of smiles. His eyes, after all, might one day save the president's life.

Parr pulled on a London Fog trench coat and said goodbye to his three daughters and his wife, Carolyn, an IRS lawyer. Then he walked across the soggy grass of his big yard and tossed handfuls of feed to the thirty chickens he kept in a coop. No matter that they sometimes dirtied his shoes, his chickens and his two-acre plot gave Parr's suburban home a rural feel and made it a refuge from the considerable stress of his job.

In his bland suit and equally nondescript coat, the fifty-year-old agent looked completely ordinary—in fact, he was anything but. An eclectic reader, he enjoyed the works of such philosophers and writers as Immanuel Kant, Thomas Merton, and Ernest Hemingway. On his commutes, alone in the car, he often pondered his favorite poem, Alan Seeger's "I Have a Rendezvous with Death," a melancholy work about a soldier in World War I whose life is destined to end on a blazing battlefield. It was this poem that inspired President Franklin Roosevelt's famous phrase "rendezvous with destiny," and President Kennedy so admired it that he often asked his wife, Jacqueline, to recite it for him. But the meaning of Seeger's famous poem was far darker than the campaign slogans it inspired, which is perhaps why it resonated so intensely with Parr, a man who relentlessly trained for a day he hoped would never come. He found the last two lines of the poem particularly powerful:

> And I to my pledged word am true,
> I shall not fail that rendezvous.

Born in 1930, Parr grew up poor in Miami, the son of a cash register repairman and a beautician. His parents divorced when he was nine; after her second marriage failed, Parr's mother married yet again, this time to a man who claimed to have slain his first wife and threatened to kill Parr's mother if she left him. For four years, Parr slept with a knife under his pillow so he could protect his mother if the hot-tempered man ever attacked, though he never did. After high school, he took a job with a local electric company and spent thirteen years working as a lineman, interrupted only by a stint in the air force. He married and then decided to attend college, ultimately earning a degree in English and philosophy; when he graduated, he interviewed with a wide range of companies and organizations, including the Secret Service.

The service had intrigued Parr for years. As a boy, he'd been enthralled by a 1939 movie called *The Code of the Secret Service*, which starred twenty-eight-year-old Ronald Reagan as the dashing Secret Service agent Lieutenant "Brass" Bancroft. Hollywood's version of an agent's workday was wonderfully fanciful: Bancroft is falsely accused of killing a fellow undercover agent in Mexico, survives a shooting, breaks out of a Mexican jail, and arrests the villain on the other side of the U.S. border. Though the movie was absurd—many, including its star, judged it to be Reagan's worst feature film—Parr never forgot Bancroft's daring exploits and for years dreamed of following in his footsteps. When the opportunity arose, he jumped at it.

Parr joined the service in 1962. He was the oldest rookie in his class; in his earliest days as an agent, while standing guard at a New York airport, he marveled at the swagger and poise of President Kennedy's Secret Service detail and decided that he wanted to be just like those agents. He even fantasized about being the lead agent in an inaugural parade and sitting in the front seat of the president's armored limousine. But from the start, he understood that he would never come close to achieving his dream without putting in years of hard work; he also knew that his educational and professional background made him something of a misfit in the straitlaced service. His first supervisor, in fact, had written in an evaluation that Parr was "not White House material."

Still, Parr was persistent and ambitious, and he loved the challenges he encountered each day. He rose through the ranks quickly, and was honored when he was chosen to serve on the vice presidential details of Hubert Humphrey and Spiro Agnew. He enjoyed devising ways to defeat potential terror threats while planning trips to war zones, former war zones, and the kinds of neighborhoods where everybody seemed to own a gun. Even visits to elementary schools were an ordeal, because nobody was above suspicion, not the principal or even the kindergarten teacher. Everyone and everything had to be checked, rechecked, and checked again. He often told friends that devising ways to protect the nation's leaders was like eating a chicken gizzard. "The more you chew it," he'd say, "the bigger it gets."

An agent's job is grueling, primarily because it requires an extraordinary ability to focus and a tremendous tolerance for boredom. Parr spent hours standing in the vacant stairwell of a hotel because the president was speaking in a nearby ballroom; he guarded a steaming cornfield because the president was scheduled to fly overhead. He suffered through stomach-shredding flights in thunderstorms on window-less cargo jets because an armored limousine had to reach Ohio or California or Alabama ahead of the president. And he routinely walked next to the president out in the open, in the so-called kill zone, where at every second he had to be prepared to throw himself in front of a bomb or bullet.

In 1979, Parr was tapped to become the lead agent of President Carter's detail. Though he no longer stood post in cornfields, he still spent plenty of time in the kill zone, and now it was his job to supervise the more than one hundred intense and highly trained men and women who shielded the world's number one target. He did everything possible to ensure that they remained vigilant; as a consequence, many had trouble leaving work at the White House gates. At home, they inspected shadows in their garages; in restaurants, they insisted on sitting in the booth that faced the door so they could immediately spot a gunman. Burnout was common. But Parr loved his job; though the work was taxing, he found it gratifying.

On January 20, 1981, Parr defied the odds and led the inaugural procession to and from the Capitol. In the morning, he rode in the front seat of the presidential limousine that carried President Carter, President-elect Reagan, and two lawmakers from the White House to the inauguration. During the ceremony, on a temporary stage on the west steps of the Capitol, Parr sat just a few rows behind Carter. After the ceremony ended, Parr watched the outgoing president walk somberly away. Then Parr turned his head and with it the focus of his attention to the new president. As Reagan left the stage, Parr fell in right behind him.

Every president presents different challenges, but in the two months since the inauguration Parr had had little trouble adjusting to the habits and routines of his new charge. Yet, as he poked around his office on this gray March morning, Parr realized that he and the president still didn't know each other well. Other senior agents had spent a lot of time with Reagan on the campaign trail or during the transition, but Parr had protected Carter in the months before and after the election. Since the inauguration, a number of agents had begun to form bonds with Reagan, who clearly enjoyed bantering with those protecting him. But Parr had been so busy with administrative duties that he hadn't spent much time shadowing the president.

Checking the day's schedule, Parr saw that Agent Johnny Guy, one of his deputies, was due to accompany Reagan to his speech at the Washington Hilton hotel that afternoon. Thinking that the trip might provide a good opportunity to get to know the president a little better, Parr went looking for Guy to tell him that he would take his place.

As MORNING LIGHT leaked into his drab hotel room, John W. Hinckley Jr. lay in bed, awake and anxious. The night before, he had gone to bed early, enormously tired after a grueling cross-country bus trip. But he hadn't slept much, perhaps an hour at most. He'd been depressed for weeks, maybe months; for a while, he'd seen a psychiatrist, but it hadn't helped. And now he couldn't shake the feeling that the fabric of his life was finally rending.

Hinckley had arrived in Washington the previous afternoon. He'd found the Park Central in a phone book where the hotel advertised its "Low Rates, AAA approved," and checked in as a "visiting student." At $47 for the night—Hinckley paid cash—Room 312 wasn't bad, with a television and decent furniture, but its brown carpet, brown-striped design on one wall, and cheap-looking floral-patterned brown comforter were hardly cheerful. Still, the place was a step up from most of the seedy motels he had called home in recent weeks.

Hinckley was not accustomed to such places. The twenty-five-year-old son of a wealthy oil executive, he had grown up in affluent suburbs near both Dallas and Denver. Unlike his older brother and sister, Hinckley had been an indifferent student. After graduating from high school in 1973, he sporadically attended college but never earned a degree. He enjoyed writing poems, stories, and songs; he also spent a lot of time playing the guitar but was too shy to perform in public or for his family. At twenty, he moved to Los Angeles with the intention of becoming a professional songwriter, but he failed at this, too. With little money or sense of direction, he had spent the past few months living mostly with his parents in Evergreen, Colorado, a wooded suburb just west of Denver.

But returning to Evergreen was no longer an option: a month ago, his parents had kicked him out of the house and refused to give him any more money. To finance his life on the road, Hinckley had stolen several gold coins from them and then sold most of his remaining possessions. His funds ran so low that he was even forced to pawn his guitar and his beloved typewriter for $50. He also sold most of his small gun collection—including a .38-caliber revolver, a Mauser rifle, and a .22-caliber handgun—to a man named Larry in a shopping mall parking lot.

Down to his last few hundred dollars, he decided to make a final attempt to reclaim his life by flying to Los Angeles and trying to sell some songs to music producers. He drove to Evergreen, parked his white Plymouth Volare in his parents' garage, and asked his mother to drive him to the airport for his Western Airlines flight.

As he stepped from the car, his mother handed him $100 in cash. "Well, Mom," Hinckley said, "I want to thank you for everything. I want to thank you for everything that you have done." It was the kind of thing people say when they don't believe they'll ever see a loved one again.

When he arrived in Los Angeles, his determination to make a new start faltered. He didn't even try to sell his music; instead, he wandered the streets of Hollywood, noticing little beyond the drunks, bag ladies, and prostitutes. That night, he had trouble sleeping, kept awake by noise from the next room and by the cacophony of Hollywood street life coming through his window.

The following morning, he pondered suicide, a subject never far from his mind. Once he had even tried to overdose on pills, but now he was imagining more creative and public ways to end his life. Recently he had become obsessed with a woman and had begun thinking about how to stage a dramatic death in front of her. He also imagined killing her and then killing himself. He couldn't decide which scenario he preferred, but either way he realized that it was pointless to stay in Los Angeles. The woman was a college student in New Haven, Connecticut; he didn't know whether she would be willing to see him, especially since she had brushed him off several times before. But it was worth the risk.

On Thursday, March 26, Hinckley packed his things; at eleven a.m., he walked to the Greyhound bus station. He decided to travel first to Washington, D.C.—he'd been there several times and was familiar with its downtown—and then catch another bus to New Haven. His ticket cost $117.80.

The four-day trip was a blur of fast food and brief stops: Las Vegas, Cheyenne, Chicago, Cleveland, Pittsburgh. Traveling through Utah, he awoke from a brief nap to find the bus hurtling through a massive snowstorm. He spent much of the trip slouched in a window seat, watching the scenery stream by or reading *The Catcher in the Rye*, J. D. Salinger's novel of teenage angst and alienation. He identified with the story's main character, Holden Caulfield, but the book was also special to him because he knew that John Lennon's assassin had pulled it from his pocket and leafed through it moments after gunning down the rock-and-roll icon. Lennon, who had been killed three and a half months earlier, was Hinckley's favorite musician; even so, he sometimes felt that he identified more with Lennon's killer than with Lennon himself.

A minister who boarded in Salt Lake City sat next to Hinckley for a day and a night as the bus traveled east. Hinckley told his seatmate that he was on vacation; lying again, he claimed that he was a college graduate and that he ran a record store in Los Angeles. When the minister asked him whether he was a Christian, Hinckley offered no reply. As the miles flowed by, Hinckley revealed few details about his life. He didn't even tell the minister his last name.

Hinckley slept poorly during the trip; by the time he arrived in Washington on Sunday, March 29, he was exhausted and hungry. He found a hotel, got some food, and spent another restless night.

Now it was Monday morning and he barely had enough energy to get out of bed. He had a little over $129 left, and he had managed to jam the jumbled detritus of his life into two suitcases. A plaid one, stacked neatly on his hotel room's foldout stand, was stuffed with an army field jacket, a black sports coat, a Best Western road atlas, two pairs of underwear, and some shirts, pants, and jeans. The suitcase also held some of his poems and short stories, as well as several of his favorite books. In addition to *The Catcher in the Rye*, Hinckley had brought along a copy of Shakespeare's *Romeo and Juliet* and a book called *Strawberry Fields Forever: John Lennon Remembered*.

Hinckley's distress was evident in some of the items he'd carried with him to Washington. Another of the books in the plaid suitcase was *Ted Bundy: The Killer Next Door*. The suitcase also held a box of ammunition containing six Devastator bullets, each nestled in a foam slot. In his smaller, tan suitcase, he had stashed a gun—an R.G. Industries model RG 14, a .22-caliber double-action revolver that had cost him about $45—and thirty-seven rounds of ammunition. The bags also held a number of tape recordings, magazine clippings, and photographs, artifacts of his obsession with the woman in New Haven.

Just after nine a.m., Hinckley dressed and left the hotel. He wandered through a bookstore and then strolled along bustling K Street. He stopped into a McDonald's and ate an Egg McMuffin. His thoughts kept returning to a simple, mesmerizing plan: he would take a bus to New Haven and end his life. Everything he had ever experienced was colliding at this singular moment in time. His money was gone. His parents would not have him back. He'd been traveling for weeks, and now he felt sure he was on his final trip.

On his walk back to the hotel, he bought a copy of *The Washington Star*, the city's afternoon newspaper. In his room, he flipped through its pages, and his eyes were drawn to page A4: "The President's Schedule." He read the schedule without excitement, put down the paper, and headed to the shower.

CHAPTER 2

THE MAN

WHEN PRESIDENT REAGAN REACHED THE OVAL OFFICE JUST after 8:50 a.m., he did not remove his suit jacket. He revered the presidency too much to display shirtsleeves in the room that had long been the epicenter of the presidential universe. It had been more than two months since Reagan's inauguration, but the space looked much as Jimmy Carter had left it on January 20. There was the same large brown oval carpet decorated with blue flowers, the same two striped couches, the same two large armchairs. Two smaller wooden chairs bracketed Reagan's desk; a polished globe stood near the window. The room's domed ceiling glowed from lights hidden behind intricate molding, and a portrait of George Washington hung above the fireplace, directly across from the president's desk.

The desk—which Carter had also used—was known as the *Resolute* desk because it had been constructed from the timbers of a British warship, H.M.S. *Resolute*, and given to the United States as a gift in 1880. Reagan, an Anglophile, loved its rugged look and rich history. It had been used by a number of presidents; Reagan enjoyed telling visitors that it was the very desk pictured in the famous photo of President

Kennedy's son John playing at his father's feet. But there was just one problem: the *Resolute* desk did not fit Reagan. The arms of his large rolling chair bumped into the desktop, making it impossible for him to slide his legs under the writing surface. When he signed a bill or an executive order, Reagan had to shift his legs awkwardly to the side. The president did not want to have the legs of his favorite chair shortened, and he wouldn't have dreamed of asking carpenters to alter the desk. Instead, he resigned himself to a bit of discomfort; the pleasure of working at the *Resolute* was worth it.

If the office did not yet have any Reagan flourishes, the president and first lady had managed to add a few personal touches. Reagan had placed several family photos on a credenza; a glass container of jelly beans, his favorite candy, stood on a coffee table next to one of the armchairs. The day before, he and Mrs. Reagan had moved some of the furniture around and put a set of miniature bronzed saddles on a display stand near a bookshelf.

As Reagan settled down to work, his three top advisors were summoned for the morning staff meeting. They were Chief of Staff James A. Baker III, Counselor Edwin Meese III, and Deputy Chief of Staff Michael K. Deaver. In most administrations, presidential power flows vertically from the president through a chief of staff. But unlike Carter and other presidents before him, Reagan delegated much of his authority, relying on his aides to shape policy and negotiate deals before coming to him for a decision or his final approval. He had left it to these advisors to organize his staff, which led to an unusual arrangement that divided control—sometimes unevenly—among the trio of ambitious aides.

Mike Deaver was closest to the president, but he was the antithesis of the hardy cowboy image cultivated by the Reagan White House. A former barroom piano player who grew up near the Mojave Desert, Deaver had a large, nearly bald dome of a head and a soft body, and bowed legs contributed to his shuffling gait. During Reagan's years as governor of California, Deaver had been his chief scheduler, a job that had brought him into close contact with Nancy Reagan. He and the Reagans had become very friendly, and Deaver stuck with Reagan after he left Sacramento, helping to manage the former governor's speaking engagements. He knew Reagan so well that others called him "the keeper of the body"; once, during the 1976 presidential campaign, he had even saved Reagan's life by dislodging a peanut from the candidate's throat during an airplane flight. Deaver, now forty-two, occupied the office closest to the president's, just beyond a subtly disguised door in one wall of the Oval Office. A public relations man and an acknowledged master of the media, Deaver was already carefully managing public perception of the president by choreographing outings and events that projected the image of a vibrant and engaged leader.

Ed Meese, forty-nine, was another member of Reagan's California inner circle who had followed the president to Washington. An amiable and cautious former prosecutor, Meese had recently retired as a lieutenant colonel in the Army Reserve. But he did not look like a soldier; instead, with his jowly face and plain gray suits, he resembled a high school math teacher. The tip of his tie usually rode an inch below his belt, and the brown case of his reading glasses almost always jutted from his shirt pocket. Like Deaver, Meese was close to Reagan, but their relationship was more professional than personal. A fourth-generation Californian, he had served as chief of staff while Reagan was governor and was skilled at synthesizing complex ideas. Early on, he'd been considered a front-runner for the post of presidential chief of staff, but his weak organizational skills sank his candidacy. Insiders called his briefcase the Meesecase, or, more explicitly, the Black Hole.

During the transition, a number of people urged Reagan to look further afield for a chief of staff, and ultimately the president-elect had surprised many by naming Jim Baker to the post. A smooth and shrewd political operator from Texas, Baker had waged two fierce political campaigns against Reagan in the previous five years. In 1976, he had played a key role in President Gerald Ford's narrow victory over Reagan for the Republican nomination; in 1980, he had managed the primary campaign of his close friend George H. W. Bush. Baker was detail-oriented and disciplined, and though he chewed Red Man tobacco and cussed like a Texas cattle rancher, he expertly played the role of quintessential Washington insider. Still youthful-looking at fifty, he spoke in a silky southern drawl and always wore nicely tailored suits and bold ties. To many, it was a sign of Reagan's supreme confidence that he would hire a man who'd been a political rival and award him such a key position. The choice proved wise, too: Baker went on to become one of the most effective presidential chiefs of staff in modern history.

Just weeks after the election, Baker and Meese hammered out a power-sharing arrangement, which the careful lawyers then put on paper. Baker controlled paper flow and personnel; Meese was responsible for domestic and national security policy. Each had the authority to walk into the Oval Office at almost any time; each also had the right to attend any meeting between the president and other government officials. Both men relied on Deaver to read and understand the president's moods, and they nearly always ran scheduling decisions by him. Thus far, the three men—each with competing interests, skills, and agendas—had been working well together. Their efforts had already earned the aides an apt nickname that described their symbiotic relationship: the Troika.

Nearly every morning, Baker hosted a daily breakfast with Meese and Deaver so they could review the day's schedule, policy issues, and political challenges. At about 7:30 on March 30, the three men had gathered in Baker's spacious office, just down the hall from Reagan's. Among other matters, they discussed a recent trip to China by former president Ford, who had carried a secret note from Reagan to that country's leaders. They also discussed how to lift the controversial grain embargo that President Carter had imposed on the Soviet Union. Though taking a tougher line on the Russians, Reagan had announced during the campaign that he wanted to lift the trade restrictions because he believed they hurt U.S. farmers more than they did the Soviets. But the geopolitical situation was making the pledge difficult to fulfill: in recent weeks, the Soviet Union had been applying intense pressure to one of its western neighbors, Poland, where the Solidarity labor movement was beginning to crack the country's communist regime, and now American irritation with the Soviet Union was once again on the rise. It was just the sort of dilemma that faces every new administration as it tries to reconcile the realities of governing with promises made during a campaign.

The Troika entered the Oval Office at precisely nine that morning. During this daily summit, Reagan and his advisors conferred about both the day ahead and any pressing issues that had been raised earlier at the Troika breakfast and at a subsequent larger staff meeting. The aides tried to keep these get-togethers brief, not least because Reagan detested long meetings and often started doodling when he became bored. Today they kept it short for another reason. In fifteen minutes, Reagan had an important call to make about the increasingly tense situation in Poland.

JERRY PARR FOUND his colleague Johnny Guy in his small office next to W-16, the agency's command post in the White House basement, directly under the Oval Office. A balding and burly agent who looked like a football lineman, Guy was one of Parr's top assistants, and the two men were quite friendly. Guy was due to travel with Reagan to the Washington Hilton that afternoon.

"I'd like to work the president today," Parr told Guy. "I feel like I need to get to know him better."

"Not a problem," said Guy. He understood the point of Parr's request; although agents were discouraged from becoming friends with their so-called protectees, they needed to understand a person's quirks and habits in order to protect him or her effectively. Conversely, it was important that the president—whom agents referred to casually as "the Man"—trust the members of his Secret Service detail and even take their orders when necessary. The only way to build that bond was to spend time with the man himself.

Guy had been granted such an opportunity when he and platoons of agents were sent to California to guard the president-elect after his victory in November. For more than a month, Guy had watched Reagan up close—lounging about his house in a robe, on official trips to the airport and at press briefings, and during private dinner parties. The agent even got a surprise preview of the president-elect's inaugural address.

One afternoon, Reagan asked Guy if they could ditch the press and visit his tailor in Beverly Hills. Reagan was restless and did not like the idea of being stalked by a horde of reporters while being measured for a new suit. Guy didn't think an "off-the-record" movement would be a problem, so he put a hat on Reagan and seated the president-elect next to him in the back of an unmarked and unarmored Secret Service sedan. Before they drove off, they stopped briefly at an encampment of reporters staking out Reagan's house for news stories.

Rolling down the window, Guy asked, "Can we get you guys some sodas or something?"

No thanks, the reporters replied.

As the car pulled away, Reagan laughed and clapped his hands. "That was just great," he said. Then, still chuckling, he reached inside his jacket pocket and extracted a sheaf of papers. "This is my inaugural address," he told the three agents riding with him. "I'd like you guys to listen to it and tell me what you think about it."

Oh no, thought Guy. This was anything but good. Guy was hardly an expert on politics, let alone historic speeches, and he knew it would be hard to give the president his full attention while trying to keep an eye on both the surrounding traffic and the follow-up car that was tailing them.

"Oh," Reagan added quickly, digging into a pocket and pulling out a stopwatch and handing it to Guy. "Do you mind timing me?"

"Sure, sir, no problem," Guy said.

The president-elect then read a draft of his first inaugural address to Guy and the other two agents while the unmarked car traveled, as inconspicuously as possible, through ten miles of heavy Los Angeles traffic. Continuously scanning the freeway outside his window and checking to ensure that they didn't lose the follow-up car, Guy had a hard time paying attention to what Reagan was saying. On an off-the-record trip like this one, his goal was to avoid any kind of incident that would draw unwanted attention to their passenger. The last thing they needed was an unscripted event or, God forbid, a car accident, especially on one of Los Angeles' notoriously congested freeways.

"So, how was it?" Reagan asked when he finished.

THE MAN ★ 31

"Excellent," Guy said. "Just excellent."

Guy's outing with Reagan that afternoon was exactly the sort of informal encounter that every security detail leader hopes to have with a protectee. He'd learned that Reagan liked to have fun; he also appreciated the fact that Reagan didn't treat him or the other agents like hired help. To his surprise, Reagan seemed like an ordinary guy.

Now it was Parr's turn to get to know the president better, and maybe the Hilton trip would provide the right opportunity. "Good luck," Guy told his boss.

RICHARD V. ALLEN arrived at the Oval Office a few minutes ahead of President Reagan's 9:15 a.m. call with Chancellor Helmut Schmidt of West Germany, during which the two leaders would discuss the brewing crisis in Poland. Allen, a gray-haired and irascible forty-five-year-old with an oval face obscured by large round glasses, was Reagan's national security advisor and one of the country's leading authorities on the Soviet Union. Though not as scholarly as his predecessors Henry Kissinger and Zbigniew Brzezinski, Allen knew as much about the Soviets and their leaders as anyone in government or academia. He had read the complete works of Vladimir Lenin and Joseph Stalin and had earned a master's degree in Soviet studies from Notre Dame before serving as a key foreign policy advisor on the first presidential campaign of Richard Nixon. He was briefly Kissinger's deputy on the National Security Council, but the two hardheaded policy experts did not get along, and Allen left in less than a year. He ventured into private industry, returned to the Nixon administration for a second stint, and then formed his own business consulting practice. A pilot, he barely survived the crash in 1973 of his small plane in Vermont. Over the years, Allen was occasionally seen as a somewhat controversial figure, but most considered him a good choice for national security advisor in an administration taking a hard line with the Russians.

A staunch anticommunist, Allen had spent years honing his arguments about the dangers posed by the Soviets. He often spoke in complete paragraphs, and his deep, naturally authoritative voice never seemed to betray any doubt about the correctness of his views. But if he was usually serious and sober, he could also be puckish and charming, especially when he performed what was generally regarded as the best impersonation in Washington of Henry Kissinger, his deep voice, German accent, and all.

Allen, who supported Reagan in the 1976 primary against Ford, became an ardent admirer of Reagan's a year later. In early 1977, Allen was mulling a bid for the governorship of his native New Jersey. After Ford's loss to Carter the previous fall, Reagan was one of the brightest stars on the Republican stage, and Allen knew that Reagan's assistance could prove critical to his own success on the campaign trail. About ten days after Carter's inauguration, Allen flew to Los Angeles, rented a car, and drove up to Pacific Pallisades to ask the former governor of California to sign fund-raising letters for his campaign. Sitting with Reagan in his living room, Allen also asked whether Reagan would be willing to come to New Jersey to campaign for him.

"Why, yes, I'd be happy to do that," Reagan replied. "But you came all the way out here to ask that? Why didn't you just call me on the telephone?"

"Well, it's not the same thing as meeting you face-to-face, Governor," Allen said.

Soon they were sipping coffee, eating sandwiches, and chatting about a wide range of topics. Reagan had read one of Allen's books—Allen had written or edited several on national security matters and communism—and the former governor peppered his guest with questions about Marxist theory, the Soviet premier, Leonid Brezhnev, and the machinations in the Politburo. The two men also had a long discussion about presidential power and how a president could shape global politics. Allen was impressed that Reagan was so well versed in foreign policy; the perception conveyed by the press was that he knew little about the world outside Hollywood.

Six hours after their conversation began, Reagan walked Allen to the front door. "Some people say I'm very simplistic," Reagan told his guest. "But there is a difference between being simplistic and simple. A lot of things are very simple if you think them through. So, keeping that in mind, here is my theory of the Cold War: we win; they lose."

The hair rose on Allen's neck and arms. For years, he had waged a losing battle with American diplomats and officials who thought the Cold War was something to be managed and survived, not won. Now he felt as if he were in the presence of an oracle. Reagan firmly believed that the United States could prevail in the Cold War—but only by beefing up the military and negotiating from a position of strength, not weakness.

During the ride to the airport and on the long flight home, Allen's mind buzzed with excitement as he thought about Reagan's yearning for a decisive victory over the Soviets. The next day, he dropped his bid for the governorship. "Here is a man," Allen told his wife, Pat, "who can really change things."

By 1978, Allen was Reagan's unpaid foreign policy advisor. He and another aide, Peter Hannaford, escorted the former governor on a trip to Asia in the spring and one to Europe in the fall to burnish his international credentials.

In Britain, they were shunned by the prime minister, James Callaghan, who apparently didn't want to offend President Carter. After a meeting with a lower-level official, Reagan was surrounded by a swarm of female office workers, many of them asking for autographs and peppering him with questions about Hollywood, actresses, and actors. Beaming, Reagan took out a pen and began signing his name and telling stories. Finally, Allen realized that he had to cut the unplanned encounter short: they were late for a meeting with the leader of the British Conservative Party, Margaret Thatcher, whom Reagan had met at least once before.

"We have to go, Governor," Allen said.

"Take it easy, Dick," Reagan replied, smiling. "These are my friends."

During the meeting with Thatcher, Reagan and the future British prime minister further cemented a bond that would fortify the two leaders through various domestic and international calamities in the years ahead. After the visit to Britain, the next stop was France, and then Reagan and Allen continued on to West Germany, where they visited the Berlin Wall.

Standing in front of the concrete barrier that separated free West Berlin from communist East Berlin, Reagan turned to Allen. When he spoke, his voice was full of passion. "You know, Dick, we have to find a way to knock this thing down." The future president's words, which he would later echo in one of his most famous speeches, hung in the air for a moment as the two adversaries of communism studied a wall that symbolized everything that was wrong with the world behind the Iron Curtain.

Since that visit to West Berlin a few years earlier, the struggle between the United States and the Soviet Union had only grown more intense. The Russians invaded Afghanistan in 1979. The United States boycotted the 1980 summer Olympic Games in Moscow. A historic arms limitation treaty died in Congress, and the United States imposed a grain embargo to protest the Soviet presence in Afghanistan. In recent weeks, Reagan and his officials had begun to ratchet up their rhetorical attacks on Moscow, accusing the Soviets of meddling in Central America and the Middle East. In January, at the president's first news briefing, a reporter asked Reagan about the "long range intentions of the Soviet Union" and wondered whether the president believed the USSR was "bent on world domination."

Reagan answered by saying that Soviet leaders had long promoted "world revolution and a one-world Socialist or Communist state." Continuing, he said, "Now, as long as they do that and as long as they, at the same time, have openly and publicly declared that the only morality they recognize is what will further their cause, meaning they reserve unto themselves the right to commit any crime, to lie, to cheat, in order to attain that, and that is moral, not immoral, and we operate on a different set of standards, I think when you do business with them, even at a détente, you keep that in mind."

Allen, standing at the back of the room, cracked a grin. Reagan's sharp words sent the Soviets a clear signal that he heartily endorsed. But during the preparations for the press conference, Reagan had carefully avoided using just this kind of inflammatory language, knowing that some of his advisors would insist he tone it down.

Shortly after the press conference, Reagan turned to Allen as they both headed for the Oval Office. "Say, Dick," Reagan said. "The Soviets—they do lie, cheat, and steal to get everything they want, right?"

"They sure do, Mr. President," Allen replied.

Reagan chuckled and said, "I thought so."

Now, in March 1981, there was serious labor unrest in Poland, a country that had been a flashpoint in World War II and whose ruling communist regime was closely allied with Moscow. Intelligence reports were suggesting that the Soviets might use their military to put down the dissent, and Allen knew there was little the United States could do to stop them. Reagan was not going to start a war over Poland—this was just one step in the long waltz of the Cold War. But before the White House switchboard connected Reagan and Schmidt, Allen advised the president to ask the German chancellor to join him in sending a stern warning to the Soviets that any intervention in Polish affairs would have serious consequences. The national security advisor understood that foreign policy was not a primary focus for the new administration; given the weak economy, Reagan's first priority was to enact tax cuts and slash spending. But Allen also knew that Reagan's most important job was keeping the country safe, and that history would ultimately judge his presidency on how he handled the Cold War and confrontations like the one over Poland.

As Allen once told an aide who complained about excessive briefing materials on national security, "This is why he has the chopper, Camp David and Air Force One, a huge fence outside the White House, and all of those damn guards armed with machine guns."

WHILE TAKING A shower on the morning of March 30, John Hinckley began to lose faith in his plan to take a bus to New Haven and commit suicide. Instead, he found himself thinking about the newspaper item he'd seen that outlined the president's schedule for the day. Reagan was to deliver a speech at two p.m. to a trade union at the Washington Hilton. Maybe he should walk over to the hotel with his little .22-caliber revolver. *If I can get close enough,* he thought, *I can end this madness.* He fantasized about getting shot and going down in a blaze of Secret Service bullets.

As he toweled off, he felt nervous and jittery. He realized that his pulse was racing, so he took some Valium. Putting on dark trousers and a blue-striped collared shirt, he wondered what he should do. His life had been descending in an ever tightening spiral, and now it had brought him to this bleak hotel room. Perhaps going to the Hilton would allow him to break this cycle, though he didn't quite know how.

Hinckley had been caught in a downward slide for a long time. Born in 1955, he spent his early years in Ardmore, Oklahoma, a bustling oil town where his father, Jack Hinckley, labored long hours repairing wells while his mother, Jo Ann, raised the family's three children. The Hinckleys moved to Dallas in 1958, and soon Jack Hinckley's oil company began doing so well that he and his wife purchased an expensive house in the affluent neighborhood of Highland Park. In grade school, John seemed pretty much like any other kid: he enjoyed sports, had a number of friends, and did reasonably well in class. But in junior high school, he began withdrawing from the world; he drifted away from his friends and spent more and more time alone in his room, playing his guitar and listening to Beatles records. In high school, he receded ever further into himself. Often compared unfavorably with his overachieving siblings, he had no close friends and never went out on a date. (Later, his mother said that when he skipped his junior-senior prom it was one of the saddest nights of her life.) He dreamed of becoming a singer and songwriter like John Lennon, and didn't see the point of higher education. "College isn't all that important for a musician," he once told his father.

In the fall of 1973, under pressure from his parents, Hinckley enrolled at Texas Tech, a large university with a sprawling campus in the dusty, hardscrabble city of Lubbock. Soon afterward, his parents relocated to Colorado; his father had grown tired of Dallas and had always wanted to live near the Rocky Mountains. After completing his freshman year at Texas Tech, Hinckley skipped a semester and then returned in the spring of 1975. His new roommate was black, and though Hinckley considered him nice enough, the experience changed him. Later, in an autobiographical essay, he would write: "It was during my years at Texas Tech that I received my education in the school of harsh reality. . . . The differences between the black and white race are too great for there ever to be an integrated America." Within three years, he'd become a white supremacist and, as he put it, an "all-out anti-Semite."

In the fall semester of 1975, Hinckley chose to live alone. He rented a sparsely furnished off-campus apartment and spent most of his time watching television, writing songs, and fantasizing about becoming a successful musician. The following spring, he dropped out of school, sold his red Camaro, and flew to Los Angeles with the hope of selling some of his songs. He rented a small apartment a few blocks from Sunset Boulevard in Hollywood and paid a few visits to music publishers. But in the end, his move to Los Angeles accomplished little: he had exchanged one drab apartment littered with fast-food wrappers for another. As before, he spent his days playing the guitar, watching TV, and going to movies.

One film in particular seized his imagination. *Taxi Driver*, released in February 1976, was the dark and disturbing story of Travis Bickle, an angry, alienated taxi driver who, after being spurned by a pretty woman, purchases an arsenal of weapons and then plots the assassination of a U.S. presidential candidate. The movie ends in an orgy of violence as the taxi driver tries to rescue a young prostitute from her pimp. Directed by Martin Scorsese and featuring a brilliant performance by Robert De Niro, the movie was one of the most talked-about films of the year, in part because it explored two of the most troubling trends of that era, urban violence and political assassination. In fact, one reason the movie rang true was because the screenwriter, Paul Schrader, had drawn on the story of the near assassination of Governor George Wallace of Alabama, who was badly wounded in May 1972 while running for president. Wallace's would-be assassin—a twenty-one-year-old busboy from Milwaukee named Arthur Bremer—had kept a journal about stalking both President Richard Nixon and Governor Wallace in the days leading up to the shooting; it was later published under the title *An Assassin's Diary*.

Hinckley was all but hypnotized by *Taxi Driver*; he watched the movie at least fifteen times. Sitting in the famous Egyptian Theatre in Hollywood, he felt as if he were watching his own life on-screen. He identified so completely with Travis Bickle that he began keeping a diary and buying guns. And, like the film's taxi driver, he developed an unhealthy fascination with a woman. In the movie, Bickle is consumed by feelings for a campaign worker and then becomes fixated on rescuing the prostitute. In Hinckley's case, he became obsessed with the young actress who played the prostitute. Her name was Jodie Foster.

CHAPTER 3

WITHOUT FAIL

HIS FEET PLANTED SHOULDER WIDTH APART, JERRY PARR DANGLED his hands loosely by his sides, ready to react the instant a paper target appeared at the other end of the firing range. The smell of gunpowder hung in the stuffy air. An ineffective ventilation fan rattled away. Suddenly the target snapped forward: it was an image of a well-dressed man aiming a large handgun right at him. His movements a blur, Parr's right hand flicked his suit jacket away from his holster and drew his gun to eye level, while his left hand reached up and grabbed the butt of his weapon. Aiming with the revolver's sights, he squeezed off two quick rounds and watched the bullets shred the target.

Parr holstered his handgun and waited for the technician to reset the target and run the drill again. The Secret Service could take no chances—assassins had to go down and not stand up again—so Parr's revolver was a fearsome and reliable weapon. A Smith & Wesson Model 19, it had a 2½-inch barrel and fired hefty .38-caliber bullets that blasted from the muzzle at 1,100 feet per second. Getting shot by one was a bit like getting smashed with a sledgehammer, only much worse: the Secret Service used hollow points, which mushroom on impact, tearing a broad channel through flesh and bone.

Parr was practicing at the Secret Service's firing range in the basement of the Old Post Office, just a few blocks from the White House. It was about nine a.m., and he was taking the monthly shooting exam that all agents on the presidential and vice presidential details had to pass in order to keep their jobs. In about fifteen minutes, Parr fired thirty rounds at targets as close as nine feet and as far away as forty-five feet. Using a two-handed grip, the agent fired first with his right hand and then with his left. Always, he pulled the trigger twice in rapid succession, a technique designed to reduce the gun's recoil and help agents stay on target. And throughout the test, Parr stood rigid and tall. Police officers, FBI agents, and soldiers all crouch when shooting. Agents on the presidential detail stand tall because they are supposed to take bullets, not avoid them.

The monthly exam was part of the Secret Service's efforts to keep its agents sharp. Originally formed in 1865 to investigate counterfeiting, the agency had started as a single small unit in the Treasury Department. By the time Jerry Parr joined, in 1962, the service had a $4.8 million budget and about 325 agents scattered across the country in fifty-five field offices. Its mission had evolved as well: though its agents still devoted considerable time to fighting counterfeiting and investigating forgeries of government checks, the service's top priority had shifted to presidential protection. Training, however, was minimal. On Parr's first day, he arrived at the twenty-member New York field office and was immediately taken to a firing range. He passed the test and was given a gun. Before he got his badge, though, the field office's top agent handed Parr the keys to a government car and ordered the rookie to take him on a drive to see if he could handle New York traffic. Parr did just fine until he hit a deep pothole, knocking his boss into the ceiling and wrecking his nice felt hat.

Parr began his job as an agent the next day. He spent much of his time investigating a range of financial crimes, but he also helped protect President Kennedy and Vice President Johnson when they visited the city. Mostly, he learned how to do his job by watching experienced agents investigate counterfeiting rings and stand guard over the president. After six months, he was sent to the Treasury Department's six-week law enforcement course, where all agents in the department's various branches learned the basics of criminal law, self-defense, and arrest techniques. Back in New York, he continued his investigations and stood post outside restaurants, hotels, and airports whenever the president or the first lady came to the city. Once Jackie Kennedy apparently ran out of money: she asked him if she could borrow $800. Parr, who at the time made less than $6,000 a year, restrained himself from laughing and politely told the first lady that he didn't have that kind of cash on him. By this time, the Parrs had two young daughters; in their small Queens apartment, husband and wife slept on a pull-out couch while their children shared the single bedroom.

In the fall of 1963, Parr was transferred to Nashville; a few days later, on November 22, President Kennedy was assassinated. Almost immediately, Parr was sent to Dallas to guard the wife and mother of Kennedy's killer, Lee Harvey Oswald, who was himself slain just two days after the president. Parr would never forget standing in a small kitchen just feet from the assassin's mother, Marguerite Oswald, listening in amazement as she boasted about becoming "a mother of history."

The next summer, Parr was sent to the Secret Service academy in Washington, where he received another few weeks of rudimentary training. He took courses in covering and evacuating the president, protecting the president in a parade and at a rope line, and investigating threats to the president—all essential training for a job he had already been doing for months. A year later, Parr was assigned to guard Vice President Hubert Humphrey. During Richard Nixon's presidency, Parr was promoted to deputy in charge of Vice President Spiro Agnew's contingent of agents; he rode with the disgraced vice president after Agnew resigned and when Agnew traveled to Baltimore's federal courthouse to plead no contest to charges of federal tax evasion. In 1979, Parr was named head of Carter's protective detail, a job he kept until Reagan was inaugurated. He now worked at the pinnacle of an active agent's career in an organization that had rapidly expanded and gradually adapted to confront a burgeoning array of threats.

During Parr's nearly two decades in the Secret Service, the agency had grown more than 400 percent: in March 1981, it fielded 1,544 agents and had an annual budget of $175 million. Its mandate had expanded significantly as well. In the wake of Senator Robert Kennedy's assassination in 1968, agents were assigned to protect presidential candidates. Three years later, they also became responsible for guarding foreign heads of state and visiting dignitaries. During the 1980 presidential campaign, agents protected seven candidates in addition to President Carter; they attended more than seven thousand rallies, fund-raisers, and other events. The service's caseload of financial investigations had also grown: by 1981, field agents were looking into more than 100,000 counterfeiting and Treasury check fraud cases a year.

But one fundamental aspect of the agency's culture had been much slower to change. Even in the mid-1970s, the service put agents to work immediately upon hiring them; only later were they provided a few weeks of training. Despite three fairly recent assassinations—John Kennedy's, Robert Kennedy's, and Martin Luther King's—agents were still not receiving rigorous refresher courses, and too often their skills eroded. This relaxed attitude toward training was dangerous: few jobs in the world require as much preparation for the unknown as that of a Secret Service agent. Only constant drilling can enable agents to react instantly in the unlikely event of a real threat.

Better training might have prevented some of the terrible tragedies that haunted the agency. For instance, the driver of President Kennedy's limousine didn't recognize the sound of gunfire after Oswald's first shot. When Kennedy was hit by the second bullet, the driver slowed down as he glanced over his shoulder to see what was happening behind him. A few seconds later, with the agent having taken no evasive action and the limousine still lumbering straight down the street, the third, fatal bullet struck Kennedy in the head. Nearly a decade later, George Wallace was shaking hands at a rope line during a campaign rally in Laurel, Maryland, when he was shot by a gunman standing in the crowd. The agents had allowed Wallace to walk up the rope line and then back down it, giving the would-be assassin time to steel his nerves and take careful aim. Wallace, hit four times, fell to the ground;

meanwhile, one agent was struck in the neck and another dove at the gunman. A third agent, startled by the gunfire, hesitated momentarily before dropping to check on Wallace's vital signs; it was the governor's wife, not an agent, who covered her husband's bleeding body. Although Wallace survived, the chaotic scramble to protect him and provide first aid was an embarrassment.

That shooting, as well as the growing threat of terrorism and the rising number of political killings around the world, forced the service to take action. The agency began by revamping its woefully inadequate first-aid training. Agents were required to take and pass "Ten Minute Medicine," a course designed to provide them with the skills needed to keep a wounded person alive for ten minutes, usually about the time needed to reach a hospital. Among other things, agents were taught how to assess internal injuries, how to treat a sucking chest wound with plastic wrap, and how to perform an emergency tracheotomy with a razor blade and a pen.

The service also borrowed a number of techniques from the military, which drilled its members to react without thinking. This revolution in training was led not from the top but by the field office in Los Angeles, where agents had been growing increasingly alarmed at the rising number of attacks on dignitaries and political leaders around the world. Over coffee or beers, they lamented not having the skills to cope with such assaults in the United States. On their own initiative and with the consent of their supervisor, the agents enlisted the Los Angeles Police Department SWAT team and began staging mock attacks at rope lines, on motorcades, and at speeches. They trained at an abandoned hospital for alcoholics in nearby Saugus, where they set off explosions, fired live ammunition, and staged ambushes on fast-moving motorcades. The exercises were so realistic that several agents who had served in Vietnam suffered nightmares and combat flashbacks. After some resistance, the service's headquarters eventually adopted a similar approach to training and began putting all agents through ever more complex drills and scenarios, each designed to teach instantaneous reactions in a crisis.

By 1981, the new training regime had become part of the service's culture. Jerry Parr, like all the veteran agents, had lost count of the number of times he had practiced throwing himself in front of a candidate at a rope line, smothering a protectee behind a podium, or shoving a president into an armored limousine. And Parr's training had taught him one thing above all: when faced with an actual threat, he could never freeze. Not for three seconds, not for one second. Without fail, he had to respond instantly.

At 9:15 A.M., President Reagan picked up the phone to speak with Helmut Schmidt in Bonn. Richard Allen and other White House officials sat in chairs near the president's desk. The call started on a sentimental note, with Schmidt thanking Reagan for sending a condolence letter after the death of the chancellor's father. Schmidt then said he hoped to deepen the ties between the two countries and that he was eager to meet with Reagan during an upcoming visit to the United States.

When Schmidt began talking about how they might better handle Leonid Brezhnev, the bellicose Soviet premier, the subject quickly turned to Poland. For months, laborers in the Solidarity movement had been agitating for more freedom in the wake of draconian economic policies and widespread food shortages; two weeks earlier, more than two dozen union activists had been beaten by police, leaving three seriously injured. Mass strikes, which could speed the country's economic decline, were planned for the next day. The work stoppages would almost certainly push the Polish government to declare martial law, which in turn would probably spark violent protests. If that were to happen, the Soviet Union, which was already leading military exercises in and around Poland, might choose to intervene. In confidential memoranda, the CIA was reporting that Soviet officials had lost faith in the ability of the Polish government to contain the crisis. For weeks, intelligence assessments had painted an increasingly bleak picture, and now the CIA believed that Poland was at a "possible turning point."

Schmidt warned Reagan that there was nothing his country could do militarily if Warsaw retaliated against the strikers or if the Soviets invaded Poland. He could apply economic pressure, though Poland was already billions of dollars in debt to West Germany. Reagan faced the same difficulty. He was not going to wage war against the Soviet Union over Poland, not least because direct conflict could easily lead to a nuclear confrontation. After fifteen minutes of discussion, the two leaders agreed to issue statements threatening to cut off financial aid to Poland if military force was used to quell the labor strife. Finishing the call, Reagan thanked Schmidt for his time.

The president spent the next hour receiving a briefing on national security and discussing a range of related matters, such as the flow of weapons to communist guerrillas in Central America and the sale of advanced military aircraft to Saudi Arabia. Then it was time for Reagan to move to the Cabinet Room for a fifteen-minute meeting with nearly three dozen Hispanic supporters to thank them for their help in the 1980 campaign. This mix of responsibilities was typical of Reagan's tenure as president: he often spent nearly as much time on ceremonial functions and meet-and-greets as on affairs of state.

This event, like every other in his day, was outlined in the script Reagan had reviewed earlier that morning:

MEETING: With Hispanic Supporters
LOCATION: Cabinet Room
TIME: 10:30AM–10:45AM
BACKGROUND: This is an opportunity to thank and encourage those who have been strongly supportive in the past.
10:30AM You enter Cabinet Room where your guests will have just completed their briefing. The press pool will enter for photos.
10:33AM You will offer brief remarks.
10:40AM The White House photographer will take photos of you with each participant.
10:45AM You thank your guests and take your leave.

Reagan arrived in the Cabinet Room ten minutes late and took his customary seat in the middle of the large wooden table. The back of his chair, which was two inches taller than those used by his cabinet secretaries, had a bronze label that read "THE PRESIDENT, January

20, 1981." In front of Reagan and the Hispanic supporters were white coffee cups in saucers. Reagan thanked the men and women for their "sizable and good showing" in the November election and said, "I know you have been told about what we are doing here in regard to getting more Hispanics in our government." Then, eyeing the journalists who had been ushered in to observe and take photographs, he continued: "But I also know that at the moment it might be better to confine ourselves to small talk here, before we get down to any real problems or issues."

Reagan smiled and turned to the clutch of journalists. "I haven't had a chance to congratulate you all—so many of you were members of the cast of the Gridiron up there that are covering us here. Have you ever thought about show business?"

The Gridiron Club dinner, an annual gala roast of official Washington, had taken place the previous Saturday evening. Journalists wore silly costumes, put on skits, and sang satirical songs, poking fun at figures such as Reagan, his wife, cabinet secretaries, and a number of politicians from both parties. At one point, the real Ginger Rogers took the stage and danced with a *Washington Post* columnist. At 11:30 p.m., after all the skits and songs were finished, Reagan took the dais and brought the house down with his self-deprecating wit and a few zingers aimed at his political adversaries.

Reagan was masterly at such events, but then he had been performing in front of audiences for years, and not just as an actor. During a long stint as a spokesman for General Electric, he had delivered hundreds of speeches at GE plants and offices across the country; over the years, he spoke to tens of thousands of the company's employees, from factory workers to executives, and the experience had taught him how to connect with many kinds of audiences.

The previous Friday, for example, he had hosted a White House luncheon for the National Baseball Hall of Fame in the State Dining Room, where he mingled and joked with the players and then gave a rousing speech that drew on his experiences as a radio announcer in the 1930s. Reagan told the ballplayers a favorite story about how, when he worked for a Des Moines radio station, he relied on telegraph feeds from the Cubs' ballpark to broadcast a play-by-play of the games. His job, which required a quick mind and a vivid imagination, was to transform short, cryptic messages into cinematic descriptions of fans catching foul balls and players turning snappy double plays. One afternoon, the wire went silent in the middle of an at bat. Dead air is a radio broadcaster's worst enemy, but Reagan didn't panic. He had the batter foul off pitch after pitch until the telegraph started working again.

"The nostalgia is bubbling within me," Reagan told the ballplayers, "and I may have to be dragged out of here because of all of the stories that are coming up in my mind." He went on to say that because he was as superstitious as any player, he had refused to mention on air that the Chicago Cubs had to win the last twenty-one games of the 1935 season to capture the pennant. "So there I was," he said, "a broadcaster, and never mentioned once in the 21 games, and I was getting as up-tight as they were, and never mentioned the fact that they were at 16, they were at 17, and that they hadn't lost a game because I was afraid I'd jinx them.

"But, anyway," Reagan added, "they did it, and it's still in the record books."

It was a great story, and it was mostly true. The Cubs did win twenty-one games in a row that year, but they lost their final two games of the season and still finished four games ahead of the St. Louis Cardinals. When telling stories, Reagan often blended truth and fiction. He was especially fond of happy endings typical of classic Hollywood movies—and no good old-fashioned baseball motion picture would end with a streaking club losing its last two games of the season.

Three days after the Hall of Fame lunch, sitting at the cabinet table with the Hispanic leaders, Reagan spent a minute or two joking with the reporters in the room and praising their performances at the Gridiron dinner. The journalists laughed and were then quickly shooed away.

Ten minutes later, his ceremonial duties finished, Reagan headed back to the Oval Office to prepare for the day's big speech.

THAT SAME MORNING, Vice President George H. W. Bush was comfortably settled in Air Force Two and flying toward Texas, where he was to deliver a pair of speeches urging passage of the president's economic policies. Politicking for his boss on a one-day trip to his home state was a typical task for a vice president, but it was still somewhat surprising that George Bush was the vice president making this trip. Only a year earlier, Bush and Reagan had been locked in a fierce and sometimes bitter fight for the Republican nomination.

As became clear during the primary campaign, the two men could not have been more different. Bush, fifty-six, was a child of privilege: the son of a U.S. senator, he had attended an exclusive prep school and graduated from Yale University. He wore Brooks Brothers suits, button-down shirts, and a watch with a preppy striped band. He kept in shape by jogging, not by riding horses or cutting wood. Unlike Reagan, Bush had seen combat in World War II. As a navy pilot, he flew fifty-eight missions and was awarded the Distinguished Flying Cross. After the war, he entered the oil business in Texas, made a lot of money, and then entered public service. He'd held a number of high-profile gov-ernment posts over the years: congressman from the Houston area; ambassador to the United Nations; U.S. envoy to China; director of the CIA. And in 1980, with the help of his good friend Jim Baker, now the White House chief of staff, Bush had attempted to snatch the nomination from Reagan, who had begun the race as the clear front-runner.

Reagan's campaign had started sluggishly. Bush weakened him, touting his own experience and "stamina"—a not-so-veiled jab at Rea-gan's age—and later attacking the former California governor's fiscal policies as "voodoo economics." After losing the Iowa caucuses to Bush, Reagan assailed the Texan for being too liberal, criticizing his oppo-nent's positions on abortion, gun rights, and taxes. By the time Bush finally conceded, both candidates held dim views of each other, which made it all the more surprising when Reagan, somewhat reluctantly, tapped Bush to be his running mate. During the run-up to the election, however, they campaigned well together, and over the past several months they seemed to have become a team. Bush had come to genu-inely respect Reagan, and the president often relied on Bush's expertise in foreign affairs and national security matters. They shared a weekly lunch, and Bush had an office in the West Wing just down the hall from the Oval Office.

The vice president often attended Reagan's morning national security briefings, but not on this day. Early that morning, CIA officials had delivered the briefing at Bush's official residence at the Naval Observatory, a half mile north of the White House. By 8:30, Bush and two aides were in a limousine heading toward the observatory's helipad; from there, they would fly to Andrews Air Force Base.

One of the aides in the limo was Chase Untermeyer, the vice president's soft-spoken and loyal thirty-five-year-old executive assistant. Untermeyer, who had worked as a volunteer on Bush's first campaign for Congress in 1966, admired the way his boss was handling his new job, one that had famously been described as "not worth a bucket of warm piss." A year ago, there had been a real possibility that Bush would become the fortieth president, yet now he had taken to this less powerful job with obvious relish, and thus far he had been working well with both the president and his aides.

As the marine helicopter lifted off from the observatory, passed over the British embassy, and skimmed below gray clouds, Bush regaled Untermeyer and others on his staff with stories about dancing with Ginger Rogers at a charity benefit the previous evening. As they boarded Air Force Two, they chatted with a couple of congressmen from Texas who were joining them for the trip. After takeoff, Untermeyer and two other aides joined Bush in his small stateroom, where they ate a continental breakfast, discussed how to fend off questions from reporters about Reagan's proposed spending cuts, and reviewed their itinerary.

The vice president's first stop in Texas was purely ceremonial: he would unveil a plaque at the old Hotel Texas in Fort Worth, where President Kennedy had spent his last night alive. Then, after a quick motorcade ride to the city's convention center, he would deliver a speech to a convention of the Texas and Southwestern Cattle Raisers Association. Following the speech, Bush would fly to Austin, where he was due to address the Texas state legislature. More of a partisan pep talk than a substantive speech about the new administration's policies, Bush's prepared remarks called for him to describe the president as "a leader with the courage of his and our convictions—a leader who thinks not of the next election but of the next generation." Aiming for a personal touch, Bush would tell the lawmakers: "I've watched him at work these first months in office. Time and again, I've seen him bring issues back to those fundamental principles which we Texans, and Americans everywhere, hold dear." After the twenty-five-minute speech, the vice president's motorcade would return to the Austin airport, from where Bush and his staff would fly back to Washington. The vice president would be home at 8:55 p.m.

Now, only a few hours into the long day, Air Force Two circled to land at Carswell Air Force Base. Untermeyer looked out his window and saw a fleet of parked B-52 bombers glinting in the bright Texas sunshine. Beyond the bombers, a patchwork of green plains seemed to stretch forever. Untermeyer marveled at the sight: in Washington, the weather had been damp and gray, but here the morning was warm and clear. Everything seemed so peaceful.

SHORTLY BEFORE ELEVEN a.m., Nancy Reagan arrived at the elegant mansion in Washington that housed the Phillips Collection, the nation's first museum of modern art. The first lady, wearing a bright red raincoat over a form-fitting gray suit with a pencil skirt, had come to the Phillips to tour its new wing and then attend a reception and social tea, where she would meet a group of volunteers in the Washington arts community. Joining her were Barbara Bush—the vice president's wife—and about two hundred other women, most of them wearing linen suits or silk dresses.

This morning's gathering resembled others Mrs. Reagan had attended since coming to the White House two months earlier. But she still felt unaccustomed to her new life: despite her years as first lady of California, she had spent most of her adulthood in the protective embrace of Hollywood high society and had not been prepared for the Washington media's intense scrutiny of her and her husband. A number of commentators were already suggesting that she had too much influence over the president, and aides sniped anonymously in the press that she could be vicious in upbraiding them for mistakes. Mrs.

Reagan was needled for admitting that she had stashed a "tiny little gun" in her bedroom drawer for protection when her husband was out of town, for her expensive wardrobe, for her decision to fly hairstylists to the inauguration, and for her ambitious plans to refurbish the White House's living quarters because she found them too shabby—all while the country's economy was suffering.

Like all first ladies, Mrs. Reagan was expected to dedicate herself to a worthy cause. An avid equestrian, she had visited a program designed to teach mentally challenged children to ride horses, and she planned to highlight the efforts of the Foster Grandparents program. She was also mulling the possibility of launching an antidrug campaign. But she was still searching for an appropriate and worthwhile focus for her considerable energies, and she often seemed tentative in her new role. The pressure was relentless: even when the Reagans escaped Washington, they never really left the White House behind. On their first trip back to their secluded ranch in the California mountains following the inauguration, Mrs. Reagan was unnerved to see dozens of Secret Service agents, police officers, military officials, and communications technicians swarming the grounds.

Still, she was where she wanted to be: at the side of her husband, the love of her life. She had met Reagan in 1949, when he was president of the Screen Actors Guild and she was just starting out in Hollywood. Then twenty-eight and named Nancy Davis, the young actress had recently signed a seven-year contract with MGM, but she was deeply worried for her new career because her name had appeared in a newspaper's listing of communist sympathizers. The Red Scare, then in full cry, was causing havoc in the film business; as head of the trade union representing movie actors and actresses, Reagan was working hard to clear the names of falsely accused union members. (Much later, it was revealed that Reagan was simultaneously an FBI informant; he and his first wife, also an actress, provided agents with the names of actors they suspected of communist sympathies.) When Nancy sought his help, Reagan quickly determined that she wasn't a communist. Through a mutual friend, he promised that the guild would defend her if a problem arose, but Nancy wanted to hear it from Reagan himself. So, that same night, Reagan took her out on their first date, a dinner at La Rue, a trendy restaurant and nightspot on the Sunset Strip. Recently divorced, he enjoyed her stories of growing up in Chicago as the daughter of a former Broadway actress and the stepdaughter of a brain surgeon. He marveled at her hazel eyes and enjoyed her laugh so much that he kept throwing out borrowed lines from George Burns and George Jessel just to hear it again. For her part, Nancy thought he was charming, and she enjoyed hearing about the Screen Actors Guild, his ranch, and his horses. They married three years later and had a daughter and then a son. (Reagan also had two children from his previous marriage.) The couple appeared together in 1957's *Hellcats of the Navy*, but Mrs. Reagan soon gave up acting to devote all her time to her husband and their children. She stood by him as he weathered good years and bad in the movie and television businesses and, later, in politics. In 1976 and 1980, she fully supported his runs for president and helped shape the campaigns.

Now she was first lady and attending a social tea with the vice president's wife on a dreary Monday in March. After a brief tour of the museum—she admired a landscape and a self-portrait by Paul Cézanne—Mrs. Reagan joined Barbara Bush near a podium in front of a painting of ballet dancers by Edgar Degas. The two women were introduced to the assembled guests; Mrs. Bush, wearing an aqua-green jacket and skirt, spoke first. "One wonderful thing I've learned," she said, "is when your leader is here, you keep your remarks very, very short. And I try not to be so fresh." Continuing, she told the gathering that "public service and volunteerism are the rent you pay for living on this wonderful earth."

Then it was Mrs. Reagan's turn. "Barbara," she said, "your leader's going to make remarks as short as yours." She went on to offer a few words about her many years of volunteering for various causes and closed by saying, "I'm a big believer in volunteer work. I think we may have gotten away from it a bit. It gives you such a wonderful feeling of satisfaction. And you do so much good."

With that, the women put on their raincoats and headed for their cars. They were both due to attend a lunch at the Georgetown home of

Michael Ainsley, president of the National Trust for Historic Preservation. There they would be joined by the wives of several members of Reagan's cabinet, among them Catherine Donovan, the spouse of the labor secretary. As it happened, while Mrs. Reagan and Mrs. Donovan were eating lunch in Georgetown, their husbands would also be together, sharing a limousine ride to the president's speech at the Hilton.

CHAPTER 4

"I'M NOT DANGEROUS"

JOHN HINCKLEY PULLED OUT A BLUE PEN AND A PIECE OF LINED yellow paper and sat down in a plain wooden chair, at a plain wooden desk, in front of a bland rectangular mirror in his room at the Park Central Hotel. He meant to declare his feelings, perhaps for the final time, to the woman he loved.

"Dear Jodie," he began in a tight script that led methodically across the page. "There is a definite probability that I will be killed in my attempt to get Reagan. It is for this very reason that I am writing you this letter now."

The words were flowing from his heart, but this was more than a love letter. It was also Hinckley's attempt to retrace and justify his obsession with Jodie Foster and to describe the steps he was willing to take to gain her attention. "As you well know by now, I love you very much," he wrote. And she did know, because this was not the first time he had reached out to Foster, an eighteen-year-old movie actress who had left Hollywood the previous fall to attend Yale University.

Hinckley had been fixated on the actress since 1976, when he'd first seen *Taxi Driver*. His obsession had grown with each passing year:

Foster seemed so intelligent and so precocious, so unlike any other movie star Hinckley had ever seen or read about. He desperately wanted to meet her, talk to her, run away with her. But any thought of actually getting in touch with her remained a fantasy until May 1980, when he read a *People* magazine profile that described her decision to leave Hollywood so that she could go to college and earn a degree. By that September, Hinckley had sold off more than $3,500 worth of stock in his father's oil company to finance an excursion to New Haven.

He told his parents he was taking a writing workshop at Yale. That was a lie; instead, he spent most of his time pursuing Foster. He located her dorm room and left her a dozen of his best poems and letters. Then he got her phone number and somehow summoned the courage to call, even tape-recording the conversations for posterity. He had expected their talks to be magical, but instead they were demoralizing. In a series of halting conversations, Foster—clearly uncomfortable and worried— tried to fend off a pitiable man-boy who was no more confident than a high school freshman struggling to ask a popular girl to the fall dance.

In their first call, Hinckley identified himself as "the person that's been leaving notes in your box for two days."

"Am I supposed to know you?" she asked.

"Well, no," he said.

"No. Oh, well, I don't . . . We have, we must not have much in common."

"Jodie, listen."

"Yes."

"I just want to talk to you. Okay?"

"I got to go out to dinner," she said. "Look, it's nice meeting you but I, I'm not supposed to talk to people I don't know, okay?"

During their next and longest phone conversation, Foster couldn't even get Hinckley's name right. "Is this John Hendrix?" she asked.

He corrected her and then said, "Jodie?"

"Yes."

"I saw you."

She soon tried to bring the awkward call to an end. "Look, I can't really be bothered with this, and I don't want, I don't want to be mean, and do you know, it just, it upsets my roommates and it upsets me. . . . You understand why I can't, you know, carry on these conversations with people I don't know. You understand that it is dangerous, and it's just not done, and it's not fair, and it's rude."

"Oh."

"All right."

"Well, I'm not dangerous. I promise you that."

A bit later, Hinckley heard snickering in the background. "What are they laughing at?" he asked.

"They're laughing at you."

"Jodie."

"Seriously, this isn't fair. Do me a favor and don't call back. All right?"

Hinckley was devastated by his inability to develop a relationship with Foster. By late October, he had returned home. He had long complained about a variety of maladies, including dizziness, headaches, pain in his arms, weakness in his legs, and heart palpitations. A few months earlier, a doctor had diagnosed him with "depressive reaction" and prescribed an antidepressant and Valium. In August, he had seen a psychologist who worked for his father's firm. After two sessions, the psychologist concluded that Hinckley was someone "who needed to get his shit together," not a deeply troubled man.

Writing was one of Hinckley's passions, and if he had allowed anyone to read his poems and short stories he would have provided clues to his distress. In recent years, his writing had grown increasingly dark, exploring such themes as suicide and patricide. In one story, a chess player kills himself; in another, a man rejects God on his deathbed, an act Hinckley portrayed as an act of courage. His most vivid descriptions were of pain: of a mind being destroyed by "dozens of ravenous lice," of "a hypodermic penis caught inside a working meat grinder," of a "few more hungry animals" chewing on a man's bones.

After he had returned home, Hinckley made a halfhearted attempt to kill himself by overdosing on the antidepressants. Within days, feeling himself near a breaking point, he had his first appointment with a psychiatrist. "A relationship I had dreamed about went absolutely nowhere," he wrote in a short autobiographical essay for the psychiatrist. "My disillusionment with EVERYTHING was complete. I gave up on myself and came back to Colorado." In the essay, he said that he cared about only two things: writing and Jodie Foster. Despite the warning signs, the psychiatrist probed no further. During their next ten sessions, which ended in February, the subject of Foster was never discussed again.

In late November, Hinckley struck back at the actress, hoping to complicate her life, or at least shake it up a bit. He sent an anonymous and threatening letter to FBI headquarters in Washington. In block letters, he wrote: "THERE IS A PLOT UNDERWAY TO ABDUCT ACTRESS JODIE FOSTER FROM YALE UNIVERSITY DORM IN DECEMBER OR JANUARY. NO RANSOM. SHE'S BEING TAKEN FOR ROMANTIC REASONS. THIS IS NO JOKE! I DON'T WISH TO GET FURTHER INVOLVED. ACT AS YOU WISH."

Over the next three months, he returned to New Haven several times and left Foster more messages and letters. In early March, before yet another trip east, he left his parents a note. "Your prodigal son has taken off again to exorcise some demons. I'll let you know where I am in a few days. This is something I have to do even though I know you don't understand."

His approaches to Foster grew more and more brazen, especially during his final trip to New Haven. "Just wait," he wrote in one letter he left at her door, "I'll rescue you very soon. J.W.H." In another, he scribbled: "Jodie, Goodbye! I love you six trillion times. Don't you maybe like me just a little bit? (You must admit I am different.) It would make all of this worthwhile." Foster turned the letters over to her dean.

Now, nearly a month after that most recent trip to New Haven, Hinckley had managed to get as far as Washington, D.C., but couldn't bring himself to make one final visit to Foster. Instead, he would find a way to impress the object of his obsession and leave a mark on the world. As he sat at the modest desk in his room at the Park Central Hotel, he had worked it out and made up his mind: he would kill the president of the United States.

"I feel very good about the fact that you at least know my name and know how I feel about you," Hinckley wrote, continuing his letter to Foster. "And by hanging around your dormitory, I've come to realize that I'm the topic of more than a little conversation, however full of ridicule it may be. At least you know that I'll always love you.

"Jodie, I would abandon the idea of getting Reagan in a second if I could only win your heart and live out the rest of my life with you, whether it be in total obscurity or whatever. I will admit to you that the reason I'm going ahead with this attempt now is because I just cannot wait any longer to impress you."

Finishing, Hinckley wrote: "This letter is being written only an hour before I leave for the Hilton Hotel. Jodie, I'm asking you to please look into your heart and at least give me the chance, with this historical deed, to gain your respect and love. I love you forever, John Hinckley."

With that, he neatly folded the letter into thirds, stuffed it into a white envelope, and labeled the envelope "Jodie Foster" before slipping it into his plaid suitcase. From the same suitcase, he removed a box containing the six Devastator bullets. Then he reached for his gun.

THE SPEECH WAS printed in all capital letters on 5¼-inch by 8-inch heavy white bond paper, just the way the president liked it. Sitting at his desk in the Oval Office, Reagan carefully reviewed the text for mistakes and typos. Sometimes he was handed the script of a talk just an hour before he was to appear on stage; this speech, though, was important, and two days ago he had spent part of his Saturday editing and rewriting the draft he'd been given by his staff.

It was now a little after eleven. In three hours, the president was scheduled to address the Building and Construction Trades Department of the AFL-CIO, in the International Ballroom of the Washington Hilton hotel. Reagan, a pro-business Republican, was a natural adversary of unions. But White House officials, especially Ray Donovan, Reagan's labor secretary, had urged the president to accept the invitation to speak at the trades department's national convention. On election day, Reagan had done surprisingly well among blue-collar workers; his political advisors had begun speaking of a new voting bloc, already being dubbed Reagan Democrats, that was generally conservative on social issues and very receptive to the president's message of lower taxes, less government, and a stronger military. The White

House wanted to broaden Reagan's appeal to such voters before the 1984 reelection campaign. Making inroads with this AFL-CIO branch—a group composed of fifteen affiliated unions with 4.5 million members—could help pave the way to more such support.

But the speech mattered to Reagan for a more personal reason: he had once been president of the Screen Actors Guild, a union also affiliated with the AFL-CIO. He fondly recalled that time and often reminisced about the guild's principles and the lessons he'd learned while squaring off against powerful studio executives. In some ways, his speech to the trades department that Monday would be a homecoming: he was the first president to be a card-carrying member of an affiliated AFL-CIO union.

The text of Reagan's talk had been drafted by Mari Maseng, a young speechwriter who had worked for Senator Bob Dole during the 1980 primary season and then joined the Reagan campaign in the fall. Maseng had produced a solid draft: she'd made all the right points about domestic and foreign policy, and she had found a good anecdote about a factory worker who had lost his job but nevertheless felt that Reagan's spending cuts should be given a chance to work, even if they might reduce his benefits and hurt his family. Maseng's boss had delivered the draft to the president on Friday; the following afternoon, Reagan read the text in his study in the White House residence and then took out a pen and rewrote the entire first section. He had spent years writing and honing his speeches, and though his new job kept him too busy to edit most of the talks he gave, he still spent time revising important addresses or those that meant something to him.

"I am pleased to take part in this Nat. Conference," Reagan wrote in his smooth and readable cursive. "I hope you'll forgive me if I point with some pride to the fact that I am the 1st Pres. of the U.S. to hold a lifetime membership in an AFL-CIO Union. Members of your organization have played & do play a great part in the building of America. They also are an important part of the industry in which my union plays a part."

Reagan then deployed a trademark bit of humor. "Now, it's true that grease paint and make believe are not tools of your members' trade but we all know the meaning of work, family and country. For 2 decades I participated in renegotiating our basic contract when it came renewal time. Here too we have much in common. Sitting at the negotiating table we were guided by 3 principles in our demands: is it good for our people, is it fair to the other fellow and to the customer and is it good for the industry?"

Drawing from a trove of hundreds of favorite quotations that he had jotted down on index cards, the president inserted one from Samuel Gompers, the founder of the American Federation of Labor, which would later become the AFL-CIO. Gompers, discussing the importance of self-reliance, had asserted that the "welfare of the workers depends upon their own initiative." Adding a gloss of his own, Reagan wrote, "Sam Gompers was repudiating the socialist philosophy when he made that statement."

The president tweaked other parts of the speech as well, scratching out most of a paragraph that began, "The American people have had enough of tinkering here and there with our massive problems." He also added a few lines asking his listeners to have faith in his plans and in themselves. "I've heard the complaints coming from those who had a hand in creating our present situation. They demand proof in advance that what we have proposed will work. Well, the answer to that is we're living with the proof that what they want to continue doing won't work. I believe what we have proposed will work because it always has."

Now, as he reviewed the final draft of the speech in the Oval Office, Reagan had a question about a potential mistake in the Gompers quotation as it appeared in the revised text. He called in his writers to discuss it; then, at about 11:30, he retired to the residence for lunch and some private "speech preparation time." He would have about two hours to himself before the motorcade trip to the Hilton.

ONE OF THE city's prime venues for presidential speeches, events, and fund-raisers, the Washington Hilton had been built in the early 1960s. Its design was intended to inspire: from above, the hotel looked like a seagull in flight. Two of its curving facades faced south, so that many rooms had a view of the Washington Monument and the city's stately skyline. To entice high-profile visitors, Hilton officials had directed the architects to include an enormous ballroom that could accommodate thousands of guests. They also designed a VIP entrance on the side of the hotel and, one floor below it, a holding room known as the bunker. From here, the hotel's most important guests could walk down a short hallway lined with presidential portraits and then enter the ballroom.

At eleven that Monday morning, Secret Service agents at the hotel were running through their final security checks. Bill Green, a slight and methodical South Carolinian who had joined the service in 1974, conducted a walk-through of all the arrangements for the event. Green was the lead advance agent for the president's trip to the Hilton; to prepare for Reagan's visit, he had drawn up a detailed security plan, determined precisely where his agents should be posted, and ensured that everyone slated to meet Reagan undergo a background check. Green and another agent inspected the ballroom, including the basementlike area under its floor, and then checked the holding room and the VIP entrance.

Green had been working on the visit since Wednesday, March 25. It was the first time he had handled security preparations for a presidential event at the Hilton, but his job had been made easier because Reagan was due to visit the hotel the following evening for the Radio and Television Correspondents Association dinner. Green read a standard security survey of the hotel written by a Secret Service agent and then observed another agent prepare for the broadcasters' function.

On Friday, he went to the Hilton and reviewed security procedures with Rick Ahearn, the lead White House advance man, as well as with hotel security officers and union representatives. Ahearn, a voluble and burly Reagan supporter who had slogged through the 1980 campaign, was in charge of ensuring that the visit went off as smoothly as possible from a performance and political standpoint. During the review, Ahearn made it clear that he was not happy with the union's plan to station the press at the far end of the room, since that would make it more difficult for photographers to take high-quality pictures of Reagan during his speech. But union officials did not want the media to obscure their members' view of the president, and since Ahearn didn't want to spark an unnecessary fight with the hosts he agreed.

Green, Ahearn, and the others then toured the hotel as Reagan would experience it, from the VIP entrance to the ballroom and back. Standing outside the hotel, Green and Ahearn discussed the arrival of the presidential motorcade. To prevent the general public from getting too close to the president, they agreed to place a rope line across the sidewalk that ran from the VIP entrance to the public entrance on T Street. This was the rope line's usual location, and it would keep people about thirty-five to forty feet away from the VIP entrance. On at least one previous visit by a foreign dignitary, the line had been placed about sixty feet from the VIP entrance. But no one felt that a similar measure was necessary for this event; besides, such a distant rope line would have required the closing of the T Street entrance, a considerable inconvenience to hotel guests. Green finished his work at the hotel that day by getting a list of the fifteen people expected to shake hands with the president before the speech, as well as an updated list of hotel employees whom he and his agents would need to check for criminal records and other potential risks.

On Saturday, Green visited the hotel for another tour. On Sunday, he made some final calls and worked on a report covering all the necessary security arrangements. At 7:30 on Monday morning, he arrived at the White House, turned in his plan, and called the District of Columbia field office for intelligence updates. He was informed that there were no threats related to Reagan's appearance at the hotel, and he was also told that the field office would be furnishing four agents as part of "protective intelligence" teams that would roam the hotel's grounds to check suspicious people. This news pleased him: earlier, he had been told that he would probably be getting only two such agents. (Later, he would be disappointed again when the field office reversed course and furnished only two agents after all.)

A little before eleven, Green drove to the Hilton in a Secret Service station wagon, which he parked near the hotel next to several other cars that were part of the president's "emergency motorcade." If there was a demonstration or a serious incident, the emergency motorcade could provide a speedy and inconspicuous means of escape.

Green then conducted his walk-through of the building to ensure that everything was ready to go. At noon, he briefed the more than two dozen Secret Service agents who would cover a variety of posts: outside the Hilton's entrance, on nearby rooftops, in the hotel's hallways, and in the area under the ballroom's floor. By the time a team of agents and officers with bomb-sniffing dogs began scouring the ballroom and other sensitive areas, Green was escorting a group of agents through the Hilton. One by one, he dropped them off at their posts, giving his most experienced agents the most critical assignments. He walked outside to verify that agents and police officers were in their proper places, then ducked back into the hotel for yet another check of security procedures. Finally, he authorized the opening of the ballroom doors to the waiting crowd of union members.

The president's arrival was now about thirty minutes away.

CHAPTER 5

THE ROPE LINE

B Y 1:10 P.M., THE PRESIDENTIAL LIMOUSINE WAS WAITING NEAR THE White House's diplomatic entrance. The 21½-foot car, code-named Stagecoach, was a black 1972 Lincoln Continental weighing 6½ tons. Covered in heavy armor plating and with windows of thick bullet-proof glass, it had a powerful V-8 engine, a rear bumper that folded into a platform capable of carrying Secret Service agents, and a self-sealing fuel tank designed to reduce the risk of an explosion. Hidden hooks allowed for secure tie-down in cargo planes, and an extra large sunroof enabled the president to stand and wave to crowds. Oddly, its rear doors opened backward.

The armored car was a necessary protection. Four presidents—Abraham Lincoln, James Garfield, William McKinley, and John Kennedy—had been slain while in office. President-elect Franklin Roosevelt and President Harry Truman had survived assassination attempts that killed others. In 1975, a quick-acting Secret Service agent stopped a woman from shooting President Gerald Ford; seventeen days later, another woman fired a shot at Ford but missed. Presidents were at their most vulnerable, of course, when away from the White House and out in the open.

Reagan was not one to dwell on the dangers of holding public office, but he knew the risks. When Robert Kennedy was killed in Los Angeles in 1968, Reagan was governor of California and running as a favorite-son candidate in his state's presidential primary. He was quickly assigned Secret Service protection. Within weeks, an agent in Reagan's detail surprised two men as they attempted to firebomb the governor's Sacramento home.

The threat of assassination was one reason Reagan had gone out of his way to keep Vice President Bush informed and brought him into so many meetings. At his seventieth birthday party in February, Reagan had leaned over and asked Barbara Bush whether her husband was enjoying the job. "Does he feel what he's doing is worthwhile? I just want to be sure he's doing enough. If the awful-awful should happen, George should know everything."

A month and a half later, on March 21, Reagan attended a black tie gala at Ford's Theatre. During a performance featuring Twyla Tharp, Tony Bennett, and Luciano Pavarotti, Reagan gazed at Lincoln's box and tried to imagine the horrific moment when John Wilkes Booth assassinated the president and then leaped to the stage. Today, no president would ever be so exposed, but Reagan well understood that, despite his armored limousine and the Secret Service detail, a determined assassin might one day kill him.

Now, at 1:45, with the president safely ensconced in the car's gray leather seats, the limousine pulled away from the White House. Riding next to Reagan in the passenger compartment was Labor Secretary Ray Donovan. Formerly a construction executive in New Jersey, Donovan had earned his position in the administration by soliciting donations and advising Reagan's campaign about politics in his home state.

Earlier that day, Donovan had spoken before the Building and Construction Trades Department of the AFL-CIO; he got a chilly reception. As the two men rode toward the Hilton, Donovan warned

Reagan to expect a tough time. But the president was unruffled. "We're used to that, aren't we?" he said, smiling.

Reagan and Donovan chatted briefly about politics before the labor secretary launched into an amusing yarn about a politically connected bar owner given a patronage job as the commissioner of weights and measures. After his first day on the job, reporters asked the new commissioner: "Sir, how many ounces in a pound?"

"Hey," the former bar owner said. "Give a guy a chance to learn his duties!"

Donovan had told the president that joke more than once over the past few years, but, as always, Reagan laughed.

Riding in the front passenger seat that afternoon was Jerry Parr. It was the same position he had occupied two months ago during the inaugural parade, and now, as then, he listened to the Secret Service radio and constantly scanned the cityscape. At the limousine's wheel was Agent Drew Unrue, an army veteran who had joined the service in 1972. Unrue was often given the stressful job of driving the hulking limousine, and even during a routine trip such as this one he was intensely focused. Knowing that he was an obvious target was bad enough, but the agent was always nervous about missing a turn or dropping the president off at the wrong entrance to the venue, the kind of mistake he would never live down.

Directly ahead of Stagecoach was a second armored limousine, a tan Lincoln that carried Dr. Daniel Ruge, the president's personal physician. Ruge or one of the doctors working for him always accompanied Reagan on trips outside the White House gates; usually Ruge sat in the second limousine, which the Secret Service would use as a spare if Stagecoach broke down. It also served as a good decoy.

Ahead of the spare limousine, riding in the passenger seat of a marked cruiser driven by a D.C. police sergeant, was Agent Mary Ann Gordon, who was responsible for ensuring that the motorcade encountered no problems on its way to and from the Hilton. Gordon, a former juvenile parole officer from Boston, was one of only a handful of female agents in the Secret Service. She had already made history when she'd chauffeured Jimmy Carter to a speech, becoming the first female agent ever to drive a president. Earlier that Monday, Gordon had driven all of the possible motorcade routes to the Hilton, to the White House, and even to George Washington University Hospital. She wanted to be sure the streets were free of construction equipment or other impediments; she also wanted to imprint the routes in her memory, because there would be no time to think or ask for directions in a crisis. Now, as they drove toward the Hilton, she kept an eye on the police motorcycles ahead of them and noted that officers were blocking traffic at all the appropriate intersections, giving them a clear corridor to the hotel.

The presidential limousine was trailed by an insurance policy—a follow-up car that carried a driver and half a dozen additional agents who wielded handguns, shotguns, and submachine guns. Code-named Halfback, the car was an armored Cadillac with running boards and a powerful engine, and the six agents riding in it were all members of the so-called working shift, which closely shadowed the president. In the front passenger seat was Agent Ray Shaddick, the shift's supervisor. Among those squeezed in the back was Timothy McCarthy, a muscular former Big Ten safety.

McCarthy, the thirty-one-year-old son of a Chicago cop, was not happy about today's assignment because of the weather—he was wearing a new Geoffrey Beene suit and didn't want it to get wet in the rain or splotchy from water dripping from Halfback's leaky roof. He had nearly gotten out of the trip but had lost a coin toss with two other agents who also wanted to skip the speech because they were behind on their expense reports.

Behind Halfback was the control car, driven by a military noncommissioned officer. Also in the control car was Michael Deaver. A member of the Troika almost always accompanied the president on official trips, and today it was Deaver's turn. Riding with him were David Fischer, the president's body man, and the military aide carrying the nuclear football.

The spare limousine, the presidential limousine, the follow-up car, and the control car together made up the "escape package," and they were never to be separated under any circumstances. Trailing the package was a staff car ferrying the president's press secretary, Jim Brady, a bear of a man respected by White House officials and the press for his work ethic, honesty, and sense of humor. Earlier that day, as he juggled a press briefing, attended staff meetings, met with the president, and schmoozed with reporters, the forty-year-old press secretary had considered skipping this event. He was always caught in a tug-of-war between his two most important constituencies: the president and the pool of White House reporters. Relatively new to Reagan's orbit of advisors, Brady was aiming to spend as much time with the president and his closest aides as possible, but he was also trying to improve his relations with the press. As the scheduled departure for the Hilton approached, Brady finally decided to travel with the president.

The string of limousines, official cars, police cars, and two police motorcycles added up to a motorcade fifteen vehicles long. With the police motorcycles leading the way, the president's limousine rumbled up Connecticut Avenue and soon took a right onto Florida Avenue. Then, after a quick left onto T Street, the big Lincoln veered into the Hilton driveway, made a sharp left, and pulled up at the VIP entrance.

The ride had covered 1.3 miles in about four minutes. It was 1:50 p.m.

A FEW MINUTES before the president's arrival, D.C. police officers Sergeant Herbert Granger and Officer Thomas Delahanty stood at the rope line, corralling seven reporters and ten spectators about thirty-five feet from the Hilton's VIP entrance. It was the officers' job to keep people away from the president and his motorcade.

At seven that morning, the two men had reported for work at the 3rd District police station to learn that they were among those being assigned to guard duty at the Hilton during the president's visit. Granger sighed—he had stood post at the hotel a number of times before, and it was boring duty. He much preferred to work the streets, especially in high-crime neighborhoods. Worse, on a day like this he would have to sweat in the suffocating department-issue raincoat. Standing at his locker in the basement of the station house, Granger picked up his bulletproof vest. He knew it would only make him perspire even more. *Hell*, the sergeant thought, *it's just the Hilton*. He tossed the vest back into his locker.

Delahanty, one of Granger's officers, was currently assigned to the department's K-9 unit, but his dog, Kirk, was ill that day, so he was available to work security. Before going to the Hilton, however, he visited the department's dog training center and also drove to police headquarters to have a new departmental photograph taken. Over the weekend, he had spotted an out-of-date picture in the newspaper of an officer involved in a recent shooting, and he didn't want his bosses handing out an old photo if he ever made the news. In the new photograph, Delahanty, forty-five, stared straight back at the camera, his tired-looking eyes framed by his square jaw and his long sideburns.

About forty-five minutes before the president's departure from the White House, Granger, Delahanty, and five other officers piled into squad cars for the short trip to the Hilton, where the sergeant deployed his men around the entrance. Granger sent an officer to stand guard on a ledge overlooking the hotel's VIP entrance, where Reagan would enter and leave the hotel, and arranged the others near the rope line and the Hilton's doors.

Not long after Granger and his officers had taken their places, a Secret Service agent emerged from the VIP entrance and yelled, "They're coming."

Granger, a former military police officer frequently assigned to demonstrations and protests, had developed a sixth sense about crowds—when they might erupt in violence; when someone might throw a brick. With the president approaching, Granger eased closer to the rope line and studied the faces of those in the small gathering, looking for signs of trouble. He saw and felt nothing.

LOOKING BACK AT the police sergeant from among the handful of reporters, photographers, and spectators was John Hinckley. His RG 14 revolver was stashed in the right pocket of his beige jacket. It was a small gun, its barrel only 1¾ inches long—the sort of weapon often called a Saturday night special because it was cheap and easy to obtain.

The firearm had no safety catch and its trigger was considered heavy, meaning that it required more pressure to squeeze than a typical gun.

The RG 14 was also relatively difficult to load. Sitting in his hotel room less than an hour earlier, Hinckley had unscrewed a knob underneath the barrel and pulled out a pin that released the gun's cylinder, which flipped out to the left on a hinge. He removed the six Devastator bullets from their box and inserted them into the round cylinder. The Devastators' tips were filled with twenty-eight milligrams of lead azide, a high explosive meant to detonate on impact. Left untouched in one of his suitcases were thirty-five hollow-point bullets and two round-nosed bullets.

Hinckley had owned this revolver only since October 13, but he had been buying guns since 1979, when he picked up a .38-caliber revolver at a Texas pawnshop. He had spent time practicing with them, too: for the past two years, he had been visiting firing ranges to hone his shooting skills.

This was also not the first time Hinckley had stalked a president. Six months earlier, stung by Jodie Foster's rejection and determined to get her attention, he had traveled to Texas to buy two revolvers and then flown to Washington to try out the idea of killing President Carter. He took a hotel room just three blocks from the White House—"Carter's fortress," as he referred to it in a postcard he sent his sister and her husband. After spotting a news story that mentioned the president's campaign schedule, Hinckley flew to Ohio. On October 2, he attended a Carter campaign rally in Dayton where he stood within arm's reach of the president, just one in a sea of about fourteen hundred screaming supporters. But he hadn't brought a gun—his three revolvers were stowed in his luggage at the city's bus station. The rally was a test run, an effort to prepare himself for the ultimate act. No agents searched him at the event, and Hinckley was astonished that he was able to get so close to the president.

Five days later, Hinckley flew to Nashville to attend another Carter rally. At the last minute, however, he changed his mind and decided not to approach the president again. Back at the city's airport, he went to security and watched as his suitcases passed through an X-ray machine. A security officer noticed what she thought was a gun in one of them;

a police officer searched the bag and found the three revolvers, as well as a pair of handcuffs and a box of .22-caliber ammunition. The guns were confiscated; Hinckley was taken before a judge and fined $62.50. He paid the fine in cash and was driven back to the airport, where he caught a flight out of town.

Hinckley felt especially lucky that day. The officer hadn't dug particularly deep into his suitcase, so he had missed his diary, which told the whole story—his obsession with Jodie Foster, his stalking of Carter in Dayton, the reason for his trip to Nashville. The first chance he got, Hinckley destroyed the journal. Then, just days after losing the three guns in Nashville, he purchased two .22-caliber revolvers at a pawnshop in Dallas.

In November, Hinckley turned his attention to the president-elect. He flew to Washington, where he was photographed in front of the White House and Ford's Theatre. He loitered for hours outside Blair House, the president-elect's official guest residence, just across Pennsylvania Avenue from the White House. With a gun in his pocket, he watched Reagan come and go, but he never mustered the resolve to pull the trigger.

Then, in December, while stalking Reagan in Washington, Hinckley learned that his hero John Lennon had been assassinated in New York City. Overcome with despair, Hinckley traveled to New York and attended a vigil. Afterward, he returned to Evergreen, where his troubles seemed to deepen. In the weeks following Lennon's death, he was swept up in a tornado of fantasies that became ever more elaborate and absurd, most of them involving Jodie Foster. He dreamed of skyjacking an airliner, forcing Foster to join him, and then compelling Reagan to resign. This narrative ended with him and Foster living in the White House. He bought a postcard of the Reagans, on the back of which he jotted: "Dear Jodie, Don't they make a darling couple? Nancy is downright sexy. One day you and I will occupy the White House and the peasants will drool with envy." He didn't send the postcard, but he slipped it into a book and saved it.

Now, having returned to Washington, he was determined to kill the president. After loading the gun in his hotel room, he'd put on his jacket and dropped the small revolver into his right pocket and a John Lennon pin into another pocket. A few minutes later, he hailed a cab and asked the driver to take him to the Hilton. On the way, he thought about what he wanted to do. He could pull out the gun and shoot; he could pull it out but then choose not to shoot; or he could just leave the gun in his pocket and walk away. He also worried that he might not get close enough to actually hit the president. Even after all of his target practice, his effective range was still only twenty to thirty feet.

Once the cab pulled to a stop near the hotel, Hinckley paid the fare, walked to the nearby Holiday Inn, and used the bathroom. Then he walked to the Hilton, where he saw cameramen and spectators gathering behind a black rope strung across the sidewalk not far from the VIP entrance. Hinckley joined the small crowd. He didn't think security seemed especially tight.

Five minutes later, the long motorcade arrived. The presidential limousine appeared at the Hilton's driveway on T Street and pulled to a stop at the VIP entrance. A Secret Service agent in a tan trench coat got out of the front passenger seat and opened the right rear door. Out stepped the president. He turned to the spectators and journalists standing behind the rope line and waved.

Hinckley felt as if the president were staring right at him. He raised his arm to wave back, but by then Reagan had already turned toward the hotel. A moment later, surrounded by a phalanx of Secret Service agents, the president walked through the Hilton's brass-plated doors and was gone.

JERRY PARR HOVERED by Reagan's shoulder as the president entered the elevator with Ray Donovan and the chief of hotel security. As Reagan and the others took the elevator to the ground level, several agents hurried down a spiral staircase to meet them. The president stepped off the elevator and then, with Donovan providing introductions, shook hands with labor leaders and smiled for the official White House photographer in the foyer of the holding room.

At two p.m., Reagan walked down the short, curving hallway lined with portraits of previous presidents and arrived at the backstage entrance to the International Ballroom. Just before he went onstage, Reagan popped out one of his contact lenses. The severely nearsighted president couldn't read a speech while wearing his contact lenses, so he had devised a unique solution: he read the text with his unaided eye and used the other to pan the crowd.

At the sound of "Hail to the Chief," Reagan strode onstage. He walked behind the head table and toward the podium, where he shook hands with Robert Georgine, the president of the trades department of the AFL-CIO. After a brief introduction, he stepped to the dais.

"Thank you all," Reagan said as the audience applauded. "Thank you. Thank you very much." The president opened his speech with a story, one he had written down on an index card long ago. He had often told a punchier version on the campaign trail, and by now it was an old standby, perfect for a group of blue-collar workers who loved sports.

"There's been a lot of talk in the last several weeks here in Washington about communication and the need to communicate," the president began. His first months in office, he said, had brought to mind an old story "about some of the basic rules of communication."

The president then told his audience about a young baseball player and his wife who invited a well-known sports announcer named Danny Villaneuva to dinner. While his wife prepared the meal, the player talked with his guest about sports. Then the couple's baby began to cry.

Warming to his story, Reagan continued: "And over her shoulder, the wife said to her husband, 'Change the baby.' And this young ballplayer was embarrassed in front of Danny and he said to his wife, 'What do you mean, change the baby? I'm a ballplayer. That's not my line of work.'

"And she turned around, put her hands on her hips"—here Reagan paused for the briefest moment—"and she communicated. She said, 'Look, buster, you lay the diaper out like a diamond, you put second base on home plate, put the baby's bottom on the pitcher's mound, hook up first and third, slide home underneath, and if it starts to rain, the game ain't called—you start all over again.'"

The room burst into hard laughter. "So," Reagan said, "I'm going to try to communicate a little bit today."

OUTSIDE THE HILTON, Drew Unrue repositioned the president's limousine, parking it about twenty-five or thirty feet from the VIP entrance with its front end aimed at T Street and its trunk close to the rope line that held back the spectators on the Hilton's sidewalk. The car's position would require the president to walk from the VIP entrance to the waiting limousine while moving roughly parallel to the rope; during this brief period, he would be fifteen to twenty feet from the spectators.

Unrue parked the limousine this way because of the somewhat peculiar design of the Hilton. The hotel sat on the northeast corner of Connecticut Avenue and T Street, and circular driveways from each street led to the hotel's entrances. Connecting the two driveways was a lane that ran past the VIP entrance. Unrue had used the T Street driveway and dropped Reagan off directly in front of the VIP entrance; if he picked up the president in the same spot and continued on, he would follow the lane out toward Connecticut Avenue. But the connecting lane was narrow and curving, and the Secret Service worried that the hulking limousine might get stuck on a curb or become trapped while trying to negotiate the sharp turn onto Connecticut Avenue. Moreover, a police car was always stationed at the top of the lane, sealing off the area to prevent attackers and protesters from driving straight toward the presidential departure area. If the officer responsible for that car didn't get it out of the way quickly during an emergency, the limousine would smash right into it.

To solve the problem, the service instructed agents driving the limousine to drop off the president, back away from the VIP entrance, and then park the car with its nose pointing toward T Street. From this position, the drivers could make a quick getaway in case of an incident. But the service's solution did have a downside: the president had to walk in the open for a few seconds until he reached the safety of the limousine's right rear door. This degree of exposure was not uncommon, and the service believed that the risks associated with negotiating the narrow lane were greater than those attending a short walk past some spectators. Besides, during the past decade the service had handled more than one hundred presidential visits to the Hilton and there had never been any reason to question this trade-off.

After watching Unrue park the Lincoln in its usual spot, Sergeant Herbert Granger decided that the rope line seemed a little too close to the president's limousine. Granger directed his officers to move the brass stanchions holding the rope back a few feet, just past a drainage grate in the sidewalk. Even with the repositioning, however, spectators and reporters behind the line—none of whom had been screened by the Secret Service—would still be about fifteen feet from the president as he stepped to his car.

Unrue, having parked the limousine, walked over to the follow-up car and began chatting with its driver. None of the agents or police officers had seen any sign of trouble. A heckler had caused a bit of a ruckus, but he was a regular on the Reagan circuit who often appeared at public events to chant antinuclear slogans. Just in case a photograph might prove useful, the hotel security chief pulled out his Olympus camera and snapped a picture of the crowd, hoping to capture the heckler's image for his files. Police officers and agents shooed a few spectators away from the president's limousine and other cars in the motorcade, although they allowed the Hilton's cafeteria manager to peek inside the armored Lincoln after listening to a persuasive plea on her behalf from a hotel security officer. Meanwhile, across T Street, agents and officers worked diligently to prevent any of the approximately two hundred onlookers from slipping across the closed street.

As departure time neared, Mary Ann Gordon, the motorcade's advance agent, inspected the line of motorcycles, police cars, and government vehicles. Everything seemed in order, so she took her place in the lead cruiser. Unrue returned to the limousine, took his seat, and switched on the car's engine. The follow-up driver started his engine and flipped on his flashing red lights. Agents and police officers began to return to their assigned posts. By now, the crowd of spectators and reporters hoping to catch a glimpse of the president had swelled to about twenty-five people.

It was 2:20 p.m.

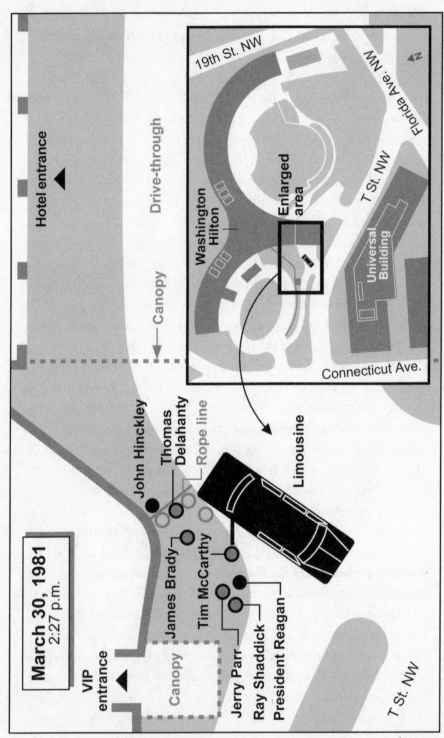

March 30, 1981
2:27 p.m.

VIP entrance

Canopy

Hotel entrance

Drive-through

Canopy

John Hinckley

Thomas Delahanty

Rope line

James Brady

Tim McCarthy

Jerry Parr

Ray Shaddick

President Reagan

Limousine

19th St. NW

Florida Ave. NW

Washington Hilton

Enlarged area

T St. NW

Universal Building

Connecticut Ave.

T St. NW

N

Frank Pompa

CHAPTER 6

2:27 P.M.

Agent Jerry Parr stood backstage, watching President Ronald Reagan finish his address to the four thousand union members sitting politely in the International Ballroom. Standing behind the familiar blue podium with the presidential seal, Reagan was bathed in bright television lights as he read from his cards between practiced glances at the audience. He was wrapping up his speech in typically optimistic and patriotic fashion: "I know that we can't make things right overnight. But we will make them right. Our destiny is not our fate. It is our choice. And I'm asking you as I ask all Americans, in these months of decision, please join me as we take this new path. You and your forebears built our nation. Now, please help us rebuild it, and together we'll make America great again."

The crowd rose to its feet, but the applause was more polite than enthusiastic. The speech had not been one of Reagan's better efforts, but he hadn't blundered and no one had heckled him or booed.

Parr moved to the edge of the stage and stood behind a swath of gold bunting as Reagan shook a few hands before walking past the head table and off the stage. The agent fell in step behind the president and trailed him down the curving hallway toward the holding room, where White House aides awaited Reagan's return.

A platoon of Secret Service agents rushed ahead. They took the stairs up from the ground level two at a time and then moved quickly out the VIP doors and into the gray, misty afternoon. One agent aimed for the rope line; another trotted along the hotel's stone wall; a third angled for the limousine's right front fender; a fourth swept around the far side of the limousine. A fifth, carrying an Uzi submachine gun in a briefcase, kept an eye on a group of spectators on a traffic island in the middle of the hotel's driveway. A sixth, Tim McCarthy, strode to the limousine's right rear door. It would be his job to open the door for the president.

Directly across T Street, Jerry Parr's wife, Carolyn, looked out her fourth-floor window and saw that the president's limousine was preparing to leave. The IRS lawyer knew her husband would be directing Reagan's security detail that day—he had called her a couple of hours ago to tell her so—and since her office happened to overlook the Hilton's VIP entrance, she'd decided to keep an eye on the motorcade and then go down to the street to watch her husband escort the president to his limousine. Now she dashed down the stairs, hoping she wasn't too late.

THE CROWD OUTSIDE the VIP doors continued to grow. The reporters and cameramen who had attended Reagan's speech were now leaving the public entrance to the hotel on T Street, about thirty feet beyond the rope line, and working their way through the waiting spectators. Some of the journalists were hoping to get video or photographs of Reagan as he left the Hilton. Others wanted to toss questions at the president—this would be as close as they got to him all day. And a few were on the so-called body watch, the morbid duty of tracking the president's every move so that if something terrible happened they could report it immediately.

Sam Donaldson, ABC's brash and outspoken White House correspondent, was on the body watch, but he also hoped to ask Reagan about the situation in Poland. Donaldson nudged his way through the crowd behind the rope line, slipping past three officials from Iowa who were in town for meetings with federal officials, an office worker who had just finished his lunch, and a cocktail waitress reporting for her shift at the hotel. By the time Donaldson reached the rope, he was standing near several union leaders awaiting Reagan's departure. One told another: "Let's count his wrinkles."

Two or three journalists and cameramen began shoving their way through the spectators. "Press, press, let us through!" a reporter shouted, trying to get to the front of the rope.

"No, we were here first!" screamed an agitated young man in a beige jacket who was standing near the two union officials. "You ought to get here on time," he yelled at the journalists. He turned to the other spectators. "They think they can do anything they want! Don't let them do that!"

There were now more than thirty people clustered behind the rope line. Three police officers, including Herbert Granger and Thomas Delahanty, stood between the spectators and the president's projected path from the VIP entrance to the limousine. One Secret Service agent moved to a spot between the rope line and the VIP entrance; a second agent stood at the curb near the limousine, keeping an eye on the crowd in case anyone tried to maneuver around the rope line and run toward the president. Meanwhile, five agents on Reagan's working shift formed a cordon around the limousine.

REAGAN EMERGED FROM the elevator after the quick ride from the holding room on the ground level. Seconds behind him, David Fischer, the president's body man, and Rick Ahearn, his advance man, ran up the wide spiral staircase. They wondered aloud why Reagan didn't just take the stairs. "It's such a short ride," Fischer said.

With each stride toward the VIP doors, Reagan accumulated a larger entourage. Just ahead of the president, Mike Deaver and Jim Brady walked out the exit. When Deaver spotted the clutch of reporters standing behind the rope line, several of whom were already shouting questions at the president, he steered the burly press secretary toward them. "Go deal with it," he said.

Stepping through the Hilton's doors, Reagan saw the same reporters who had caught the attention of his deputy chief of staff. He would not be taking any questions, though—not today. Lately he and his advisors had been trying to be more disciplined; answering random questions from journalists rarely served their purposes. But the president did plan to make one dramatic gesture. With his back to the reporters, he would step onto the edge of the limousine's door frame and boost himself up to wave to the spectators across the street.

JERRY PARR SLID a step behind the president as they moved away from the VIP entrance and strode across the slick hotel driveway. Glancing up, Parr saw dark scudding clouds; then he scanned the crowd of reporters and spectators behind the rope line as well as those across the street. His eyes swept the limousine and the driveway. All the agents and police officers were positioned properly. Behind Parr, Ray Shaddick carried a fiberglass panel covered in leather, which was used to shield the president whenever he approached a crowd.

Everything was in order.

Walking eighteen inches behind the Man, Parr guided Reagan toward the limousine. As always in such situations, the agent was busily plotting his response in case of an emergency. If an attack had occurred just after they'd walked through the VIP doors, Parr would have pulled the president back into the safety of the hotel. Now, halfway to the limousine, his plan changed: if something happened, they would dive into the armored Lincoln.

As they approached the limousine, Tim McCarthy, Parr's point man, opened the Lincoln's right rear door. Looking toward the dozens of spectators lining T Street, Reagan smiled, raised his right arm, and waved. A woman to his left shouted, "Mr. President, President Reagan." The president swiveled his head toward the rope line, raised his left arm as if to acknowledge her, and seemed to mouth the word "Hi."

Eyeing the crowd, Parr began gliding to a point just off Reagan's left shoulder, where he would serve as a barrier between the president and anyone who might try to attack him from that side. As he continued to guide Reagan toward the door, Parr heard what sounded like gunfire.

Pop. Pop.

Instantly, Parr's left hand grabbed Reagan's left shoulder. His right hand reached for the president's head, and his torso twisted into a human shield. He drove Reagan toward the open door of the Lincoln, his legs pumping like a running back pounding through a defensive line.

He heard another *pop*, then another.

All in a seamless motion—part programmed, part improvised— Parr grabbed and twisted, shoving Reagan forward. Out of the corner of his eye, he saw Tim McCarthy turn and spread his arms wide to protect the president.

Parr heard another *pop* and felt Ray Shaddick's strong hands ramming him and the president through the limousine's doorway.

One final *pop*.

They tumbled into a heap on the transmission hump. Parr's mind raced, instantly ruling out firecrackers, balloons, pranks.

He knew it was gunfire. Someone was trying to assassinate the president.

JOHN HINCKLEY COULDN'T believe his luck. After the president's arrival at the Hilton, Hinckley had walked into the hotel's lobby and loitered there for a while, the gun still in his jacket pocket. Then he'd returned to the rope line and waited with the others in the crowd, at one point shouting at some journalists who were pushing to get into better position. A few minutes later, Hinckley saw Reagan emerge from the VIP entrance. Unbelievably, the president was completely out in the open— and Reagan would pass right in front of him.

Hinckley felt exceedingly calm. Standing between the hotel's wall and a cameraman, he reached into his jacket's right pocket. But even now he wondered whether he should pull out the gun and start firing. Two police officers turned away toward Reagan; a Secret Service agent looked down at the ground. Nobody was paying any attention to him; the cameramen and reporters were focused on the president, as was everyone else in the crowd.

There was no time to think. He knew only that he would never get another chance as good as this one. He pulled the gun from his pocket.

As he did, he saw himself dying in a fusillade of Secret Service bullets. And then he crouched, gripped the revolver's handle with both hands, and aimed.

Goodbye, he thought. *Goodbye to myself.*

He pulled the trigger. Blue flame spat from the gun.

THE FIRST PERSON hit was Reagan's press secretary, Jim Brady, who'd been standing a few feet from the rope and just in front of the president. Hinckley's bullet smashed into Brady's head, and the press secretary toppled. He fell so close to Hinckley that he nearly landed on him.

Officer Thomas Delahanty had turned away from the crowd to check Reagan's progress toward the limousine when he heard the sharp sound of gunfire. Instinctively, he pivoted to shield the president, but then he fell hard to the ground, wounded in the back by Hinckley's second shot. "I am hit!" he screamed.

The sight line between Hinckley and the president was now clear. Hinckley's third shot sailed over Reagan's head.

Positioned at the limousine's rear door, Agent Tim McCarthy whirled to face the gunfire. He assumed a blocking stance and spread his arms, becoming an extension of the armored door. As the president and Jerry Parr vanished behind the agent's body, Hinckley's fourth shot hit McCarthy in the chest, spinning him to the ground.

The fifth bullet slapped the bulletproof window of the backward-opening limousine door as Reagan and Parr flashed behind it.

The sixth shot cracked across the driveway.

It was 2:27 p.m. Just 1.7 seconds had elapsed since Hinckley's first shot, and now three men lay wounded.

SITTING AT THE Lincoln's wheel, Drew Unrue couldn't believe what was happening. He heard gunfire through the open door and watched his friend Tim McCarthy fall; then Jerry Parr and the president landed in a heap on the floor between the limousine's front and rear seats. He saw agents and police officers draw their guns as spectators scattered. Unrue wanted to slam his foot on the accelerator and speed away from the hotel, but the limousine's backward-opening rear door hadn't been closed and might shear off if it hit an obstacle. An age seemed to pass before Ray Shaddick finally shut the door. Unrue's foot was already moving for the gas pedal when Parr screamed, "Let's get out of here! Haul ass!"

Unrue aimed the heavy limousine for T Street and with his right hand flipped the switch that activated the car's lights and siren. As he peeled away, he replayed the sight of Tim McCarthy falling to the sidewalk near his rear right wheel. *God, don't let me run over Timmy*, prayed Unrue. *I hope I don't run over Timmy.*

AGENT DENNIS MCCARTHY—no relation to Tim McCarthy—had been scouring the crowd of reporters and spectators behind the rope line, looking for trouble, as the president walked through the VIP doors. Then he heard what he thought were firecrackers—until he saw bodies falling and spectators ducking and people running for their lives.

But where was the gun? Suddenly he saw it: a black pistol in the hands of a man who was crouching between a photographer and the wall and inching toward the president as he fired. Desperate, the agent hurled himself at the pistol. *I have got to get to it,* his mind screamed. *I have got to get to it and stop it.*

As he slammed into the attacker and they fell to the ground, the gunman kept pulling the trigger. Despite the screaming and tussling and commotion, McCarthy could clearly hear the hammer *click, click, click*ing against the revolver's now-spent cylinder.

Sergeant Herbert Granger was facing the president when he heard the first cracks of gunfire. Whipping around, he spotted a blond man in a combat crouch. The gunman was holding a small revolver with both hands and firing at the president, tracking his target from right to left. Granger lunged toward the shooter, but his body felt strangely sluggish, as if he were moving through syrup. He heard screams and his own grunting, but they echoed in his ears like an audiotape being played on its slowest setting. He was puzzled by the gunman's blank and emotionless expression; then he watched as an elderly man in a yellow sweater raised his arms and slammed them down on the neck of the assailant. "Kill the son of a bitch!" the old man yelled. "I'll kill you!" Meanwhile, another man was throwing wild punches at the shooter.

Granger's vision narrowed. It seemed to take forever to reach the gunman, but he arrived at almost the same moment as Dennis McCarthy. Then a flurry of agents and officers crashed into them, propelling McCarthy, Granger, and the gunman into the stone wall with such force that the sergeant's Timex watch shattered.

At the bottom of the pile, Dennis McCarthy handcuffed the attacker, who offered no resistance. McCarthy scrambled up from the sidewalk, his mind repeating a single thought: *We have to keep him alive, we have to keep him alive.* Now his job was to protect the assailant instead of the president—there mustn't be another Lee Harvey Oswald.

A roiling mass of people—agents, police officers, journalists, and spectators—converged on McCarthy, Granger, and the gunman, many of them screaming or shouting.

"Get out of the way!"

"Back up, back up!"

"Get me a squad car!"

"You motherfucker!"

"Call an ambulance!"

A police car appeared, and a scrum of agents and police surrounded the would-be assassin and surged toward the car's rear door. McCarthy punched a man who stepped in their way. Another agent scrambled inside the squad car but couldn't get the right rear door to open. Outside the car, officers couldn't budge the door either—it was jammed.

"Let's move him to another car," McCarthy yelled. They hustled their suspect toward another police car that had just stopped on T Street, and after McCarthy opened the right rear door he jumped inside, dragging the gunman behind him by his handcuffed wrists.

A second later, they were joined by Dennis McCarthy's partner, Agent Danny Spriggs. He too was thinking about Oswald. They had to get the gunman away from the scene, but they needed to find someplace safe. Where to go? Spriggs ruled out the service's Washington field office—located on busy L Street, it would be too crowded with civilians, and escorting the shooter through the office's public lobby would be a nightmare. No, they should go to D.C. police headquarters. It was built like a fortress, and it had an underground garage and a secure cell area. "Head to police headquarters," Spriggs told the officer driving the cruiser.

McCarthy thrust his prisoner's hands onto the grate that separated the front and back seats. He wanted to keep those hands where he could see them.

"I think my wrist is broken," the man said. "Can you loosen the handcuffs?"

McCarthy exploded. "You are fuckin' lucky that's the only god-damned thing that is broken!"

AT THE FIRST sound of gunfire, Agent Jim Varey watched Reagan being thrown into the limousine and then turned to find the gunman. But when he saw that the assailant was already under a pile of agents and officers, his attention shifted to the three men lying on the ground. One was his friend Tim McCarthy; another was a police officer. The third was Jim Brady, the president's press secretary, who lay at the agent's feet. Brady was moaning and blood was already pooling on the concrete by his head.

Varey dropped to his knees and put his face right up to Brady's where it lay on the sidewalk. "Can you hear me?" he asked.

Brady twitched, and Varey thought he heard him say yes.

"Don't move," Varey said. "Help is coming."

Rick Ahearn, the presidential advance man, had been standing near Reagan when the shooting started. Now he rushed to Brady's side and helped apply pressure to the press secretary's wounds. Stunned, Ahearn felt blood and bits of brain oozing into his hands. He felt as if he were holding his friend's head together.

AGENT MARY ANN Gordon leaped from the front passenger seat in the lead police cruiser when the shooting started and sprinted toward the president. She stopped when she realized that the Lincoln's doors were shut and the limousine was already speeding off. She turned and started back toward the lead police car, but it was now too far away. She looked around and saw the spare limousine right in front of her. She opened the left rear door and darted inside. "Let's go!" she yelled to the driver.

Dan Ruge, who was standing near the spare limousine when the gunfire erupted, moved toward the scene of the shooting and carefully studied the clothing of each of the three wounded men. He was looking for the president's blue suit: every morning, he committed the president's wardrobe to memory in case of an emergency like this one. Ruge didn't see the suit.

A Secret Service agent was shouting at him. "Doctor, get in that car!" The agent pointed to the spare limousine, which was about to pull away. Ruge turned from the scene and hurried into the car's back seat, just as Mary Ann Gordon climbed over the front seat and took her place next to the driver.

The spare limousine raced after the president's Lincoln.

AFTER RAY SHADDICK pushed Jerry Parr and the president into the back of the limousine and shut its door, his first impulse was to jump into the front passenger seat. One agent always rode shotgun in the presidential limousine, and Parr was already in the passenger compartment with Reagan. But Shaddick didn't want to risk opening the door for another gunman; besides, all of Stagecoach's doors were now locked tight and the president was secure inside. Shaddick turned and took a quick inventory of the scene: Brady was down and so were a cop and his man Tim McCarthy. Shaddick wanted to help them, but his job was to guard the president, not deliver first aid. He ran to the armored follow-up car.

He scrambled into the Cadillac's front passenger seat and picked up the car's radio handset. "We've had shots fired, shots fired," he said. "There are some injuries."

Shaddick told the driver of the follow-up car to pull away. As he did, two other agents jumped on board. One climbed through the open right rear door, picked up an Uzi, and took a position on the left running board. The other agent, who had sprinted alongside the departing presidential limousine, hopped on the opposite running board and was handed an Uzi by another agent inside the car. The car sped off, just seconds behind the presidential and spare limousines.

THE ASSAILANT'S GUN had only just stopped firing; it was still 2:27 p.m. Spectators ran for cover. Agents and police officers, revolvers in their hands, shouted warnings and instructions. Reporters pulled their notebooks out and began looking for people to interview. Television cameramen continued shooting video; photographers kept snapping pictures.

All around them, people were frightened and upset—a number of them were crying. Questions started flying through the crowd. Is this part of an exercise? Is the president all right? Are there other gunmen? Is this really happening?

Across T Street, spectators and bystanders stood frozen, staring in bewilderment at the scene and the fleeing limousines and cars. But one woman sprinted straight toward the melee. It was Carolyn Parr, who had been standing directly across the street when the world turned to chaos. As she ran, she prayed that Jerry was safe. Seeing an agent holding an Uzi and standing with his back braced against the hotel's stone wall, she ran toward him.

"My husband!" she screamed. "My husband!"

The agent pointed up the street. "He's with the Man," he yelled, his submachine gun pointed into the air. "He's okay! He's okay! He's in the car!"

CHAPTER 7

"I CAN'T BREATHE"

A S THE PRESIDENT'S LIMOUSINE HURTLED AWAY FROM THE HILTON, Jerry Parr glanced out the rear window. He counted three men down and wondered who had been hit. Turning, he noticed the telltale marks of a projectile's impact on the right rear door's bullet-proof window. Parr had no idea what was happening. Was this a terrorist attack? Was the world at war? It occurred to him that he might have been hurt, too, but he gave himself a quick once-over and decided he was fine. He took a deep breath, turned to the president, and helped him into the limousine's right rear seat. Reagan sat slumped forward—he looked like an exhausted basketball player taking a breather on the bench.

"Were you hit?" Parr asked.

"No, I don't think so," Reagan said. "I think you hurt my chest when you landed on top of me."

Parr quickly examined Reagan's mouth and nose for damage or obstructions, then ran his hands along the president's white shirt and through his hair. He felt nothing unusual. He inspected his own hands. No blood. *Thank God.*

Parr fumbled for the radio strapped to his belt, but it wasn't there. In the scramble for the car, it had been ripped away from his earpiece and sleeve microphone. Parr swiveled to Unrue. "Give me the radio."

Unrue handed him the microphone, its cord connected to the dashboard.

"Rawhide is okay, follow-up," Parr radioed Shaddick in the follow-up car. "Rawhide is okay."

"Halfback, roger," Shaddick replied. "You want to go to the hospital or back to the White House?"

"We're going, we're going to Crown," Parr said, using the code name for the White House.

"Okay," Shaddick said.

A few seconds later, Parr turned back to Reagan. Despite his assurance that he was all right, the president looked as if he was in pain.

"I think you hurt my rib," he growled. "I'm having trouble breathing."

"Is it your heart?" Parr asked.

"I don't think so," Reagan replied.

Reagan was pressing his left arm hard against his chest. Reaching into his right jacket pocket, the president pulled out a paper napkin that he'd taken from the hotel's holding room. He wiped it on his lips. When he pulled the napkin away, it was coated in blood.

"I think I cut the inside of my mouth," he said.

Half kneeling, half sitting in the speeding limousine, Parr leaned in and studied the napkin. Then he spotted more blood on the president's lips.

HUNCHED FORWARD IN the driver's seat, with the limousine's sirens wailing and its hood-mounted flags flapping in the wind, Drew Unrue tried to keep calm and alert as they sped down Connecticut Avenue. There was no traffic, because D.C. police had shut down all the intersections in anticipation of the president's departure from the Hilton.

Unrue's big worry, though, was that he would hit something. As they sped away from the hotel, he had swerved just in time to avoid crashing into a stalled police car. Then, as they raced down Connecticut Avenue, a woman pushed a stroller into their path. Unrue dodged left, barely missing her. "Don't hit anything," Unrue repeated to himself as he checked his mirrors and watched the road ahead. "Don't make this worse."

It didn't help that they were alone. They'd pulled away from the Hilton so fast that they'd left the rest of the motorcade behind. Unrue checked the rearview mirror again but still didn't see the follow-up car.

He forced his mind to slow down. This was the most important drive of his life, and he could not afford to make a mistake. *Don't compound this,* he thought.

He scanned the road ahead and then took another quick look in the rearview mirror. This time he spotted the spare limousine and the black follow-up car, both racing to catch the Lincoln. At least he was no longer alone.

A few moments later, the spare and the follow-up car drew up behind them. Unrue saw two agents, their Uzis drawn, clinging to the armored Cadillac's running boards. About a mile from the Hilton, the tan Lincoln pulled to the right and allowed Halfback to race ahead and settle in behind the president's limousine, in its proper spot.

D.C. police officers were not far behind, and soon at least one squad car and several motorcycles sped ahead of the Secret Service vehicles, taking the lead. The president now had a makeshift motorcade.

IN THE BACK of Stagecoach, Jerry Parr examined the president. Not only was his face gray, his lips seemed a little blue. Clearly Reagan had been hurt in some way—was a rib broken? And whatever his injury, could it be treated by doctors at the White House?

Parr spun quickly through his options, wondering whether they should return to the White House or head straight to the nearest hospital. But what if the assassination attempt was part of a coordinated attack? What if there were other assassins out there? In that case, the White House was the safest place on earth, and that was where he should go. Besides, if he decided to take the president to a hospital and he hadn't been seriously injured, the visit might unnecessarily panic the country or trigger a financial crisis. Moreover, the hospital wouldn't be guarded, so he would be putting the president at great risk, especially if coconspirators were lurking there, waiting, if need be, to finish the job.

Still, what if Reagan was badly injured? Going to the White House could be disastrous; they'd be much better off at the nearest trauma center, in this case the one at George Washington University Hospital.

Parr weighed the two options. Neither seemed particularly good.

He looked again at the president. Having soaked the napkin with blood, Reagan was now pressing his handkerchief to his lips. Parr examined the blood more closely. He noted that it looked frothy, which meant that it was probably oxygenated and coming from the president's lungs. This was no cut lip—the president had likely suffered some kind of lung injury.

"I think we should go to the hospital," Parr told Reagan.

"Okay," said the president.

Parr turned forward and hollered at Unrue. "Get us to George Washington as fast as you can."

Unrue picked up his radio microphone. "Gordon, Unrue," he said, speaking to Mary Ann Gordon in the spare limousine.

"Go ahead, Drew," Gordon responded.

"We want to go to the emergency room of George Washington," Unrue said.

"That's a roger," Gordon said.

"Go to George Washington *fast*," Unrue said.

Parr grabbed the radio microphone from Unrue and asked Ray Shaddick if he had received that last transmission. Shaddick replied that he had.

"Get an ambulance, I mean, get a stretcher out there," Parr said. "Let's hustle."

Lights flashing and sirens screaming, the motorcade streaked across L Street. They were now about a mile from the hospital.

IN THE FRONT passenger seat of the spare limousine, Mary Ann Gordon tried to reach the lead police car by radio. "We're going to GW hospital," she told the police sergeant.

But she received no reply and wasn't sure the sergeant had heard her. Worse, if the motorcycles and squad car missed the turn onto Pennsylvania Avenue for the trip to the hospital, the presidential limousine would be exposed. She needed another vehicle to get in front of Stagecoach to help clear traffic and act as a battering ram if confronted by assailants. Gordon also didn't want Unrue to worry about how to get to GW.

"We have to get in front of the limo," Gordon told her driver. He immediately swept around the follow-up car, accelerated past the president's limousine, and pulled in front of it.

As Connecticut Avenue turned into Seventeenth Street, Gordon looked ahead and saw the police cars and motorcycles continue straight for the White House. The spare limousine made the sharp right onto Pennsylvania Avenue; a moment later, Gordon spotted a Secret Service sedan ahead of them. It was the so-called route car, which always preceded the motorcade by five minutes to ensure that the streets were free of trouble. Its driver and the agent riding with him had heard the radio transmissions about the decision to go to the hospital and were now clearing a path through traffic. His siren wailing, the driver of the route car honked his horn, flashed his headlights, and sped through each intersection ahead of the motorcade.

The president's limousine had just six blocks to go.

ONLY JERRY PARR knew why the motorcade was racing to the hospital. Mary Ann Gordon and Ray Shaddick had no idea what had happened; even Drew Unrue, who assumed Reagan had been injured while being pushed into the car, didn't know how seriously the president had been hurt.

Reagan's top aides were also at sea. Two of them were already on their way to the hospital: Mike Deaver and David Fischer, along with the president's military aide, were riding in the control car, just behind the makeshift motorcade. After the shooting, Deaver had scrambled for the door of the president's limousine but couldn't open it. Then he spotted Fischer, the president's body man, huddled nearby and pointing at the control car. "We have to get to that car!" Fischer yelled at Deaver.

A minute or two later, as they careened down Seventeenth Street,

Fischer reached over and squeezed Deaver's hand. "Everything is going to be okay, Mike."

Fischer saw the limousine turn in what seemed to be the wrong direction, down Pennsylvania Avenue and away from the White House. The control car made the same pivot, and soon Fischer realized that the president's motorcade must be heading toward the hospital.

Now Fischer was sure something terrible had happened. Holding back tears, he started to pray, for Reagan and for the men left behind at the Hilton. He couldn't stop his hands from shaking.

A FEW BLOCKS away, in the Secret Service command post underneath the Oval Office, Agent Joe Trainor was monitoring traffic on police and Secret Service radios and a stack of scanners. Once Ray Shaddick reported the shooting, the radios went berserk, and he had called a supervisor into the room to help him. Trainor could barely make out what people were saying through the screeching of sirens. As soon as he learned that the president's limousine was on its way back to the White House, he spoke by phone with the uniformed division of the Secret Service. He had to make sure the limousine could get inside the White House perimeter quickly. "Open all the gates," he told an officer.

A minute later, when Trainor heard that the motorcade was heading to George Washington University Hospital instead, he picked up the phone again and asked the White House signal operator to patch him through to a special telephone in GW's emergency room.

"Hold on for a second," the operator said.

While he waited, Trainor heard Shaddick's voice speak from the radio in front of him asking if he had heard the transmissions about going to GW.

Trainor replied that he had and that he was calling GW now.

Just then a woman answered the phone Trainor was holding to his ear. He presumed it was a nurse in the emergency room.

"This is Agent Trainor at the White House," he said. "The president is en route to the emergency room."

"Has he been shot?"

"I'm not sure," Trainor said. "I don't think so. Three other people may have been wounded and are also en route. Tell every doctor to get to the emergency room. And please make sure a stretcher is ready at the entrance."

As the motorcade neared GW, Drew Unrue asked Jerry Parr if they should head the wrong way around the traffic circle in front of the hospital to save time. "No, go around the circle," Parr said. He didn't want to risk crashing into oncoming traffic.

Tires squealing, the Lincoln sped around the circle and jerked to a stop in front of the emergency room doors, its right side facing the hospital entrance.

Parr looked out the window. No one was waiting for them.

The two agents with Uzis jumped from the running boards of the follow-up car, and Ray Shaddick leaped from its passenger seat. Shaddick opened the back right door of the presidential limousine; Parr slipped past the president and got out first, then put his hand out for the president. Reagan shook his head, as if to say "I can do it myself."

I guess he wants to be a cowboy, Parr thought, momentarily reassured that the president seemed to be strong enough to get out of the limousine under his own power.

Mary Ann Gordon and Dan Ruge emerged from the spare limousine, and a moment later Mike Deaver, David Fischer, and the military aide got out of the control car. They all moved quickly toward the president's limousine.

Reagan climbed out of the Lincoln and stood up. He steadied himself and hitched up his pants, a reflex that Deaver and Fischer had seen hundreds of times.

So far, so good, thought Deaver.

Fischer felt less sanguine: he thought Reagan looked sick and gray. But Fischer could see that his boss was determined to walk unaided through the ER doors.

Parr took a position to the president's left, Shaddick to his right. Others stood nearby while an agent went ahead to run interference and scout for trouble in the hospital's hallway.

Surrounded by his guards, the president shuffled uneasily through the hospital's sliding glass doors. It was 2:30 p.m.

BEFORE THE PRESIDENT'S arrival, it had been a typical afternoon in the busy emergency room of George Washington University Hospital, a 512-bed medical center near downtown Washington. Nurses in green scrubs and doctors in white lab coats worked under the yellowish haze of fluorescent lights, checking on a dozen or so patients suffering from colds, broken bones, and more serious maladies. They treated at least one person who had overdosed on drugs and another who'd experienced a stroke. In a secure room, they evaluated a psychiatric patient who seemed deeply troubled. The tiled floors and walls, which gave off a faint odor of disinfectant, echoed with the din of hospital chatter—nurses questioning patients about their pains and headaches and fevers, doctors providing diagnoses of illnesses and injuries.

In Trauma Bay 5, a curtained-off area on the northeast side of the ER crammed with equipment and supplies, Dr. Joyce Mitchell, an attending emergency-room physician, was examining an elderly woman who had suffered a heart attack. The woman had arrived in the ER that afternoon and been stabilized; she was now resting on a gurney near a wall of shelves stacked with medical equipment, gauze pads, medication, monitors, tubes, instruments, and clean sheets. As Mitchell prepared to transfer the woman to intensive care, a police radio crackled in the hands of a nearby officer who was taking a report.

The policeman pressed the radio to his ear and listened for a few seconds. Then he spoke in a loud, angry voice. "I'm tired of my buddies getting shot down!"

"Please," an ER nurse said. "Keep your voice down."

The officer became more upset. "There's a cop down, there is a cop down at the Hilton!" he shouted. "The president was there."

Mitchell knew that anyone shot at the Hilton could be coming their way. She immediately turned to Kathy Paul, an experienced emergency room nurse, and said, "Maybe you should set up the other room for a trauma patient. It sounds like somebody has been shot at the Hilton."

The elderly woman on the gurney was wheeled to a nearby room, and a nurse drew a curtain that divided the trauma bay into two units, 5A and 5B.

A moment later, a small white telephone began to ring at the ER nurses' station. Tucked away in the corner of the desk, it was the special White House telephone, which was never to be touched unless it rang. It was a direct line to the White House signal operator, installed sometime in the 1970s to speed communication between the White House and its closest emergency room.

A busy clerk at the nurses' station ignored the ringing. Wendy Koenig, a nurse doing paperwork within reach of the phone, watched and listened as it rang once, then twice. On the rare occasions when the white telephone rang, it usually stopped after a couple of rings—perhaps someone at the White House had dialed the wrong number. But this time the phone rang a third time. Koenig answered.

Before she could say a word, a gruff male voice told her that the presidential motorcade was on its way to the hospital. Then the line went silent.

Koenig's face turned white. "The presidential motorcade is on its way," she told the assistant nurse in charge of the unit, Judith Whinerey.

"That means the president is coming here," Whinerey said. "Let's assume it's the president."

Whinerey, who had been gathering her things to leave for a doctor's appointment, picked up the phone and got her doctor on the line. "I have to cancel," she told her. "The president is coming here. Turn on your television."

Whinerey hung up and began calling the heads of every department and specialty in the hospital. If the president really was coming to GW, she wanted the hospital's most experienced doctors on hand in the ER. Her hands trembled as she flipped through the hospital's phone book. "I'm so nervous that my hands, they won't stop shaking," Whinerey told a clerk as she cradled two telephones to her ears. "You have to help me."

"You'll be fine," the clerk replied. "I can't help you. My hands are shaking, too."

A minute later, the White House telephone rang again. This time, the clerk at the nurse's station picked it up.

"We have three gunshot wounds coming in," a voice said. Again the line went dead. Wendy Koenig hurried to the trauma bay to get intravenous lines and equipment ready for arrivals. Joyce Mitchell and Kathy Paul headed toward the emergency room's entrance. All over the hospital, pagers chirped and loudspeakers barked the names of doctors who were needed immediately in the ER.

Near the nurses' station, Frederick White, a Secret Service administrator who happened to be in the ER on personal business, watched the commotion and stood up after he heard a nurse announce, "Attention everyone, the president's motorcade is on its way here!" White approached the nurse, identified himself, and suggested they clear the emergency room. She agreed, and White helped usher about a dozen patients from the ER into a hallway. He then walked to the emergency room's entrance and told a security guard to hold open the sliding glass doors in case the president had to be rushed inside. As White stood just outside the open doors, he heard the sound of sirens approaching from Pennsylvania Avenue; a moment later, he saw the president's limousine race around the traffic circle. Right behind it was the follow-up car—and when he saw the two men clinging to the running boards and holding Uzis, he knew something awful had happened.

KATHY PAUL WATCHED as President Reagan hobbled through the open glass doors. He and his entourage walked over a rubber mat with arrows pointing to the emergency room, then passed an admissions area and approached another set of glass doors.

Paul stepped to the president's side and braced her right hand under his left arm. She thought he looked terrible—ashen and very sick. She noticed a spot of blood on his lips.

"This is the president, let's get to the emergency room," a Secret Service agent yelled.

"I feel like I can't breathe," Reagan told Paul. "I can't breathe."

"Come this way," she answered, gently coaxing the president toward the trauma bay.

Joyce Mitchell, the ER doctor, felt suddenly overwhelmed by the knowledge that she was in charge. Collecting herself, she addressed the Secret Service agents accompanying Reagan. "Was he shot?" she asked.

"No, we think he got an elbow in the ribs," one agent said.

"Maybe broke a rib when we pushed him into the limousine," said another.

Mitchell wasn't convinced; the president looked so bad that she thought he might be having a heart attack.

Bob Hernandez, a paramedic who had earlier brought in the cardiac patient and had just finished writing up a report, stepped out of a small office and into the hallway. His partner followed him. Seeing the president and several Secret Service agents walking toward him, Hernandez froze. As it happened, the two men had trailed Reagan in their ambulance during the inaugural parade, and they had been told that a sudden move near the president might cause the Secret Service to pounce. Now, they both stood like statues until Reagan was within arm's reach.

Studying the president as he shuffled forward, Hernandez immediately noticed several things: Reagan's legs wobbled and his steps seemed uncertain; his eyes were glazed and he seemed to be staring off into the distance; his arms were locked at his sides. Hernandez thought the president was on the verge of collapse.

An agent yelled for a wheelchair, but he was too late. Just as they passed through the second set of glass doors, Reagan's eyes rolled to the back of his head, his legs buckled, and he toppled toward the floor. Jerry Parr and Ray Shaddick caught him before he hit the ground.

"Don't make him walk!" one of the paramedics shouted.

Parr and Shaddick grasped the president's arms. The two paramedics held his legs, as did Kathy Paul. With Joyce Mitchell hovering alongside, the clutch of medical personnel and agents lifted 196 pounds of dead weight and rushed the president into the ER. Turning left, they surged past the nurses' station and several examination rooms. Once they reached the trauma bay, they gently placed Reagan on a gurney.

Paul was dizzy. Her hands were shaking. She couldn't believe her own eyes: the president of the United States was having a heart attack right here in the ER! She realized that she was pleading silently, repeating the same thought over and over. *Please don't die, please don't die, please don't die. Not here. Not today. Please don't die.*

Hernandez, the paramedic, was convinced the president wasn't going to make it. He looked like a heart attack victim in the final moments of life. *My God, he's Code City,* Hernandez thought—paramedic jargon for someone about to die.

Paul, still struggling to keep calm, leaned over and spoke into Reagan's ear. "We're going to cut your clothes off and stick some needles into your arms to pump in fluid and draw blood."

"I feel so bad," Reagan said. "I really feel awful. I can't breathe."

Paul loosened the president's tie, ripped apart his white shirt, and began slicing at his suit with scissors so nurses and technicians could insert intravenous lines and take Reagan's blood pressure. Paul noticed blood on the president's left hand. She still couldn't stop her own hands from trembling, and she felt her skin getting hot and splotchy.

Another ER nurse elevated the foot of the bed to force more blood toward the president's heart and head. A technician who had just arrived in the trauma bay helped Kathy Paul cut off his suit jacket. The technician then jabbed a three-foot-long IV line into a vein in Reagan's right arm and snaked it to his heart so that it could supply fluids and measure how the heart was functioning. A smaller line was inserted into a vein in his left arm. The nurses and the technician were following standard ER procedures: strip, insert IVs, start fluids.

"I've got a line!" the technician shouted.

At first the technician was so busy that she didn't look at her patient's face. As usual, she had responded to the emergency call by getting to the trauma bay as fast as she could and then going right to work. But now she noticed that several men in suits surrounded the patient, and that some of them had radio plugs jammed in their ears. She also thought one or two of them were holding guns. Finally she looked closely at the patient's face and realized that it was President Reagan. Dizzy and disoriented, she swiveled, grabbed a pack of smelling salts from a box on a shelf, and inhaled. A moment later, she returned to the president's side.

Herndanez pulled off Reagan's shoes and socks and began yanking at his pants, hoping to pop the button. But his trousers wouldn't budge.

What are these, made of steel? he wondered as he kept tugging. When they finally came off, Hernandez's partner cut away the president's boxer shorts with a pair of bandage scissors. He left the shredded undershorts on the table; the rest of the president's clothes had already fallen into a pile on the floor.

Wendy Koenig had helped cut away the president's shirt, and while doing so she noticed that it was stitched with the monogram "RR." When she looked into Reagan's ashen face, she saw that he was laboring to breathe and seemed about to go into shock. *He's barely hanging on,* she thought. *He's going to die.* Her hands started shaking. She fought back tears. Suddenly her mind flashed on two images. In the first, it was 1963 and she had just come home to find her dad sobbing in front of the television. The second was a vivid and recent nightmare in which Reagan had been wheeled into the ER and then died from a heart attack.

Now, trying to refocus, Koenig wrapped a blood pressure cuff around the president's left arm, put her stethoscope under the device, and began to inflate the sleeve to constrict blood flow. She released the pressure and listened for the telltale thump of Reagan's systolic blood pressure. But she couldn't hear anything above the din in the trauma bay.

"I can't get a systolic pressure," Koenig told the nurses and doctors around the gurney.

Koenig repeated the procedure. Again, she heard nothing.

"Oh, shit, try it again!" Mitchell shouted. "Try again!"

SINCE ENTERING THE ER, Jerry Parr had stayed as close as possible to the president. As the nurses and technicians cut away Reagan's clothes, he'd turned to Ray Shaddick and said, "Set up a perimeter." He also told a nurse to prevent any unnecessary hospital personnel from coming into the ER.

But now there was nothing left for Parr to do. He watched the flurry of activity around the president; he heard a nurse trying to take Reagan's blood pressure yell, "I can't hear anything!"

He felt sick, helpless. What had happened? What had gone wrong? When he pushed the president into the limousine, had he caused one of Reagan's ribs to puncture a lung or some other organ? Had he caused a heart attack? He felt nauseous and terrified. If the president died, it would be his fault. He shouldn't have pushed him so hard.

Watching the nurses struggle to take the president's blood pressure, Parr felt overwhelmed by an awful thought: *Oh, my God, we have lost him. We've lost another one.* Parr had never been a religious man, but he felt something surging within him. *Lord be with him,* he prayed.

Then the agent stepped up to the gurney and gently patted Reagan on the head. He didn't want the president to feel alone, so he leaned over and looked him in the eyes. *Let him live,* Parr prayed. *God, let him live!*

CHAPTER 8

THE TRAUMA BAY

A GENT GEORGE OPFER, THE HEAD OF NANCY REAGAN'S SECRET Service detail, was looking forward to a productive afternoon. It had been an easy day so far, and the first lady wasn't scheduled to leave the White House grounds again, which meant he would have time to catch up on paperwork. But as he eased into a chair at a desk in W-16, the Secret Service command post beneath the Oval Office, he wondered about the first lady's abrupt departure from a lunch in Georgetown a little while earlier. Something had been bothering Mrs. Reagan— she didn't seem sick, just anxious and unsettled—and she had told Opfer to take her home. He had promptly escorted her from the luncheon. By the time he drove inside the White House gates at about 2:20 p.m., Mrs. Reagan seemed calmer.

The first lady immediately went upstairs to meet with her decorator and the White House usher about her plans for renovating the residence. Opfer returned to the command post, where he planned to spend the next couple of hours scheduling his team of seven agents. Happily, the week ahead was fairly routine. The first lady's next major engagement wasn't for two days, when she would be attending a lunch with the wife of Lloyd Bentsen, a Democratic senator, at Mrs. Bentsen's home.

Opfer—a lean, blond New Yorker who sometimes received fan mail from young women who'd spotted his photograph in the newspapers when he happened to be standing next to Mrs. Reagan—had been assigned to guard the eventual first lady even before the November election determined who that would be. When Reagan triumphed, one of the service's top agents, John Simpson, asked Opfer to pay him a visit. In June 1968, Simpson had led a team assigned to protect Reagan when he was an undeclared candidate for the Republican nomination, and he'd become friendly with the Reagans over the years. He knew Opfer would be apprehensive about guarding Mrs. Reagan, who had a reputation for being demanding and sometimes less than understanding when things didn't go her way, so he offered some advice: "Don't listen to the stories, because they are wrong. Make your own evaluation when you get out there. And one more thing: the Reagans really are a modern-day love story. So be prepared for that."

In November 1980, while protecting Nancy Reagan at the couple's Pacific Palisades home, Opfer had his first encounter with the president-elect. Mrs. Reagan introduced the two men; Reagan looked Opfer in the eye and said, with a bit of an edge in his voice, "Well, George, make sure you take good care of her."

The hair on the back of Opfer's neck stood up. Intentionally or not, there was something a little threatening in Reagan's delivery, as if to let Opfer know that mistakes would not be tolerated. Opfer imagined being shipped off to some remote field office if he screwed up.

Now, as he sat in the command post and jotted notes on his scheduling forms, his earpiece suddenly came alive with radio traffic: there had been a shooting at the Hilton and the president was being rushed back to the White House. Opfer looked up and saw a supervisor and an agent frantically working the radios and phones in the communications area.

Opfer bolted from his chair and rushed over to see what was happening. The agent at the bank of radios said the president "had shots fired at him," and the supervisor told Opfer to inform Mrs. Reagan that there had been an incident at the Hilton. As he raced for the stairs, he heard over his radio that the motorcade had changed course and was heading to GW. He knew the agents wouldn't divert to the hospital without a good reason, which meant the president was almost certainly injured.

Now Opfer was desperate to reach Mrs. Reagan before she heard about the incident from someone else. He was certain that if he arrived even a few seconds behind the news, he'd be chasing the first lady across the White House driveway as she ran for the hospital. If he had learned one thing in the past few months, it was that Mrs. Reagan was her own woman. Especially in a crisis, she would never take orders from him. So it was critical that he get to her right away, approach her with extreme care, and somehow manage the situation as it evolved. Above all, he had to protect her from acting impulsively and putting herself in harm's way. He knew she would stop at nothing to be at her husband's side.

Opfer's heart pounded as he took the stairs two at a time to the third floor of the residence and the White House solarium. As he neared the door to the solarium, he tried to calm down. Then he put on his best poker face, opened the door, and walked up the ramp leading into the room.

As Opfer entered, the first lady was talking to Ted Garber, the Reagans' decorator, and Rex Scouten, the chief White House usher. When Opfer caught Mrs. Reagan's eye, the first lady seemed puzzled; then as she walked toward him, her expression became anxious, and suddenly he felt certain that she knew that something awful had just happened.

In his calmest and most measured voice, Opfer told her, "There was a shooting when the president was departing the Hilton hotel. My information is that your husband was not injured, but others have been shot. The president is going to the hospital."

The first lady's eyebrows furrowed and she instantly seized on the obvious question. "George, why would they be taking him to the hospital if he wasn't hurt?"

"It's just precautionary," he replied, hoping that this invention would allay her fears until he could learn whether a trip to the hospital would even be safe. For one thing, he worried that other assailants might target Mrs. Reagan or anyone trying to approach the hospital; for another, he knew nothing about the president's condition. If he'd been seriously wounded, it might be traumatic for the first lady to see him.

"Besides," the agent added, "maybe he is insisting on seeing the condition of the other people who were wounded."

Before Opfer could utter another word, he was looking at Nancy Reagan's back. She was hurrying for the elevator.

"I'm going to the hospital," she said. "If you don't get me a car, I'm going to walk."

"No, let's wait and see what happens," Opfer said, following her. "It's a madhouse over there. He'll probably be coming right back to the White House any minute."

"No, I'm going to the hospital," she said.

"Once we get the all clear, I'll take you over," he said.

"No, I'm going now," she replied.

There was no point in arguing. "Okay," Opfer said. "How about this, give me a couple of minutes to have the cars ready and we can go."

"Fine," she said.

With Opfer leading the way, they took the stairs down to the ground floor. Then they headed for the diplomatic entrance to the White House, where the first lady's two-car motorcade would assemble. He could hear Mrs. Reagan right behind him—she was nearly clipping his heels.

"George, when are we going?" He heard a note of panic in her voice.

"As soon as the cars are ready," he answered.

By now Opfer had radioed instructions to prepare the motorcade. When the two agency sedans pulled up outside the diplomatic entrance, Opfer took his place in the front passenger seat of the first black car. Mrs. Reagan, wearing her red raincoat, sat in the back and was joined by her spokeswoman. Opfer made sure the doors were locked, as much to keep the first lady in as to keep danger out.

The two cars pulled out of the White House and onto Pennsylvania Avenue for the short ride to the hospital. The radio in Opfer's ear fed him a steady stream of information, but since the radio's frequency was unsecured the reports weren't very specific. He still didn't know how badly the president had been hurt.

Only a block or two from the White House, the small motorcade encountered heavy traffic and came to a stop. They were stuck for just a few minutes, but to Opfer the wait seemed interminable.

Soon two hands gripped Opfer's shoulders from behind. "When am I going to get there to see him?" the first lady asked.

"We're moving," Opfer replied. "We'll get there soon."

A minute later, she seized his shoulders again. "George, I'm going to get out and walk. I need to get out and walk."

"No, no, we can't do that, it's not safe," Opfer said.

"I need to walk," she said. "I have to get there."

At last the traffic eased and they began making good progress. As soon as they reached the ER entrance, Opfer opened the car's rear door. He watched a blur of red raincoat run for the emergency room doors and then hurried to catch up.

IN THE CHAOS of the emergency room, Dan Ruge, the gray-haired and decorous White House physician, remained remarkably composed. As soon as he saw an opening, he stepped up to the gurney carrying the president and used one of his delicate fingers to find an artery in one of Reagan's feet. The president's pulse was steady, a good sign.

Before coming to Washington, Ruge, a neurosurgeon by training, had been a colleague of Loyal Davis, Nancy Reagan's stepfather. Ruge hadn't wanted the job of White House physician, but he accepted it after Davis, a respected neurosurgeon in Chicago, convinced him that the Reagans needed an experienced doctor to prevent anything "foolish" from being done to the president during his time in office. Now Ruge was being put to the test, and though he worried that Reagan had suffered a heart attack, he didn't have enough information to make a confident diagnosis. But it was not his job to treat the president; his first concern was that the doctors at GW not give Reagan special care. Exotic tests, diagnosis by committee, flying in experts from another city—such measures would take time and could put the president's life at even greater risk. As he stepped back from the gurney, Ruge was

determined to ensure that Reagan wasn't treated like a VIP. He immediately began telling doctors to handle the president exactly as they
would any other patient in his condition.

Only a few feet away, Mike Deaver and David Fischer were watching the unfolding emergency in stunned horror. The leader they both
revered seemed to be in terrible trouble.

Seeing Ruge, Deaver signaled him to come over. "Tell me what's
happening," he said.

"I don't know," Ruge replied. "Maybe he had a cardiac."

Deaver and Fischer were dumbstruck. They'd both watched the
president's speech at the Hilton; he had been so vibrant and alive, and
now he was pale and sickly and possibly having a heart attack. It was
too much for Fischer; tears streaked down his face.

Watching the frenzied efforts of the trauma bay's doctors and
nurses, Deaver recalled hearing about the chaos at Dallas's Parkland
Hospital, where John F. Kennedy had been rushed. Realizing that providing accurate information to the White House would be critical, he
ran to find a phone so he could call Jim Baker; Fischer followed. Deaver
had trouble getting through to the swamped White House switchboard, but an operator finally answered and transferred him to the
office of the chief of staff. An assistant picked up the phone.

"Find Jim," Deaver said. "Have someone hold this line open."

A moment later, Baker got on the phone.

Deaver quickly recounted what had happened at the Hilton and
then said, "We don't know what the problem is. It may be a heart attack."

Deaver turned to Fischer. "Go find out what's going on in there."

After Fischer hurried back to the trauma bay, a hospital worker in
green scrubs approached Deaver. "Do you know the name of the patient
in the emergency room?" he asked.

"Yes."

"Would you give me his name, please?"

"It's Reagan. R-E-A-G-A-N."

"First name?"

"Ron."

The hospital employee kept scribbling.

"Address?"

"Sixteen hundred Pennsylvania."

The man's pencil stopped moving.

"You mean . . . ?"

"Yes, you have the president of the United States in there."

THE VOLUME OF noise in the trauma bay was now so high that Wendy Koenig gave up on using a stethoscope and instead placed a finger over the brachial artery in the president's left arm, just below the blood pressure cuff. She inflated the device a third time, desperate to get a reading. Koenig released the air and waited; she sensed more than actually felt the bump as she watched the needle descend on the cuff's pressure gauge. Reagan's systolic blood pressure was about 60; his normal reading would be about 140. This was bad news: a reading of 60 indicated that he was in shock, and, as Koenig knew, most seventy-year-olds who came to the ER in a condition similar to Reagan's did not survive.

Only five or six minutes had elapsed since the assassination attempt. Nurses and technicians were pumping crystalloid fluid, a salt solution, into Reagan's body to boost his sagging blood pressure and reduce his chances of slipping further into shock. He had three IV lines running into his arms, and doctors had already ordered universal donor blood from the hospital blood bank.

Joyce Mitchell, the ER doctor, noticed the pile of clothes under the gurney and realized that Reagan's shirt was spotted with blood. She told an orderly to rush the shirt to the laboratory so they could determine the president's blood type. Another nurse drew blood from Reagan so it could be taken to the same lab. A moment later, another doctor turned to Jerry Parr: did he know the president's blood type?

"O positive," Parr replied.

By now, trauma surgeons were on their way to the emergency room. One of the first to arrive was William O'Neill, a thirty-year-old surgical intern who had been consulting with the family of a patient in a fourth-floor hallway when his pager started beeping. He politely excused himself and ran for the ER.

As he neared the nurses' station, two men in suits grabbed the five-foot, six-inch O'Neill and lifted him into the air. "Who are you?" they demanded.

"I'm Dr. O'Neill. I'm on the trauma team."

The agents flung O'Neill toward the trauma bay, where he found several doctors and nurses working frantically on a patient lying face-up on a gurney. His skin was gray and his lips were caked with blood. O'Neill, already experienced enough to make quick and fairly accurate assessments of new patients, thought the man might not survive.

All at once, O'Neill understood the scene around him. There was a reason the ER was so alive with activity: the well-dressed men he'd just encountered on his way here were Secret Service agents, and the man on the gurney was the president of the United States. He took a close look at the gray face of his patient and confirmed his identity.

O'Neill turned to the Secret Service agent who seemed to be in charge. "What happened?"

"There was a shooting and I shoved him into the car," the agent said. "I think he may have broken a rib."

O'Neill heard someone say that Reagan's blood pressure was now 80, already 20 points better than when it was first measured. The fluids were working.

The doctor leaned over the gurney. "Hello, Mr. President, how are you doing?" he asked. "Where are you hurting?"

"I'm having a hard time breathing," Reagan replied.

"Mr. President, do you know what happened?"

"Not really."

Other doctors joined O'Neill at the president's side, including Drew Scheele, another intern, who had been observing a surgery but wanted to see what was causing all the commotion in the ER. As he entered the trauma bay, he spotted the remnants of a nice blue suit on the floor. *What a waste of an expensive suit,* Scheele thought. He walked up to the gurney, made a quick assessment of the patient's condition, and placed an oxygen mask on the man's face.

The patient stared up at Scheele. "Am I dying?" the man asked through the mask.

"No, you're going to be fine," answered Scheele. In fact, he could see that the man was in serious condition; he had no idea whether the patient would live or die. He still hadn't focused on the man's face and so had no idea who he was.

G. Wesley Price, a surgical resident, arrived soon after Scheele. Price had already had a long night and day. A twenty-five-year-old man, shot several times in the abdomen, had died in surgery early that morning; afterward, Price had continued with his usual duties, checking on patients and working in the pathology lab. Just minutes earlier, he'd been in the lab when he heard sirens on Pennsylvania Avenue. Looking out an open window, he saw a motorcade speeding toward the hospital. He sprinted downstairs to the emergency room, where a crowd was gathering in the far corner by the trauma bay.

"Who's the patient?" Price asked a nurse.

"It's the president!" the nurse replied.

"You're kidding," Price said. He walked the final ten feet into Bay 5A and there was Reagan, now naked, lying on a gurney. Bags of fluids were suspended above him, and a urologist had already inserted a Foley catheter to remove his urine.

As he entered the room, Price spoke to Judith Whinerey, the assistant head nurse. "Who is in charge?" he asked.

"You are," replied Whinerey. Turning, she shouted to everyone in the bay, "Everybody, Dr. Price is here."

Price, a thirty-one-year-old fourth-year resident, was now the most senior surgeon in the room. The nurses and O'Neill told him what they knew: Reagan had walked into the ER and collapsed. His blood pressure was low, and they were giving him fluids and waiting on blood from the hospital blood bank.

"I can't breathe," the president said again. "My chest hurts."

Price leaned over his patient. "Hello, Mr. President, I'm Dr. Price." He pulled out his stethoscope and pressed it to the right side of the president's chest. It was difficult to hear anything in the din, but Price detected a light rush of air and decided the right lung sounded normal. But when he moved the stethoscope to the left side of Reagan's chest, he heard nothing, which meant the left lung wasn't functioning and had probably collapsed.

"I don't hear very good breath sounds on the left side," Price said. "We'd better roll him over."

As nurses and doctors gently turned Reagan onto his right side under the trauma bay's bright lights, Price noticed what appeared to be a small slit in the president's skin. Half an inch long, it was about five inches below the left armpit. A few drops of blood dribbled out of the wound.

Price turned to the Secret Service agent standing nearby—Jerry Parr—and asked what had happened. Parr briefly described the shooting and the chaos at the Hilton. As Parr finished, Daniel Ruge introduced himself to Price and told him that the president had coughed up blood on the way to the hospital.

Price looked again at the wound.

As he did, Drew Scheele—a Vietnam War veteran who had himself been shot in combat—leaned in. "That's a gunshot wound," the intern said.

Price nodded and turned to Parr and Ruge. "He's been shot."

Ruge leaned down and informed the president that he'd been wounded. "Everything is going to be okay," Ruge told him.

Price had treated many gunshot wounds to the chest and knew that the first order of business was to insert a tube to drain blood and air, one or both of which must be collecting in the chest cavity. Pressure was almost certainly preventing the left lung from inflating; draining the blood and releasing the air would allow the lung to reexpand. Price thumped the president's chest with his fingers but heard only a dull thud through his stethoscope, a sure sign that the chest was filling mostly with blood; air would have produced a hollow sound.

A gunshot wound, a collapsed lung, and a chest cavity filling with blood—there was no time to lose. Price asked O'Neill for the chest tube kit, which contained everything they needed for inserting the tube and was stored on a nearby shelf for easy access. Then he began preparing to make the necessary incision in the president's chest.

＊　＊　＊

ED MEESE HAD been conducting a meeting in his office when one of his aides burst in and told him what had happened at the Hilton. Meese and his visitors turned to see the "board," a small computer screen that told top White House officials the location of the president. It suddenly flashed: "En route to GW Hospital."

Meese hurried down the hall and found a cadre of staff members assembling in Jim Baker's office. One of Baker's assistants announced that Deaver was back on the line from the hospital. Baker put his phone to an ear; Meese picked up another line.

Deaver had terrifying news. "He's taken a shot in the back," Deaver said.

"Shit," said Baker.

"Jesus," said Meese.

A moment later, Baker and Meese heard Deaver pass the phone to Ruge, who informed them that the president seemed to be losing blood. Shocked, Baker jotted "P hit/fighting" on a slip of paper.

Lyn Nofziger, one of Reagan's most trusted aides, entered the crowded office. "We need to tell the public that the president has not been wounded," Nofziger told Baker, who was still on the phone and taking notes on his conversation with Ruge.

Baker gave Nofziger a stern look and held up his hand. Everyone immediately knew what the chief of staff was signaling: the president had in fact been wounded. The room went silent.

After finishing the call, Baker conferred with Meese and Nofziger. The three men agreed that they should all go straight to the hospital. A White House spokesman, Larry Speakes, would join them.

By now the phone was ringing constantly. A staff member informed Baker that Secretary of State Alexander Haig was waiting to speak to him. Baker picked up the phone and told Haig that the president had been shot in the back.

"It looks quite serious," Baker added.

Haig said he would leave the State Department right away and come to the White House. He told Baker that he would arrange to have the other cabinet secretaries assemble in the Situation Room; he would also call Vice President Bush.

"I'll be in touch with you as soon as I reach the hospital," Baker replied. Then he, Meese, and Nofziger hurried toward a waiting car.

DAVID GENS, ONE of GW's four chief residents of general surgery, had been reviewing medical journals in the cluttered third-floor on-call room when his pager started beeping. Soon he was on the phone to the ER. A normally unflappable clerk answered the phone, and Gens overheard him screaming: "You want four units of uncross-matched blood STAT?"

Gens hung up the phone and sprinted out the door. He knew that someone needing four units of uncross-matched blood was in bad shape; ER doctors weren't even taking the time to type-match the patient's blood for a transfusion. Trauma surgery was like this—moments of tedium interrupted by crisis and the attendant flood of adrenaline. Gens was addicted to the rush: slight and intense, he had caught the trauma bug five years earlier, when, as a medical student, he had held a beating heart in his hands while another surgeon stitched closed a stab wound in the pumping organ. He liked the combination of quick thinking and delicate hands that trauma required, and it thrilled him when he sometimes saved a life that had seemed lost just minutes earlier.

On his dash to the ER, Gens was joined by Paul Colombani, another chief surgical resident. As they took a shortcut through the urology suite and crossed the threshold of the ER, Colombani looked out the hospital doors to his left and noticed a black limousine parked in the driveway. It had the presidential seal on one of its doors. "Look," Colombani said, pointing to the car, but in the rush the meaning of the seal was lost on Gens.

As they entered the ER, Gens and Colombani were intercepted by Joyce Mitchell.

"Quick, come here," she said waving them toward the two trauma bays. "The president's been shot," she said, pointing to 5A, the left bay. Then, pointing to the right, she told them that a second shooting victim was in 5B. Gens moved toward the left bay, Colombani toward the right.

When Gens arrived at the president's side, he found Wesley Price standing to Reagan's left. At the foot of the bed was William O'Neill, holding medical instruments. Another surgical resident who had arrived in the ER a minute or two earlier was standing nearby.

By virtue of his seniority as a chief surgical resident, Gens was now in charge of the president's care.

"What do you have?" asked Gens.

"It's the president of the United States," one of the residents answered. "Looks like he's been shot."

"What's his blood pressure?"

"It's 110," the resident replied. This was already a major improvement.

"Keep the fluids going until we get the blood," Gens said, before turning to Price. "Did you hear any breath sounds?"

"No."

"Go ahead with the chest tube," Gens told Price, confirming that they would be following standard protocol for such a wound. With any luck, the lung would soon reinflate and clamp down on nearby blood vessels, thus stanching most of the bleeding. Whatever the problem, chest tubes usually took care of it: 85 percent of the time, surgery was not required after this type of trauma.

Price scrubbed Reagan's lower left chest with Betadine, an antibacterial solution, and covered the surrounding area with sterile towels. He injected Xylocaine, an anesthetic, near the president's fifth rib. Next he would slice open the skin and underlying tissue, after which he would burrow a hole large enough to allow him to insert a No. 36 tube, which was about half an inch in diameter. Then he would push the tube deep into Reagan's chest cavity and begin to drain the accumulating blood.

Approximately seven minutes had passed since the president had walked through the emergency room doors.

CHAPTER 9

STAT TO THE ER

D R. JOSEPH GIORDANO LEANED AGAINST THE WALL OF THE HOSPI-tal's sixth-floor vascular laboratory, watching a nurse strap a blood pressure cuff around a patient's penis. The nurse hadn't wanted to work alone with the man, so she'd asked Giordano to attend the proce-dure. Giordano was a new breed of surgeon—a bit softer around the edges, he was kind to nurses and considered this sort of professional babysitting just another duty among many. He was the type of surgeon who learned his patients' names and was obsessed with their outcomes. On many nights, the surgeries and patients invaded his dreams, star-tling him awake, sending his hand flashing reflexively for the phone on the nightstand. "How was the blood pressure?" he would ask the nurse on duty. "Any bleeding?"

He practiced vascular surgery, a demanding specialty that focused on repairing damaged blood vessels. That morning, he had removed a gallbladder, and he would perform another half dozen operations before the week was over. His vascular work was enough to keep him more than busy, but it wasn't his only job at GW.

Giordano joined the hospital's staff in 1976 after a stint in the U.S.

Army. A few weeks before his arrival, GW's brusque chief of surgery called Giordano into his office and told him that the director of the emergency room had quit. He needed his new vascular surgeon to take over management of the ER.

"By the way," the chief of surgery said, "the handling of trauma patients down there is a real mess. See if you can fix it."

Giordano was stunned—he knew next to nothing about emergency medicine. Soon he was reading everything he could in medical journals and newspaper stories, seeking to learn more about a specialty that was still considered a backwater by the medical establishment. In the 1960s and 1970s, internists, gynecologists, even psychiatrists shared ER duty at most hospitals. The emergency room is one of the most intense and chaotic units in any hospital, but in those days it was often run by an intern or a nurse. Few civilian doctors had extensive training in trauma care; most hospitals didn't have appropriate equipment. Administrators questioned the cost of ER medicine, which was often very high. Many ambulance systems were a hodgepodge of city shuttles and contracted morticians who picked up patients in converted hearses. Studies from that era showed that a soldier wounded in Vietnam had a better chance of survival than a man shot on a U.S. street corner.

As Giordano discovered, GW was no different. He spent a few weeks observing the ER and saw inexperienced interns leading inefficient medical teams. Chains of authority were conflicting and confusing. Care was often slow and haphazard. And when badly injured patients received inadequate treatment, follow-up was so lacking that it was nearly impossible to identify mistakes and assign responsibility.

His research taught Giordano that saving the lives of trauma victims required speed and coordination among doctors and nurses, and that this was particularly important in the effort to prevent the onset of shock, an insidious and deadly condition. A seriously injured person often bleeds profusely; blood flow to organs is reduced, and with it the oxygen supply. Deprived of oxygen, the heart, lungs, kidneys, and liver fail. Doctors had only recently discovered that they could reduce the impact of shock and save more lives by pumping patients full of fluid and blood and surgically stopping the bleeding. Only then, after stabilizing a patient's blood pressure and eliminating heavy bleeding, should a trauma surgeon repair damaged organs and tissue. Gradually it became clear that if doctors prevented shock from setting in during the hour after a serious injury—a window of time that became known as the golden hour—survival rates improved dramatically.

Giordano wanted to observe this new approach to the treatment of trauma victims in action. Fortunately, a hospital in Baltimore, only thirty-nine miles up Interstate 95, was breaking new ground in trauma care. Officially called the Maryland Institute for Emergency Medical Services but more commonly referred to as Shock Trauma, the hospital was founded and run by R Adams Cowley, an innovative surgeon who was waging war on shock. With Cowley's permission, Giordano spent a month in 1976 working at the state-of-the-art trauma center.

He was deeply impressed by the speed and precision of the center's doctors and nurses, and by their comprehensive approach to treating patients, many of whom arrived in state police helicopters. As soon as a patient entered Shock Trauma's assessment and resuscitation area, a team of experienced doctors and nurses went to work, inserting three IV lines—not just one—and delivering as much fluid as possible to stabilize blood pressure and prevent shock. The medical crews didn't wait to type blood; they loaded patients full of universal-donor blood. X-rays were taken by a machine parked in the emergency room, not one down the hall in the radiology laboratory. Prepackaged kits for specific procedures lined the shelves, shaving precious seconds off response times. Shock Trauma's mantra was to treat first, definitively diagnose later.

With the help of Craig DeAtley, an energetic twenty-six-year-old physician's assistant, Giordano turned around emergency care at GW. He created specialized trauma teams, which consisted of doctors and nurses who already worked in the hospital. He established strict treatment protocols and gave surgeons and anesthesiologists pagers so they could respond promptly whenever they were needed in the ER. And because the Baltimore hospital received many more patients than GW, he mandated that every one of GW's surgical residents spend a three-month rotation at Shock Trauma to learn how the system worked and to sharpen their skills.

Giordano and DeAtley also overcame opposition from some doctors in other departments who feared losing turf; they faced down skepticism from cost-conscious administrators at the George Washington University Medical Center, which oversaw the hospital, the university's medical school, and the staff who worked at both of them. But once the two mustered sufficient support for their project, Giordano began to reconfigure the emergency room itself. The hospital, completed in 1948, was a massive six-floor bandbox-style concrete building that occupied an entire city block. Its layout was antiquated, and the emergency room, at just three thousand square feet, was tiny for a big-city hospital. With so little space, Giordano couldn't create a Shock Trauma–style center; instead, he cordoned off a 150-square-foot area in one corner of the ER and dedicated it exclusively to trauma care. He bought high-tech medical equipment and suspended it from two large pods in the ceiling, saving space and making doctors and nurses less likely to trip over wires and tubes snaking through the trauma bay. He set up shelves in the bay and lined them with prepackaged kits for every imaginable procedure, just as at Shock Trauma. He shaved about three minutes off the time required to move a patient from the ER to the operating rooms by having maintenance workers knock out a wall and install a doorway to provide a more direct route.

Within two years of Giordano's arrival at GW, the hospital's emergency room was providing much better supervision, training, and treatment. In 1979 the District of Columbia's government designated GW as an official trauma center, adding it to a growing list of such units across the country. GW had long been the Secret Service's first-choice hospital if someone in or near the White House needed medical attention; now it actually could provide appropriate care in the event of an emergency.

THAT MONDAY, AS he stood in the vascular laboratory and watched the pressure cuff inflate, Joe Giordano was already many hours into another exhausting day. His days and nights at GW were often frantically busy: though he had handed off the responsibility of running the ER to another capable doctor, he was still in charge of the hospital's trauma teams. Whenever a major trauma case arrived, whether at three p.m. or three a.m., he tried to get down to the ER. Between his vascular practice and his trauma duties, he was always on the run, which was probably why, with a receding hairline and a perpetual five o'clock shadow, he looked at least a half decade older than his thirty-nine years.

Just after 2:35 p.m., Giordano heard his name being called over the hospital intercom system. "Dr. Giordano, STAT to the ER. Dr. Giordano, STAT to the ER." That was unusual. He couldn't remember the last time he had been paged over the intercom—the ER usually called him on the phone. Something big must be happening.

Because of his long involvement in managing GW's trauma teams, Giordano had been aware that a president might one day come through his doors, and in fact he had envisioned the moment a number of times. Even so, the scene he confronted when he reached the trauma bay was startling: a scrum of about fifteen doctors, nurses, and Secret Service agents stood in or near the bay, and the din of many voices reverberated off the ER's tiled walls. But once Giordano slipped through the crowd and reached Reagan's side, he felt strangely calm.

The first thing he noticed about the president was not the gunshot wound but his hair. It seemed too dark and thick to be natural. *I wonder if he dyes it*, Giordano thought. Then he focused his attention on his patient and the doctors treating him.

"How are you doing, Mr. President?" Giordano asked.

"I'm having trouble breathing," Reagan replied through his oxygen mask.

Giordano felt Reagan's femoral arteries on both sides of the groin. The pulse was strong. Bags of crystalloid fluid drained into the president's arms, and his blood pressure was hovering around 100 or 110. After being introduced to Dan Ruge, Giordano asked for Reagan's normal pressure.

"One forty over eighty," Ruge said.

David Gens, who had been at the president's side for about three minutes, gave Giordano a brief report on the situation. He explained that Reagan had been shot in the left lung, that they had not found an exit wound, and that the injured lung seemed to have collapsed. Gens then told Giordano that Wesley Price had just injected Xylocaine and was about to insert a tube that would drain blood from the president's chest.

Without hesitating, Giordano looked at Gens and Price and said, "You better let me do this one." Normally he would have let them handle the procedure—in fact, he hadn't inserted a chest tube in years. But he thought it would be irresponsible to put such pressure on the two residents. If mistakes were made, he wanted to be the surgeon to own them.

Giordano asked for the chest tube and a No. 10 scalpel. The scalpel, made of high-grade steel, was about as heavy as a fountain pen but so sharp that it cut through skin with the slightest pressure. Giordano told Reagan to relax and then went to work.

He began by slicing into the skin about eight inches below Reagan's left armpit and pulling apart the tissue with his gloved fingers. He gently pushed a Crile clamp, a skinny scissorlike device, into a two-inch gap between two ribs. With his fingers and the clamp, he pried away fat and muscle, mining a hole into the president's chest cavity. The space was slightly too small, so he had to force the clear plastic tube through. He slid it eight inches into Reagan's chest and sutured it into place before attaching it to a Pleur-evac device, which suctions out and collects blood. Blood started pouring into the Pleur-evac's plastic container.

As the tube began to relieve some of the intense pressure in the president's chest, Reagan became calmer. An anesthesiologist gently patted his right shoulder and leaned down to his ear. "Everything is going to be okay," he said.

Looking up from the gurney, Reagan spotted Jerry Parr, one of the few familiar faces within view. "I hope they are all Republicans," he said through his mask. Parr smiled, but he was too anxious to laugh. Reagan would repeat the line later, to better effect.

One nurse monitoring the president's vital signs was startled by his attempt at humor; given his condition, she didn't think it was a good time to be joking around. Another nurse was amazed at how calm Reagan seemed. And everyone working around the gurney was impressed by his courtesy.

"I don't mean to trouble you," the president said to one of his doctors, "but I am still having a hard time breathing."

WHEN NANCY REAGAN rushed through the hospital's emergency entrance, trailed by her Secret Service agents, Mike Deaver was waiting for her.

He broke the bad news right away. "He's been hit," Deaver said.

"But they told me he wasn't hit," Mrs. Reagan said.

"Well, he was. But they say it's not serious."

"Where? Where was he hit?"

"They don't know," Deaver said.

"I've got to see him," she said. "Mike, they don't know how it is with us. He has to know I'm here!"

As she approached the ER, Mrs. Reagan spotted Dan Ruge in the hallway.

"Oh, Dan," she said, nearly in tears as they embraced.

The scene around the first lady was chaotic. Secret Service agents and police officers ran past her in the hallway; police radios squawked as officers and hospital security teams chased away medical students, onlookers, and even reporters. (At least one journalist had already been discovered hiding by a bank of telephones.) Mrs. Reagan and her agents were ushered into a small office near the ER. There she was joined by several friends and associates who had rushed to the hospital, including Senator Paul Laxalt of Nevada, a longtime Reagan supporter and advisor.

One of Mrs. Reagan's friends gripped her hand; then he began to sob. The first lady did not break down, but her mind flashed back to November 22, 1963, when she'd been driving down San Vicente Boulevard in Los Angeles and heard a radio report that President Kennedy had been slain. She prayed that history would not repeat itself, and she kept telling herself that the hospital's doctors knew what they were doing and that she had to stay out of their way. But she desperately wanted to comfort her husband. She was not accustomed to being kept away from him, especially under such dire circumstances. To anyone who would listen, she pleaded, "I want to see my husband."

WHEN JEFF JACOBSON, a neurosurgical resident, heard the trauma team being paged, he rushed to the ER. There was a slight chance that the bullet had hit Reagan's spinal cord; Jacobson's task was to determine whether he had suffered any nerve damage. Jacobson worked his way through the throng of doctors and nurses and began to assess the president. He asked him to move his left hand, left arm, right hand, and right arm, and then his legs. The surgeon tapped the president's knees and ankles with a rubber mallet, then ran a pinwheel over his extremities. Reagan reacted perfectly to all the tests.

As Jacobson stepped away from the president's gurney, he noticed a second patient in the trauma bay: this was Jim Brady, the president's press secretary. As nurses and technicians cut off Brady's clothes, inserted IV lines, and put an oxygen mask on his face, Jacobson performed a cursory inspection of Brady's head, which was swaddled in bloody bandages. The press secretary's left eye was swollen to the size of an egg, and blood and brain matter oozed from the wound just above the eye. Clearly, the injury was devastating, but Brady was breathing on his own and moaning, two good signs.

Also attending Brady was Paul Colombani, who had rushed down the stairs with David Gens. Colombani quickly checked the press secretary's chest, lungs, abdomen, and extremities but found no other wounds. He stepped back to allow Judith Johnson, an anesthesiologist, to go to work. To ensure that his brain was getting enough oxygen, Brady needed to be put on a respirator as soon as possible. Johnson asked Brady whether he was getting enough air.

Yes, he said, trying to remove the mask.

"No, you've got to leave it there," Johnson said.

Brady's blood pressure was high and his pulse was racing. Johnson ordered a nurse to administer the drugs that would put the press secretary to sleep and paralyze his body. It would then be easier for Johnson to get a tube down Brady's throat and take over his breathing with a machine or a respiration bag.

Brady was large and had a short neck, both factors that made it more difficult to "tube" him. Johnson had to get it right the first time: failure would waste precious seconds or minutes, allowing carbon dioxide to build up in Brady's blood and brain. Repeated attempts to insert the breathing tube might also make Brady vomit, sending debris into his lungs that could obstruct his air supply and later lead to infections.

With Jeff Jacobson and Paul Colombani standing by, Johnson stood over the front of the gurney; then she gripped Brady's jaw, swiveled his head, and aimed the breathing tube at the back of his tongue. The tube went in on the first try. Doctors immediately increased his air supply to 100 percent oxygen and raised the head of Brady's gurney to a 45-degree angle, hoping to reduce pressure on the press secretary's brain.

ARTHUR KOBRINE, ONE of GW's top neurosurgeons, was reviewing X-rays in a room near the ER when his beeper went off. Walking down the hall, Kobrine spotted Dan Ruge, an old friend who had been his teacher years ago at Northwestern University's prestigious medical school.

"Art, I'm glad you're here," the president's doctor said. "There's someone in the back you have to see."

"Is it the president?"

"It's not the president, but it is somebody who I think is going to need your services."

Kobrine moved toward the trauma bay and spotted Reagan lying on a gurney in Bay 5A. Turning right and stepping into Bay 5B, Kobrine immediately saw that Brady was in very bad shape. His first cursory examination confirmed his sense that the press secretary's chances of survival were slim.

A fellow surgeon who'd been observing the initial treatment of Brady pulled Kobrine aside. "I hope you are not going to operate on this guy," the doctor said. "It wouldn't be good for your career."

Kobrine shrugged off his colleague; of course he would operate. If he didn't, Brady would die.

✻　✻　✻

SHORTLY AFTER BRADY arrived in the ER, paramedics wheeled in a third gurney, this one carrying Agent Tim McCarthy. But the trauma bay was bedlam, and there was no room for a third patient in any case. McCarthy's gurney was parked against a wall in the ER.

Stephen Pett, a thoracic surgeon, saw McCarthy curled on the cart and took charge of his care. Pett grabbed an orderly and wheeled McCarthy into ER Room 3, a small space with an exam table. Nurses cut off McCarthy's clothes and started running IV lines into his veins. Pett, who specialized in chest injuries as well as heart and lung problems, carefully examined McCarthy's body and found a small bullet wound in his right chest.

After cleaning the area with antibacterial solution and injecting anesthetic, Pett made an incision and inserted a chest tube. Only a trickle of blood emerged. Pett and another doctor then inserted a catheter into McCarthy's abdomen. This time, blood poured out. The bullet had entered McCarthy's chest, but had somehow passed into his abdomen and was now probably lodged somewhere in his flank. A doctor called for an operating room to be prepared for surgery.

Through it all, McCarthy was stoic. He seemed more concerned about the president than about himself.

Standing at McCarthy's gurney was Paul Colombani, who had left the trauma bay and come to Room 3 to help treat the agent. In a few minutes, he would join the surgical team operating on McCarthy.

"What happened?" Colombani asked.

"I got in front of the shooter," the agent said simply.

As McCARTHY WAS being prepared for surgery, doctors at the Washington Hospital Center, GW's crosstown rival, were examining Thomas Delahanty, the wounded police officer. He'd been brought to WHC because the paramedics at the scene feared that GW would be too crowded with the other victims. In agony from the bullet wound in his back, he had left deep bite marks in the leather slapjack shoved into his mouth to help him fight the pain. While lying on the sidewalk, he had asked for a priest.

The bullet was nestled near Delahanty's spine. The trauma team called in a neurosurgeon, who concluded that, with the bullet so close to the spinal cord, an attempt to remove it might do more damage than the actual wound. Doctors gave Delahanty pain medication, cleaned the wound, and pumped him full of antibiotics. Then they sent him to another part of the hospital to rest. For now, there was nothing more they could do.

WITHIN FIFTEEN MINUTES of the assassination attempt, the man who had caused all this havoc arrived at D.C. police headquarters. Hands cuffed, he sat between Agents Dennis McCarthy and Danny Spriggs as the police cruiser they had commandeered at the Hilton pulled into the basement parking garage and came to a quick stop outside one of the underground entrances.

Their suspect between them, McCarthy and Spriggs tumbled from the cruiser and then rushed toward the door and into the station's cell block. McCarthy had his gun out: even in a police station, he was not going to let someone get close enough to kill the would-be assassin.

Once in the cell block, McCarthy shoved the gunman against a wall. Spriggs patted him down for weapons and pulled a number of items from his pockets. A police officer put him in a cell and slammed the door shut.

McCarthy took a seat outside the cell and trained his eyes on the assailant. No one was going to get near the blond man, nor would he have an opportunity to kill himself—not while McCarthy was guarding him.

Spriggs retreated to a small room and spread the contents of the man's pockets and his black leather wallet across a table. He studied the array of items with intense interest. A Texas driver's license informed Spriggs that his suspect's name was John W. Hinckley Jr.; his age was twenty-five and his address was in Lubbock. From a Colorado ID card, Spriggs learned that Hinckley was five ten and weighed 175 pounds, had blue eyes, and lived in Evergreen. Spriggs also inspected three business cards, two belonging to doctors in Lubbock and another to a psychologist in Denver. He flipped through several photographs of a young woman, all of which appeared to have been clipped from magazines; two receipts for three handguns and some ammunition; and a card proclaiming the right to bear arms under the Second Amendment. From Hinckley's pockets came $129.08 in cash and coins, and a four-inch-wide John Lennon pin. It was about the strangest assortment Spriggs had ever pulled from a suspect's pockets.

THREE FLOORS ABOVE the station's cell block, the D.C. homicide office was eerily empty. As soon as they'd received word of the shooting, supervisors had dispatched every available detective to the Hilton, to GW Hospital, and to Washington Hospital Center. Only one detective had remained behind: Eddie Myers, a thirteen-year department veteran. It was Myers's job to formally take the suspect into custody and bring him upstairs for questioning.

Myers, his silver badge clipped to the lapel of his beige suit, went down to the cell block and found the gunman sitting on a bench. From a distance, the suspect was good-looking. A thatch of sandy hair covered most of his ears, and thick bangs dipped down to his eyebrows. He was obviously careful about his clothing and appearance: his blue-striped shirt was open at the collar, and he was as calm and nonchalant as a man waiting for an appointment with his doctor. With his bright blue eyes, he looked a bit like a musician in a boy band. But seen up close, his face was flat and empty of emotion.

"You have the right to remain silent," Myers told Hinckley. "I don't want to discuss anything about what happened down here. I'm going to take you upstairs to my office, where we can talk."

"Watch out for my wrist," Hinckley said. "I think they broke it."

"We'll be careful with your wrists," Myers said, handcuffing Hinckley behind his back and then taking him up a rear elevator to the third floor. With Dennis McCarthy trailing, Myers led Hinckley through the empty homicide office and into a small, white, windowless room used by detectives to interrogate murder suspects. Myers sat Hinckley down on one of the room's three chairs and cuffed his left hand to the small metal table, freeing his right hand to fill out forms. Sitting across from Hinckley,

Myers pulled out a form that advised the suspect of his right to remain silent and to consult an attorney. Hinckley said he understood his rights.

"Do you wish to answer any questions?" Myers asked.

"I'm not sure. I think I ought to talk to Joe Bates."

"Who is Joe Bates?"

"He's an attorney, in Dallas, Texas."

Myers left the room to find someone who could track down the lawyer. He soon returned; with any luck, he could get Hinckley to decide an attorney was not necessary.

"I simply want to hear your side of the story," Myers said. Then, trying to get his suspect to loosen up, he said, "You must be a Democrat."

Hinckley chuckled.

"Whatever you tell me I am going to tell the court," Myers said, adding, "We don't have to talk about the shooting."

"I don't know anything about any shooting," Hinckley replied.

Despite this denial, Hinckley expressed concern about his own safety. Myers assured him that the police would protect him.

At the moment, the urgent need was not to prove Hinckley's guilt but to find out if coconspirators were about to strike other targets. The best way to discover whether Hinckley was part of a larger plot was to get him to tell them, so Myers was eager to keep Hinckley talking. With Dennis McCarthy looking on, the detective rolled an arrest report into the room's typewriter. Saying he needed to take care of some paperwork, Myers began asking Hinckley questions about his background.

As Myers slowly pecked away at the typewriter, using his two index fingers, Hinckley provided his correct name, date of birth, and social security number. Among other things, he told Myers that he had recently arrived in D.C. on a bus from California and had been staying at the Park Central Hotel. Myers's low-key approach seemed to be working: Hinckley even mentioned his arrest in Nashville.

Myers left the room again for a minute or two and inspected the contents of Hinckley's pockets, which had been brought upstairs. He thought the magazine photos of the woman, who looked as if she could be a model, might get Hinckley to open up.

"Who's the girl in your wallet?" Myers asked when he returned to the interrogation room.

"She's a friend of mine," Hinckley said.

"Why did you do this?"

"When you find my room, you'll know why."

Hinckley seemed to have no interest in saying more. Myers continued filling out the arrest report, noting that Hinckley was being charged with assault with intent to kill a police officer. The detective was about to add the charge of attempting to kill the president when he paused and turned to McCarthy.

"How do you spell 'assassinate'?" Myers asked.

"I'll spell it for you," Hinckley interjected. "A-S-S-A-S-S-I-N-A-T-E."

Myers was floored. The detective thought he had seen it all: drug deals gone wrong, violent domestic disputes, gambling-fueled rages, abductions, rapes, murders. A few years earlier, he had questioned a cop killer; in the end, the man coldly admitted, "Yeah, I killed that motherfucker. He was trying to be a hero." Myers had studied the eyes of sobbing husbands who had killed their wives, of mothers who had identified the bodies of their own children, of thugs who had committed terrible crimes without apology or remorse. But nothing had prepared him for John Hinckley, an emotionless enigma, a man who was both worried about his safety and eerily calm. At first, Hinckley had seemed to want to talk, to tell the story that would apparently be instantly obvious to anyone who "found his room." But then he went no further. He simply wouldn't open up—except to spell a word, and correctly at that.

CHAPTER 10

"MY GOD. THE PRESIDENT WAS HIT?"

HOSPITAL PERSONNEL CONTINUED TO POUR INTO GW'S EMERGENCY room; doctors and nurses now stood guard with Secret Service agents at the entrances to keep the area from becoming even more crowded with people who didn't belong there. The noise level was higher than ever; at times, agents and nurses and doctors had to shout to be heard. Even so, the necessary work of trauma care was getting done.

The president seemed to be doing better. He was receiving universal donor blood, and doctors were speeding it into his system by kneading the blood bags dangling from hooks above his gurney. His blood pressure had risen to about 160, high enough that doctors decided to reduce his fluids. But blood kept flowing from his chest. Within a few minutes, the Pleur-evac had collected more than half a liter, then nearly a liter. The crimson stream was steady, and it was not slowing down.

Joe Giordano and David Gens watched it with concern; perhaps the president had suffered a second injury. They rolled him over to inspect his body for more wounds, but found none. Gens "milked" the chest tube to get a sense of the blood's temperature. The stream was warm, meaning that it came from deep inside the president's body, another bad sign.

Because the blood was flowing so fast, Giordano suspected that the bullet had ruptured an organ or an artery. Short of surgery, there was only one way to spot such damage. "We better get a chest X-ray," Giordano said.

A technician wheeled over an X-ray machine and positioned its camera above the president's chest. The platoon of doctors and nurses around the gurney stepped back six feet as the technician pressed the trigger on a small cord. Then the technician collected the X-ray cartridge and rushed off to radiology.

As the minutes ticked by, the president's blood kept flowing. The Pleur-evac was now filled with over a liter of blood, more than 15 percent of Reagan's total volume. Whatever the problem was, the chest tube wasn't solving it. Giordano was running out of options—it was time to call a chest surgeon and get him to take a look.

Speaking as much to himself as to the others in the trauma bay, Giordano said, "We need Ben Aaron."

NOT WANTING TO stoke panic, Secretary of State Alexander Haig ordered his driver not to use his official car's lights and sirens as they sped down Constitution Avenue toward the White House. The former general sat in the sedan's backseat, his right leg crossed over his left, his right foot bouncing up and down, a sign that he was deep in thought. Sitting next to him was his executive assistant, Woody Goldberg. "We have to send a message to all of our posts about what is happening," Haig told Goldberg. "We are not going to have another Kennedy situation. If there is a conspiracy, we have to let the American people know."

As a young military aide, Haig had helped plan Kennedy's funeral, and he'd long suspected the Soviet Union or Cuba of playing a role in the killing. The former NATO commander also had firsthand experience with assassins: two years earlier, he had nearly been killed when terrorists bombed his motorcade in Brussels. Lately, such acts of political violence seemed to be happening with alarming frequency all over the world.

Upon their arrival at the White House, Haig and Goldberg hurried to Jim Baker's office. Baker—along with Ed Meese, Lyn Nofziger, and Larry Speakes—had already left for the hospital, but the office of the chief of staff was serving as an unofficial headquarters for various officials involved in the response to the assassination attempt. His square jaw clenched, the tail of his trench coat flapping, Haig entered Baker's office, marched toward his desk, and gruffly asked to be connected to the vice president. Aides looked confused. "How do we do that?" one asked.

When the White House switchboard eventually got Bush's plane on the line, the connection was poor. Moreover, Air Force Two did not have scrambled voice communications; since anyone with a shortwave radio set could potentially listen to their conversation, Haig had to be vague when informing the vice president about the shooting.

Standing at Baker's desk, Haig held the phone tight to one ear and put his free hand over his other ear to block out the noise in the office. When Bush came on the line, the secretary of state spoke loudly: "Mr. Vice President, this is Secretary Haig. We had a serious incident and I'm sending you a message by secure line. I recommend you return to Washington as soon as possible."

Haig heard only static in reply.

"Do you read me, over," Haig said, his voice rising. "This is Al Haig, over."

Still there was no reply.

"This is Secretary Haig, over!"

Again Haig heard nothing but static.

"George, this is Al," Haig bellowed. "Turn around! Turn around!"

Realizing that the bad connection made any communication with Bush impossible, Haig ended the call by saying, "I'll have a message to you shortly."

UNTIL NOW, THE vice president's trip to Texas had been going exactly as planned. After his speech in Fort Worth, Bush returned to the airfield; at about 2:45, with Major Stetson Orchard at the controls, Air Force Two lifted off the runway.

Minutes later, as the plane flew toward Austin, Orchard and his copilot received a radio call from an air traffic controller. "Are you continuing to Austin or diverting to Washington?" the controller asked.

"We're heading to Austin, as scheduled," responded the copilot. He turned to Orchard with a raised eyebrow.

At that moment, one of the plane's radio operators burst into the cockpit. "We just got a high-priority message," he said. "You may not want to land in Austin." The operator scurried off to find someone on the vice president's staff.

Meanwhile, in an aft compartment of the plane, a Secret Service agent was getting a sketchy report about an assassination attempt over the radio headset plugged into his ear. He passed the information to the head of Bush's detail, Agent Ed Pollard, who unclipped his seat belt and raced to Bush's cabin. After knocking on the door, he entered and said, "Sir, we've just received word about a shooting in Washington. There is no indication that the president has been hit. Word is that two agents are down. That's all we have right now. But I'm going to make some calls and see if I can get some more information."

"Oh, no," said Bush, stunned. "Where did it happen?"

"Outside the Washington Hilton."

A few minutes later, Bush got word that Haig was on the line, but after picking up the phone he had heard little but static. Soon Haig's message emerged from Air Force Two's secure teletype machine: "Mr. Vice President: In the incident you will have heard about by now, the president was struck in the back and is in serious condition. Medical authorities are deciding now whether or not to operate. Recommend you return to D.C. at the earliest possible moment."

Sitting in a high-backed chair in his small wood-paneled cabin, Bush began to sort through his thoughts about Haig's message. His first concern, of course, was for the president's health and safety; he also hoped that someone was comforting Nancy Reagan. As he tried to imagine how his responsibilities might change due to the crisis, the vice president remained calm. He felt prepared for this day. Yes, there was a brewing crisis in Poland, and yes, there were several other urgent items on the administration's agenda. But the vice president had attended many of the president's most important meetings, and he'd kept up with all the information in his briefing books. Bush felt confident that, if called upon, he could navigate the conflicting advice of aides and allies and make the necessary decisions.

By now, others on Air Force Two, including members of the vice president's staff and three congressmen, were learning about the assassination attempt from a television in the plane's conference room. Sitting on a couch and crowded around the kidney-shaped desk installed by President Johnson, they watched news reports on a black-and-white set mounted on a bulkhead. Information was still incomplete and scattered; TV reception was poor anyway, and the screen filled with static whenever the pilots used their radios. But when Frank Reynolds, a respected anchor at ABC News, assured his viewers that Reagan had escaped injury, everyone in the small room felt great relief.

"Mr. Reagan was not hit," Reynolds reported. "He was bounced around as the Secret Service agents maneuvered or flung—I think is probably the right word—flung him into the car to get him out of there." Sitting to Reynolds's right was Sam Donaldson, who had come to the studio straight from the scene of the shooting.

Reynolds was handed a note on a yellow piece of paper. "Here we have a report," he said as the broadcast cut to a replay of the shooting. "The president was not wounded." When the camera returned to Reynolds, Donaldson could be seen leaning toward the anchorman, studying the piece of paper. Then Donaldson pointed at a word and said quietly, "He was."

The anchor paused and looked at the paper again. "He was wounded!" Reynolds said, slapping his right hand to his forehead. "My God. The president was hit?" The question was directed to a producer off camera. "He's in stable condition. All of this information . . . The president was hit. He was hit in the left chest, according to this. But he is in stable condition."

After another pause, Reynolds continued. "The information we have been telling you is incorrect. We must redraw this entire tragedy in different terms. The president was hit today. He was hit in the left chest. But we are told he is all right. He is at George Washington University Hospital."

ACROSS THE STREET from the hospital, Dr. Benjamin Aaron, head of GW's cardiovascular and thoracic unit, was at his desk, filling out paperwork. His office, on the tenth floor of the building where the medical center's physicians worked when not operating or on rounds, was entirely free of decoration. On the wall behind him, the shelves were filled with slide carousels and various medical books, including *Grant's Atlas of Anatomy*, a classic text that he had picked up in a remainder pile back in medical school. The only personal touches, if they could be called that, were on the desk: a black coffee mug decorated with a bright red heart and a paperweight in the shape of a duck.

Aaron had returned to his office at about two p.m. Except for a short nap, this was his first moment of peace since early that morning. Just after midnight, he had received an urgent call at home and returned to the hospital for emergency surgery on a male patient who was bleeding badly two weeks after receiving a new heart valve. Aaron opened the man's chest, drained the blood, and stopped the hemorrhaging; afterward, he caught some sleep on a hospital cot. Next he performed a five-hour coronary bypass operation, followed by two hours of rounds, during which he checked on his patients.

Despite a grueling schedule of surgeries and clinical work, Aaron didn't look or feel the worse for wear. While serving as a surgeon in the U.S. Navy for twenty-two years, he had become superbly disciplined. He had honed his body into the human equivalent of a surgical machine: he jogged at least four miles nearly every day and, by willing himself not to be tired, he could work for forty-eight straight hours without sleep. He had conquered hunger in much the same way. A few years earlier, Aaron had realized that although he was always famished at lunchtime, he never had time to eat. His solution was to simply force himself to forget about lunch, and he was never again hungry for a midday meal.

Now, as Aaron worked on his reports, he turned on a small radio on his desk and heard an announcer say that there had been a shooting at the Washington Hilton involving the president, but that Reagan had not been hurt. Aaron wondered whether some of the victims might be coming his way; sure enough, he soon heard sirens and a few minutes after that his pager started beeping. When he called the operator, she told him he was needed immediately in the emergency room.

Aaron threw on a lab coat, took the elevator to the ground floor, and strode across the street to the hospital. Entering the emergency room, he found pandemonium. Walking down a narrow hallway toward the trauma bay, he turned to his left and spotted a man being treated in Room 3. Even from a distance of ten feet, Aaron could see a neat bullet hole in the victim's right chest. Ahead of him and to his right, in Trauma Bay 5B, he saw a second victim lying quietly on a gurney, his head wrapped in bandages. His years in the military had trained Aaron to quickly triage patients; he gave this one little chance of survival.

A surgeon grabbed Aaron's arm and steered him toward Bay 5A. Secret Service agents stepped aside as he slipped through the bay's curtains. Glancing at this third victim, Aaron recognized him right away.

Aaron could see that the president was in a good deal of pain. Joe Giordano told him that Reagan's blood pressure was improving and that they had inserted a chest tube a few minutes ago.

"He's responding very nicely," Giordano said—but, he pointed out, Reagan was still bleeding profusely. Checking the Pleur-evac, Aaron saw that it held 1.2 liters of blood.

As Aaron surveyed the situation, he thought of the doctors who had treated President Kennedy in Dallas. He also thought about the physicians of the three earlier presidents who had been shot and who had died, either from a devastating wound or from appallingly poor care. A born-again Christian, Aaron believed that everything happened for a reason, and now, as he studied the president, he uttered a silent prayer. He didn't ask for a miracle or ask God to spare Reagan. Instead, he simply asked for a chance to save the president's life. *God*, he prayed, *please don't let the president be irretrievable.*

As THE TRAUMA bay buzzed around him, Aaron watched the blood pouring from Reagan's chest. He touched the tube leading to the Pleur-evac;

it was warm. He looked up and exchanged a knowing glance with David Gens: the blood was obviously coming from deep within Reagan's chest. And the blood was not only warm but also dark. That meant it was probably streaming from a pulmonary artery. These arteries, which directly connect the heart with the lungs, are large and if breached tend to bleed until surgically repaired.

Since the president was stable and responding well to fluids and transfusions, Aaron decided to allow a few more minutes to pass in the hope that the bleeding would stop on its own. He asked whether anyone had ordered an X-ray; Giordano said that one had already been taken and that it should be coming back from the radiology suite momentarily.

Standing next to Aaron, Gens looked closely at Reagan's lips through the clear oxygen mask and for the first time saw the blood on them. Gens also noticed spots of blood on his teeth. Leaning close to the president's ear, Gens asked him what had happened.

"I coughed up blood in the car ride over," Reagan said through his mask. "I am still having trouble breathing, but it is better since you inserted the tube."

"You are going to be all right, Mr. President," Gens said.

As a precaution in case Reagan's condition began deteriorating rapidly, the trauma team attempted to insert a large-bore IV line into his right jugular vein. This would allow them to quickly pump more fluids into the president.

Again Gens leaned close to Reagan and spoke to him. "We're going to put a line into your jugular vein in the neck, and in order to do that, I'm going to lay you flat."

Earlier, the president's gurney had been elevated to a 45-degree angle, which alleviated some of the pressure in his chest. The plan to lower the bed again seemed to make Reagan anxious. "But I'm short of breath," he said. "If I'm lying down, it'll be more difficult to breathe."

"It's only for two minutes at the most," Gens said.

Once the gurney had been lowered and the president was horizontal, a surgeon tried to slip a needle into the neck vein. When he couldn't find the vein on the first attempt, he tried a second time and failed again. Reagan began complaining of increasing chest pain. After two minutes, the surgeon abandoned the attempt, and nurses returned the president to the 45-degree position.

By now, the X-ray image of Reagan's chest had been developed and brought to the trauma bay. Back in the radiology suite, Dr. David Rockoff had closely studied the film. The left lung seemed to have re-expanded, which was good news. But when Rockoff examined the image of a bean-shaped piece of metal that was presumably the bullet, he couldn't determine its precise location. The bullet might be lodged in the lung, near the heart, or even in the heart itself. There was also the terrifying possibility that the bullet had nicked and weakened the aorta. If that had happened, the artery could rupture at any moment.

Now, holding the image aloft for Aaron in the trauma bay, Rockoff commented that the chest tube was in a good position. But the metal fragment seemed small and deformed, which suggested that the bullet might have fragmented either before entering the president or upon impact. If it had somehow broken apart inside the president, there could be other pieces of shrapnel somewhere in his body.

Rockoff also told Aaron that he didn't know the caliber of the round. Turning to a Secret Service agent, Rockoff asked: "What caliber bullet was it?"

The agent, who hadn't heard any specifics about the weapon or the bullet, asked another agent to find out. Using a phone near the trauma bay, that agent called the FBI, which had confiscated Hinckley's gun.

After the agent hung up a few moments later, he reported—erroneously—that it was a .38-caliber bullet. Rockoff was shocked: a .38 is a sizable shell, and the object on the X-ray was too small to be a .38. This suggested that it was indeed just a fragment. Rockoff and Aaron believed that if there was more shrapnel inside the president, it was most likely in his abdomen, where any number of organs and blood vessels could be hemorrhaging. Concerned, the trauma team ordered another X-ray, this one of the president's belly.

EVER SINCE ARRIVING at the hospital, Nancy Reagan had been politely pestering doctors and nurses about when she would be permitted to see her husband. The hospital's acting chief of surgery, Dr. Neofytos

Tsangaris, was deputized to act as the liaison between the first lady and the trauma team; when Tsangaris asked whether Mrs. Reagan could come to the trauma bay, he was told that the president's doctors needed more time. For one thing, they hadn't completed their evaluation of their patient. But they also wanted to clean up some of the blood and fluids on the floor and cart away some of the cut-up clothes. They didn't want the messy and chaotic scene to upset the first lady.

Once the doctors decided to allow Mrs. Reagan to see her husband, Tsangaris retrieved the first lady and led her to the far corner of the ER and the trauma bay. Accompanying her were Paul Laxalt and George Opfer.

When Mrs. Reagan entered the bay through its parted curtains, she was badly shaken by the sight of her wounded husband lying on the gurney. IV lines stretched from his arms and a clear oxygen mask covered his face. His skin was shockingly pale, and the first lady immediately spotted the caked blood on his lips. She also noticed that his new blue suit—the one she had had made for him—was a shredded mess, crumpled in the corner of the bay. Laxalt, beside her, saw a frightened look in Reagan's eyes; Opfer thought the president looked terribly gray.

But when Reagan saw his wife as she reached out to comfort him, his spirits seemed to lift. Even though he was still struggling to breathe, he pulled up the oxygen mask and reprised a famous remark made by boxer Jack Dempsey after he lost the heavyweight championship in 1926.

"Honey," the president said, "I forgot to duck."

Reagan then turned to Laxalt. "Don't worry about me, I'll make it."

Mrs. Reagan gently put the oxygen mask back on. "Please, don't try to talk," she said.

The first lady kissed the president's cheek and left the bay. It was time for the trauma team to get back to work.

THE CHEST TUBE wasn't stopping the bleeding; the Pleur-evac now held 1.8 liters of the president's blood. Looking down at his patient, Ben Aaron knew it was time to make a decision. Should he operate or not?

As he considered his options, Aaron was particularly concerned about two issues, neither of them medical. First, the surgeon wanted to get Reagan out of the trauma bay. It was too crowded and too noisy, and he had too little control. Aaron had dominion in only one place: the operating room. Reagan would be safer there because Aaron would be in full command, and the throng of spectators and hangers-on would be much smaller. Second, even if the bleeding stopped and the bullet seemed secure, Aaron felt queasy about the political ramifications of leaving a fragment of metal lodged in the president's chest. Having studied the first X-ray, Aaron was fairly confident the bullet wasn't in the heart itself. Even so, leaving it near the heart and other important organs would almost certainly cause anxiety in the country and the world.

Aaron made up his mind: he would operate. He informed Joe Giordano and the other doctors on the team, and then bent down to the president.

"Mr. President, there is a lot of blood coming from your chest tube," Aaron said. "We know the bullet is in your chest. But we don't know what has been injured. Because the blood continues to come, we think it would be safest to take you to the operating room. We don't think you are in any immediate danger. But we think that is the safest course, going to the operating room."

The president nodded. "Whatever you think is best," he said from behind his oxygen mask. "I leave it up to you."

By now, the surgeons knew that the second X-ray revealed no shrapnel in the president's abdomen. Even so, Giordano and Gens worried that the bullet might have penetrated Reagan's diaphragm, a muscle less than a half inch thick that separates the abdomen from the chest cavity. If it had pierced the diaphragm, it could have penetrated an organ such as the stomach or spleen before passing back through the diaphragm and lodging in the chest. The doctors also feared that a seventy-year-old being thrown violently into a limousine might have sustained a rupture of his liver, appendix, or kidneys. The only way to find out whether there was bleeding in the abdomen was to administer a peritoneal lavage, or "belly tap." In this procedure, a surgeon would cut a small slit near the belly button, open up the abdominal cavity, insert a small plastic catheter, pour in a liter of saline, and let it swirl around before draining it. If there was even a drop of blood in the abdomen, the saline would turn pink.

Giordano and Gens advocated a belly tap, but Aaron wasn't sure it was necessary. The X-ray showed the bullet was lodged in the chest, not the abdomen. If he detected a problem in the president's belly during surgery, he could fix it through the chest incision. But he also respected Giordano and Gens and wanted to avoid dissension among the trauma team, especially since they had been working together smoothly thus far. Because Aaron was now Reagan's primary surgeon, it was his call whether the team should perform the procedure. In the scheme of things, a belly tap was rather harmless; also, the president was currently stable and his vital signs were decent. Aaron kept his doubts to himself and consented to the lavage.

Gens tried to take Reagan's blood pressure, but the ER was still so noisy that he couldn't hear anything through his stethoscope. As he inflated the cuff and slowly let out the air, he placed a finger over the radial artery in the president's left wrist and waited to feel the tell-tale thump. The president's blood pressure was still 160, high but acceptable under the circumstances.

As Gens prepared to leave for the operating room, he suddenly wondered whether anyone had told the president why he was in the hospital. The surgeon—a loquacious and earnest man who often lost track of time while talking to patients about everything from their conditions to sports—leaned close to Reagan's ear and asked, "Mr. President, do you know what happened?"

"No," Reagan said.

"First of all, you were shot in the chest, and the bullet has torn your lung apart and you are leaking blood and air," Gens said.

Reagan looked surprised.

"We have to do two things," Gens went on. "First, we have to do what we call a peritoneal lavage to see if there is any blood in your belly. If there is blood in your abdomen, we will do an abdominal incision to see what is bleeding. If there is no blood in your abdomen, then we turn you to your side, and Dr. Aaron will perform what we call a chest incision. He will then fix your lung. You are going to be okay. You are short of breath because of your injury, but you are going to be all right."

Before being taken to the operating room, Reagan got the attention of Cyndi Hines, a technician who was monitoring his IVs, fluids, and blood pressure.

"What do you think?" the president asked her.

Hines smiled. She was pretty sure she knew what he was really asking: Am I going to be okay, or am I going to die? Patients, afraid to pester the doctors, asked her that question all the time. "I think you are doing all right," she replied gently. "They are taking you to the OR. If you were really bad, they would be opening you up right here. I really think you are doing fine."

The president grinned at her through his mask.

CHAPTER 11

OPERATING ROOM 2

A T 2:57 P.M., EXACTLY THIRTY MINUTES AFTER THE ASSASSINATION attempt, doctors and nurses began wheeling President Reagan feet-first out of the trauma bay. A Secret Service agent had already surveyed and secured the route to the operating room: it led down a hallway, past the urology department's examination rooms, through the sprawling recovery room, and then down another corridor. The president would be taken into Operating Room 2, which was at the far left side of a hallway running between a total of thirteen operating rooms.

A couple of minutes earlier, Ben Aaron had informed Mrs. Reagan of the imminent surgery. Meeting with the first lady, Mike Deaver, and several family friends in the small office where they had been waiting for further news, Aaron explained that although the bullet had apparently not touched the president's heart, it had come to rest in his lung.

"Here's what we're going to do," Aaron said. "We're going to take him and do an abdominal tap to find if there's any blood in the abdomen. If there is, that's a serious problem. If that is negative, we're going to roll him over and open him up and check everything out, including his heart, because you can't really be sure until you get in there, and try to get the bullet out and stop the bleeding."

"How do you stop the bleeding?" Mike Deaver asked.

"Well, we'll clamp it or suture it, or if it isn't necessary, it could be a wound that would heal itself," Aaron replied.

After telling Mrs. Reagan he would keep her informed, Aaron politely excused himself and left to change into his surgical scrubs. The first lady was escorted to the trauma bay, where doctors were getting ready to move the president. She walked straight to her husband's bed and clasped his left hand, despite a recently inserted arterial line that jutted from the top of it.

Now, as the trauma team began rolling their patient toward the OR, Dr. Sol Edelstein, the director of the emergency room, took his place at Reagan's feet, his back to the hallway down which they would be traveling. Edelstein, who had just arrived at the hospital after racing from his home in suburban Maryland, deliberately shuffled backward as slowly as he could. Partly, he wanted to act as a speed brake to prevent IV and blood lines from being jostled as the gurney moved down the hallway. But he also hoped to instill calm and a sense of purpose. Rushing led to mistakes, and there could be no errors today.

As the procession moved slowly down the narrow hallway, Mrs. Reagan continued to hold the president's left hand. David Gens clasped the first lady's waist and pulled her close to the gurney so she wouldn't bang into objects in the hallway. "Watch your legs, they might get hit," he said protectively. "Watch your legs." He could see that Mrs. Reagan was frightened.

The gurney inched between the nurses' station on the left and the examination rooms on the right. Rounding a corner, the procession encountered Jim Baker, Ed Meese, and Mike Deaver, as well as two other aides. Baker and Meese had arrived at the hospital only a few minutes earlier; upon entering the emergency room, they had spoken to a doctor who told them that the president was in bad shape and might be bleeding to death. Shell-shocked, they were waiting anxiously for a chance to see him for themselves.

Despite his condition and all the commotion, Reagan spotted his

Troika immediately. Speaking through his oxygen mask, the president got in the first word. "Who's minding the store?" he asked.

Then he winked at Baker.

The gurney rolled on, its route to the OR crowded with doctors, nurses, Secret Service agents, and police officers. The trip seemed to take a long time, and when the procession finally reached Operating Room 2, an anesthesiologist couldn't find a handhold on the gurney that would enable him to guide it through the doors. In the end, he grabbed one of Reagan's feet to pull him into the room.

At the door to the OR, David Gens turned to Mrs. Reagan and gently told her that she had to say goodbye. "You can't go any further," he said.

The first lady leaned over and kissed her husband on his forehead. "I love you," she said.

ONLY A FEW minutes before the president's trip to the OR, Arthur Kobrine had visited the radiology suite, where a CAT scan machine was taking X-rays of Jim Brady's brain. Kobrine, who would soon be operating on the press secretary, carefully studied each image of his patient's head as it appeared on a small monitor in the lab. Halfway through the CAT scan's run, he stopped it; he had seen enough. The images revealed bullet fragments scattered across the front of Brady's brain and a huge blood clot forming in the right frontal lobe. The damage was devastating, and Kobrine didn't want to waste any more time before getting Brady to the OR.

Brady's wife, Sarah, had rushed to GW from the couple's home in Arlington; now a social worker opened the radiology suite door and told Kobrine that she was waiting outside. The surgeon found Mrs. Brady sitting in a chair in the hallway and took a seat next to her. Speaking very directly, Kobrine informed Mrs. Brady that the bullet had passed through her husband's brain; he then described the operation he was about to perform and spelled out its dangers. Calmly, he told her the prognosis wasn't good: her husband might not survive the operation.

"You have to save him," she said, holding back tears. "He has a little boy. Please."

For a moment, Kobrine turned away. He knew the situation was too dire to make any promises. Instead, he simply said that he would do the best he could.

Returning to the radiology suite, the surgeon marshaled his troops and exhorted them to move quickly. Turning to a Secret Service agent standing nearby, Kobrine told him, "You are going to push through the crowd. We're going to go down the hall, turn left, and go down to the operating room. We are not stopping. We are just going. Just push people out of the way."

While Kobrine steered the gurney carrying the press secretary from behind, the agent took a position in front and began to stiff-arm and block people, moving them aside. Just as they began making good progress, the agent abruptly stopped, and Kobrine nearly toppled over Brady.

"God damn it, I told you not to stop for anything," the surgeon yelled at the agent.

"Sir, that is the president rolling in front of us," the agent replied. "We have to let him go first."

SITTING ON A wooden bench in a locker room after donning his green surgical scrubs and blue Nike running shoes, Ben Aaron adjusted his eyeglasses and mapped out the operation in his mind. It was not a particularly demanding procedure: he would make an incision in the president's side, cauterize and suture any wounds, and probe the left lung in search of the bullet. But no chest operation is simple. Even healthy patients die from unexpected complications, and Reagan's surgery presented its own challenges. The patient was seventy years old, and he had been thrown roughly into the limousine, had been in or near shock, and had lost a significant amount of blood. Given all the stresses the president had endured in the past half hour, Aaron worried that he might go into a rapid decline after being put to sleep.

Aaron stood up, took a deep breath, and headed for the operating room. With his years of experience, he knew how to block out any apprehensions and focus entirely on the task at hand. When he entered the OR, he would be all business. His approach to surgery left no room for doubt, earning him comparisons to the advisory on a jar of mayonnaise: he kept cool and didn't freeze.

Joe Giordano had taken time to gather his thoughts as well. Shortly after inserting the tube into Reagan's chest and turning the case over to Aaron, Giordano took refuge in the doctors' lounge and sat down at one of its tables. He tried to absorb what had happened over the past few minutes; at one point he turned to another doctor—an ophthalmologist—and said, "I just put a chest tube in the president of the United States." He said nothing more before getting up and walking back to the ER.

David Gens didn't wait to reach the locker room to put on his scrubs—to save time he removed his street clothes and donned his surgical greens inside the closet in which the scrubs were stored. He washed his hands and arms thoroughly and then hurried into the operating room, the first surgeon to arrive. It was always a good idea to have one surgeon scrubbed and ready as soon as a patient had been wheeled into the OR—that way, someone would be on hand in case the patient suddenly began to fail.

Jerry Parr and several other agents were also in the OR. With the help of a surgeon, the agents screened everyone entering the room so that no spectators could slip in. The agents amused the doctors and nurses: Parr had put his scrubs on backward over his suit, and other agents had put their scrubs on incorrectly as well. Hair peeked out from under their surgical caps; pant cuffs jutted from under the scrubs. At least one agent was wearing surgical booties over his bare feet instead of his shoes.

From his position just a few feet from Reagan, Parr surveyed the room. A large adjustable lamp hung overhead, and the shelves on the walls were filled with medical equipment. Metal tables with rollers carried trays upon which surgical instruments had been neatly arrayed. Parr noticed a windowed observation deck overlooking the operating room. He sent another agent to investigate; the door to the deck was locked and a police officer had already been stationed behind it.

By the time the surgical team had assembled, the crowd of doctors, nurses, and agents was so large that some of those present couldn't see the patient through the throng. The room quickly became quite warm, and the noise level rose as several conversations occurred at once and equipment was prepared for the surgery.

Gently, doctors transferred the president from the gurney to the operating table. A nurse squeezed Reagan's hand. Manfred "Dutch" Lichtman, an anesthesiologist, leaned down and said, "We're going to be putting you to sleep now."

"How are you going to put me to sleep if I can hardly breathe now?" Reagan asked. The tone of his question was almost academic, as if he were trying to figure out the mechanics of how he'd be able to breathe once he was put to sleep.

Lichtman assured the president that he would have no difficulty breathing during the operation and then prepared to administer the anesthetics.

As if responding to a cue, the president rose up on one elbow and dramatically pulled the oxygen mask from his face. Salvaging a line that had fallen flat in the emergency room earlier, he said, "I hope you are all Republicans."

Nervous chuckles quickly became laughter; the tension in the room evaporated. Standing near the foot of the operating table was Joe Giordano, who happened to be a die-hard liberal. "Today, Mr. President," Giordano said, "we are all Republicans."

An ophthalmologist was summoned to pluck out Reagan's contact lenses. He found one in the president's right eye and removed it by hand. He saw nothing in the left eye. Perhaps Reagan had not replaced it after his speech; it might also have popped out when the president was pushed into the limousine, or it might have been removed in the ER.

An anesthesiologist injected drugs into an IV line and within seconds Reagan's eyes closed. Lichtman began the intubation process, which would make it possible for a machine to breathe for the president. First, he pressed his thumb and forefingers on a small ring of cartilage near Reagan's Adam's apple to close off the esophagus; this prevents vomit from getting into the windpipe and lungs, an important precaution because the president had just eaten lunch. Next, another anesthesiologist, George Morales, inserted a breathing tube into the president's throat and slipped it into his trachea. A small balloon was inflated at the tip of the tube, sealing it into place. Using bags, anesthesiologists began pumping air into Reagan's lungs; as surgery progressed, a machine could also be used to supply air.

For a moment, silence filled the room.

It was just after 3:08 p.m.

AN HOUR EARLIER, Richard Allen, the national security advisor, had been taking a rare midday swim at the University Club, an exclusive athletic facility near the Soviet embassy. As he completed his twentieth lap, his military driver, Joe Bullock, tapped him on the head and said he was needed at the White House because "something terrible has happened." Allen bolted from the pool and was still buttoning his shirt when he dashed out the club's doors.

When Allen's driver pulled into the White House grounds just after 2:50 p.m., he nearly collided with the sedan ferrying Jim Baker and Ed Meese to the hospital. Inside, Allen's first stop was the office of the chief of staff, where he witnessed Al Haig's futile attempt to talk with the vice president on Air Force Two. Then the two men and a number of other Reagan aides headed for the Situation Room, where they could consult in a secure setting.

Located on the ground floor of the West Wing, the Situation Room was in fact a group of offices and high-tech communications areas where staff members monitored a steady stream of diplomatic cables and intelligence bulletins from around the world. The complex had been built in 1961 after President Kennedy grew frustrated by the slow arrival of information during the Bay of Pigs crisis. Two decades later, information from all over the government flowed into the Situation Room through secure phone lines, clattering teletypes, and advanced fax machines.

Central to the complex was the part the press and public thought of as the Situation Room, a cramped, wood-paneled conference room illuminated by bright fluorescent lights. At the center of the room was a nine-and-a-half-foot polished hardwood table surrounded by comfortable striped chairs on rollers. Mounted on the wall was a small color television, and there was a receptacle for a secure telephone. Richard Allen, whose office was just a few steps away and who used the conference

On March 30, 1981, President Ronald Reagan delivered a speech to a branch of the AFL-CIO at the Washington Hilton hotel. The president, a former union leader in Hollywood, thought the address was important enough to rewrite the beginning by hand. Reagan began his twenty-minute speech just after two p.m.

At 2:27 p.m., just seconds before a would-be assassin opened fire on Reagan and his entourage, the president waved to spectators across the street. Walking on the president's right, wearing a light-colored raincoat, was Secret Service agent Jerry Parr, head of Reagan's protective detail.

Hoping to get to know Reagan better, Jerry Parr had switched shifts so he could accompany the president to the speech. Parr saved the president's life that day—twice.

That morning, John W. Hinckley Jr. spotted Reagan's schedule in a local newspaper and at the last minute decided to go to the Hilton and attempt to kill the president. Clearly visible in back of several journalists and onlookers, Hinckley was inadvertently captured in this photograph by a hotel security official concerned about a noisy heckler.

Federal agents and D.C. police detectives were confounded by Hinckley's calm demeanor as they pressed him for information in the hours after the shooting. In this photograph taken by an FBI agent at the bureau's Washington field office, D.C. police detective Eddie Myers is keeping a close eye on his suspect.

Hinckley bought this R.G. Industries model RG 14 for about forty-five dollars at a Texas pawnshop in the fall of 1980, soon after three other handguns were taken from him at the Nashville airport following his stalking of then president Jimmy Carter. Before leaving for the Hilton, Hinckley loaded the revolver with explosive bullets.

Secret Service agents and D.C. police officers rushed at Hinckley as he unleashed a fusillade of bullets, but they were too late. Hinckley got off six shots in just 1.7 seconds; his bullets struck four people, including the president.

AP Images

Respected by reporters and White House staff members alike, press secretary James Brady made a last-second decision to attend Reagan's speech at the Washington Hilton hotel. He was the first person wounded by one of Hinckley's bullets and suffered a devastating head wound.

AP Images

That morning, D.C. police officer Thomas Delahanty had this official photograph taken in case anything bad should ever happen to him. Stationed at the rope line, he had just turned to orient himself to the president when he heard gunshots. He was struck in the back by Hinckley's second shot.

Secret Service agent Timothy McCarthy had hoped to avoid duty at the Hilton so his brand-new suit wouldn't get wet in the rain. After opening the limousine's door, McCarthy heard gunfire; swiveling, he became a human shield for the president. He was struck in the chest by Hinckley's fourth bullet.

AP Images

After a frantic car ride from the White House, Nancy Reagan rushed into the emergency room entrance of George Washington University Hospital, where she learned that her husband had been wounded. A few steps behind Mrs. Reagan's left shoulder was Secret Service agent George Opfer, who had told the first lady about the shooting.

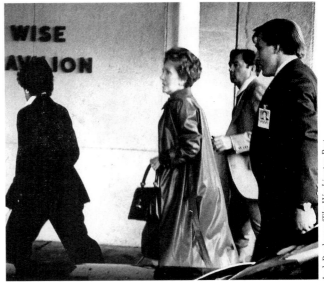

Jack Buxbaum/The Washington Post

Frank Johnston/The Washington Post

At a press conference a few days after the shooting, Dr. Benjamin Aaron, who had performed surgery on the president, pointed to a spot on Dr. Joseph Giordano's left side to demonstrate where Hinckley's sixth bullet had struck Reagan. Giordano, head of GW's trauma teams, had led a recent effort to improve the hospital's emergency medical care.

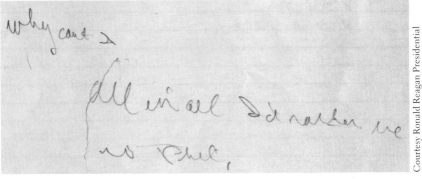

Courtesy Ronald Reagan Presidential Foundation

In the hours after his surgery, Reagan jotted a number of notes to doctors and nurses, and this was one of his first. The president also wrote about his difficulty breathing. "Why can't I…"—visible just above "All in all I'd rather be in Phil."—was almost certainly the beginning of a question about why he couldn't breathe.

Lyn Nofziger, a gruff White House aide, provided the first confirmation that the president had been wounded to reporters during a press conference outside the hospital. Watching Nofziger was Larry Speakes, a deputy White House press secretary. Nofizger later told reporters about the jokes delivered by the president while he was in the emergency room.

Secretary of State Alexander Haig addressed reporters in the White House press room and famously asserted that he was "in control." Standing next to Haig was National Security Advisor Richard V. Allen, who struggled to contain his shock when Haig mangled the order of presidential succession during the briefing.

The atmosphere in the Situation Room—a secure conference room on the ground floor of the White House—was tense throughout the afternoon, and the attention of the country's leaders was often riveted on slow-motion replays of the shooting on the conference room's single television.

Before issuing a statement to the press shortly after eight o'clock that evening, Vice President George H. W. Bush (left) conferred with top Reagan administration advisors. Clockwise from Bush's left are Edwin Meese, James Baker, Caspar Weinberger, Fred Fielding, and William French Smith.

President Reagan, hugging the first lady, waved to a crowd of supporters who cheered his return to the White House on April 11, only twelve days after the assassination attempt. One advisor later commented that Reagan resembled a championship golfer strolling toward the eighteenth green.

On April 28, 1981, just four weeks after nearly being assassinated, the president delivered an address to a joint session of Congress following what one reporter called a "rafter-shaking ovation." With his behavior immediately after the shooting and this speech to Congress, Reagan turned a near tragedy into a political triumph.

room more than anyone in the administration, had personally ensured that the room contained no other televisions or even a phone. He didn't want distractions: the room was a place for serious consultation, not mindless chatter.

At about 3:15 p.m., Allen sat down at the conference table across from the television. Haig took a seat across from him. Others joined them, including Donald Regan, the Treasury secretary; Fred Fielding, the White House counsel; and David Gergen, the White House staff director. Soon they were joined by William French Smith, the attorney general, and Dan Murphy, Bush's chief of staff.

Everyone in the room was anxious to know what was happening at the hospital, but reports were scattered and incomplete. The White House Communications Agency was setting up a command post in GW, but for the moment the hospital's phone lines were overwhelmed and sometimes went dead. In the meantime, Allen and Haig began analyzing a flood of information coming into the White House about the gunman, the status of U.S. forces around the globe, and the current movements of the Soviet military. They also asked Gergen to draft a statement that would reassure the American public and the world that the government was functioning smoothly despite the crisis.

By now, Allen and the others had heard from Jim Baker, who called from the hospital to report that the president had walked into GW under his own power, was in stable condition, and was being examined by doctors. According to Baker, surgeons were still weighing whether to operate. Allen had been relieved to learn that Reagan's condition was stable, but he also knew that any gunshot wound had to be taken seriously. He prayed that the president would pull through.

Now, as he worked at the conference table, Allen's attention was drawn to the television, where a newscast was replaying the shooting. "Oh, Jesus, God," Allen said. The sight of James Brady lying on the sidewalk was particularly wrenching; the two men were neighbors in Arlington, and Allen often gave the press secretary a ride to work. In recent months, they had become good friends.

After the video replay ended, the national security advisor leaned toward Fielding, his closest friend in the administration. "Remind me to tell you a sensation, an incredible sensation I had," Allen said. "I had a premonition."

On his way to his swim at the University Club, Allen's car had pulled alongside another. The driver of the other car had looked a bit shady, and for no reason at all Allen suddenly felt vulnerable. *You know,* he thought, *that guy could take me out if he wanted to.* Allen, who had declined government bodyguards, was a devout Catholic and an optimist, and he was not inclined toward paranoia. In fact, he couldn't recall another time he had felt so exposed.

Haig, too, had watched the news report, but now he turned away from the television and brought everyone back to the work at hand. What's important, Haig said, is that everybody stay together. "We'll decide here what the hell we are doing. That's the best way, always."

Haig was particularly concerned lest any officials try their hand at "playing public relations"—to avoid creating panic, it was critical that the administration speak with one voice. But Haig and Allen both understood that this would be difficult, since the press secretary was gravely wounded and his backup, Larry Speakes, was with Baker and Meese at the hospital. That left Gergen and Frank Ursomarso, the director of the White House office of communications, to deliver the news. Each had dealt extensively with the media but never under such trying circumstances.

A moment later, Gergen appeared and passed a hastily drafted statement to Haig, who began to read it aloud. "'This is to confirm the statements made at George Washington Hospital that the president was shot once, in the left side, as he left the hotel,'" Haig said, jotting notes as he went. "'His condition is stable. We are informed by James Baker that a decision is now being made . . .'"

Haig paused, obviously unhappy with the rest of Gergen's sentence.

Allen jumped in: "'. . . as to the course of medical treatment'?" he asked. "Are we going to say the word 'operate'?"

"'Whether or not to operate now to remove the bullet,'" Haig said slowly, pausing as he made corrections on Gergen's draft.

After a few more minutes of work, the brief statement was nearly finished. Before it was done, though, Haig made sure that it mentioned that the secretary of state was among those in the Situation Room.

OUTSIDE THE HOSPITAL, a growing horde of reporters was becoming impatient for news. At least two journalists had already slipped into the hospital and had had to be escorted out by officials. Scores of others prowled the grounds, interviewing patients, employees, bystanders—anybody who might have something to say about the shooting and Reagan's condition.

Jim Baker knew that the administration had to provide some information about the president before things got out of hand. Skeptical that Larry Speakes, the deputy press secretary, could handle the assignment, Baker deputized Lyn Nofziger—a top political aide who had also made his way to GW—to talk to the media. Though Nofziger had handled press for Reagan when he was the governor of California, he was not an ideal spokesman in the television age. Gruff and quick-witted, he had bags under his eyes, wore a ragged goatee, and favored rumpled sports coats and loosely knotted ties. Still, he had a sharp mind, and he was easily the most experienced and unflappable public relations staffer at the hospital. Standing in front of a line of reporters not far from GW's emergency entrance, Nofziger clutched notes he had scribbled on the back of pink hospital record sheets. A Secret Service agent shadowed his every move.

"We have this information," Nofziger said, his voice grave but confident. "The president was shot once in the left chest. The bullet entered from the left side. He is conscious. He is in stable condition. That is literally all I can tell you at this time."

"The president?" a reporter asked.

"The president."

"Was anybody else shot?"

"Off the wires, I understand that three people were shot, including Jim Brady, the press secretary. I do not know how serious that wound is. . . . I have no information on the condition of the other persons."

"Was the president's heart endangered by the shot?"

"No."

Nofziger began walking up and down the line of journalists, punctuating each answer with a quick movement of his right hand.

"Is the bullet still in his body?"

"Yes."

"Is he in surgery?"

"At this moment, he is not undergoing surgery," Nofziger said, although he had just seen Reagan being wheeled to the operating room. "I don't know whether he will."

"Is he conscious?"

"Yes."

"Did he seem seriously injured?"

"Obviously a wound in the chest is a serious wound."

IN OPERATING ROOM 2, Wesley Price, one of the doctors who had initially treated the president, prepared Reagan's abdomen by bathing the area from his ribs to his groin in antiseptic. Though the belly tap itself would require only a small incision, Price sterilized a large part of Reagan's body in case the surgical team encountered unanticipated problems. If they found damage below the diaphragm, for instance, they might decide to perform immediate abdominal surgery. As for the president's chest wound, Ben Aaron was also preparing for the unexpected. He had ordered that a heart bypass machine be placed on standby, just in case Reagan's heart had been nicked by the bullet and needed to be repaired.

Before the surgery got under way, a nurse changed the Pleur-evac container. It now held 2.275 liters of blood, about 35 percent of the president's total blood volume. David Gens, standing at the foot of the operating table, was shocked. The bleeding hadn't significantly slowed since they'd inserted the chest tube.

At 3:26 p.m., an hour after Reagan had been shot, Joe Giordano asked for a No. 10 blade and made an inch-long vertical incision just two inches below the president's belly button. He then sliced through three layers of tissue and fat before poking through the peritoneum, the thin sheet of tissue that encloses the abdomen. Using forceps, he passed a needle trailing surgical thread through the tissue, creating a so-called purse-string suture, like the cord on a duffel bag. He inserted a small catheter into the hole and pulled tight on the thread, drawing the wound taut around the thin tube.

Another surgeon injected a liter of sterile saline solution through the tube and into the president's abdomen. Nurses and doctors jiggled the president's body to ensure the saline made its way around all the organs. If the solution came back clear, the president was probably free from abdominal injury. If it came back red or pink, the surgical team would learn that his wound was even more serious than they had believed.

For the moment, there was nothing to do but wait.

CHAPTER 12

A QUESTION OF AUTHORITY

T ABOUT 3:30, RICHARD ALLEN SLIPPED OUT OF THE CONFERENCE room and walked to his office, just outside of the Situation Room's communications area. Joining him was the secretary of defense, Caspar Weinberger, who had arrived minutes earlier from the Pentagon. Together, they took a call from Ed Meese at the hospital.

Meese reported that the president was unconscious and that doctors were going to perform surgery, although Meese did not want that information to be made public yet. He then reminded Weinberger that the secretary of defense had command authority over all U.S. forces— that is, in absence of the president and vice president, Weinberger could deploy troops, planes, and nuclear weapons under certain circumstances or in response to an attack. The three men then discussed how to frame statements issued by the White House. They agreed to be as candid as possible, but they also wanted to downplay the extent of the crisis. It would be a mistake, they felt, to unnecessarily worry the American public or to send enticing signals to enemies.

"What we want to do is to mainly indicate that he is not in any major danger," Meese said.

"You think this an appropriate time now to [communicate] with foreign governments?" Weinberger asked.

"I would think so, you might want to talk to Al [Haig] about that, but I think we don't want to have any thought of any kind of a vacuum," Meese said.

An aide handed Allen a draft statement that the administration intended to issue to U.S. embassies around the world; the statement would then be delivered to foreign governments. Allen began to read it to Meese. "'You will have heard that on March 30th there was an attempt on the life of President Reagan,'" Allen read. "'Although he was injured in that attack, his condition is stable. You should inform the government that in spite of this terrible event, the government in Washington continues to carry out its obligations to its people and its allies.'

"Is that statement all right," Allen asked, "for a temporary?"

"Yeah, okay," Meese said.

Weinberger didn't like it. "I wonder if the last sentence is more alarmist than it should be," he said.

Meese suggested that they simply leave it out and then added that they should include a line indicating that the president "was stable and conscious following the injury."

After finishing the call, Allen and Weinberger returned to the Situation Room, where Allen informed Haig and the others that doctors were beginning to operate on the president. "But it's not for publication," Allen added.

Concerned that they might need the country's nuclear war plans and codes, Allen requested that a duplicate nuclear football be brought to the Situation Room. When it arrived, he stashed it by his feet. He also obtained an authentication card. (Reagan's military aide had the president's football at the hospital, and the FBI had recovered Reagan's nuclear code card. On Air Force Two, Bush had his own authentication card and his own military aide carrying a football.)

Just as Allen and Weinberger began discussing the alert status of U.S. forces, David Gergen appeared on the television mounted on the room's wall. He was at the podium in the White House press room, before a large crowd of reporters.

"This is to confirm the statements made at George Washington hospital that the president was shot once in the left side this afternoon as he left the hotel," said Gergen, who stumbled over a few of his words and looked a bit shaky as he read his notes at the podium. "His condition is stable. A decision is now being made whether or not to operate to remove the bullet. The White House and the vice president are in communication. . . . We have been informed by Jim Baker that the president walked into the hospital. I would also like to inform you that in the building at the moment are the secretary of state, the secretary of the Treasury, and the secretary of defense, and the attorney general, as well as other assistants to the president."

"What building, the hospital?" a reporter asked.

"No, in this building," Gergen replied.

"Do you have any condition on Brady?"

"I'm sorry, we do not."

To Allen, it was like watching a train wreck. Gergen looked wide-eyed and nervous. In a crisis such as this one, Allen knew, it was imperative that the government project confidence.

When Gergen started taking questions, the normally unflappable advisor seemed to struggle to provide useful answers and then had trouble bringing the session to a close. Watching, Allen said aloud, "Don't take any more questions. He's not in any state for that. Get off the platform."

Haig swiveled in his chair to look at the TV screen. "I didn't think he was going to do that," he said. "I thought the press guy was going to."

"He *is* the press guy," Allen said. "We haven't got a press guy."

As Gergen carried on, Haig and Allen turned their attention back to the message they were preparing for foreign governments.

"Al, they want something about the president being stable," Allen said.

"That's right," Haig said. "'His condition is stable and he is conscious. . . . The vice president . . .'"

"We don't need to say any more," Allen said. "'The vice president is en route—'"

"'From Texas,'" interjected Weinberger.

"No, we're not saying from Texas," Allen said. "'The vice president is en route.'"

"'Will return to Washington this afternoon,'" Haig said.

"'At 6:30,'" said Dan Murphy, Bush's chief of staff.

"'Is returning to Washington,'" Haig said.

"'Is returning to Washington,'" Allen repeated.

Sitting at the end of the table and reviewing some notes, William French Smith, the attorney general, abruptly changed the subject. "Anybody interested in who did it?" he asked.

JOHN HINCKLEY, LEANING against the wall of a small white interview room in Washington police headquarters, stared blankly at a Polaroid camera held by Secret Service agent Stephen T. Colo. It was 3:50 p.m., and as Colo took seven instant photographs of the would-be assassin, he pondered the young man standing before him. Hinckley was unlike any suspect the agent had ever confronted. He didn't seem crazy: he wasn't ranting or twitching or wearing a tinfoil hat. He didn't seem hardened, sad, or scared. He looked boyish but strangely plain, and his face was utterly without emotion.

Hinckley was silent while the photos were being shot, but as Colo turned to leave he spoke, complaining that his throat and wrists hurt.

The agent said nothing and continued out the door.

Colo, who was detailed to the service's Washington field office, had been one of the two dozen agents assigned to guard Reagan at the Hilton. That morning, however, he had been told that, instead, he should finish the paperwork documenting an accident involving his government-issued car. After the shooting, Colo had been dispatched to police headquarters to act as a liaison among local authorities, the FBI, and the service.

His supervisors couldn't have picked a better man for the assignment. Colo, a native of New Jersey, had spent three years on the D.C. police force before joining the Secret Service in 1976. Since then, he'd remained in Washington, where he had investigated fraud artists, hardened criminals, and a number of men and women who wanted to kill the leader of the free world. He had also questioned scores of suspicious and unstable characters who appeared at the White House. His work for both law enforcement agencies had given him considerable insight into troubled minds.

When he arrived at D.C. police headquarters soon after the shooting, Colo was surprised by the acrimony and chaos in the homicide office. FBI agents were battling with police officers over jurisdiction, and the officers were yelling back. Several officers who clearly hadn't visited homicide in years wandered among the desks, curious about the man who had shot the president. Police radios crackled with news from the scene at the Hilton.

Colo tracked down Eddie Myers, the homicide detective who had tried to question Hinckley, and Myers gave him permission to take some Polaroid photographs of the suspect. Colo planned to check the pictures against those already in the agency's files; he also wanted to pass a few of the photos to other investigators who would then show them around town to see if anyone recognized the gunman.

About an hour after Colo took his pictures, the bureau won the jurisdictional dispute with the D.C. police. At 5:15 p.m., FBI agents took Hinckley to their field office in southwest Washington. Two agents, showing professional courtesy toward the Secret Service, asked Colo to join them on the ride. They also invited Detective Myers.

Colo sat next to Hinckley, who spoke not a word on the short trip to the bureau's field office. Hinckley had still refused to say anything to anyone about the shooting or his motive. Myers and other investigators had grown increasingly sure that Hinckley was a disturbed loner; he had a psychologist's business card in his wallet, after all. But Colo and the FBI agents were not so sure. Terrorists and killers, many of whom were part of elaborate plots, were often disturbed. And all three agents had seen too many investigations founder when someone rushed to judgment; before reaching any firm conclusions, it was always best to track down every possible lead. And they had no time to waste. Co-conspirators might be hiding in the city and waiting for the right moment to strike again, or they might use the coming hours to flee the country. As they sped toward the FBI's field office, the agents knew there was only one way to find out quickly whether their suspect had acted alone. They would have to get him to crack.

IN THE SITUATION Room, the secretary of state was becoming increasingly agitated. As other officials discussed how to properly calibrate the administration's public statements or worried about the gunman's potential associations, Haig remained concerned about how to control the flow of information to the public.

"We're going to be on a straight line from the hospital," Haig said. "So anything that is said, before it's said, we'll discuss at this table, and any telephone calls that anybody is getting with instructions from the hospital"—his voice rose to a near shout—"come to this table first!"

Then Haig smacked the table hard with a hand—*thwap!* "Right here! And we discuss it and know what's going on."

Richard Allen elbowed Fred Fielding and threw a glance over at Haig. The two men had often talked about the retired general's theatrics and his endless conflicts over turf. Now, in the midst of a crisis, Allen was alarmed by Haig's aggressive tone and his table slap, which seemed completely out of place at such a sober moment. He wondered if they foreshadowed more problems to come.

To many outsiders, Haig had seemed like the perfect secretary of state when the president nominated him to the post the previous December. During his years in the army, he had risen quickly through the ranks, earning a number of decorations; later, as President Nixon's chief of staff, he earned the respect of many for his part in holding the government together during the Watergate scandal. From 1974 to 1979, he served as supreme allied commander of NATO forces and became well known in European capitals. A staunch conservative who took a hard line toward the Soviet Union, he was tough, intelligent, and fearless.

Richard Allen, however, was not an admirer. Allen had worked briefly with Haig during the Nixon years and considered him too blunt and bullheaded and volatile. As well, he felt that the backbiting culture of the Nixon White House had permanently damaged Haig's ability to collaborate with others. On a more personal level, Allen was privately concerned that a heart bypass operation in April 1980 had made Haig even more erratic.

Only weeks into Reagan's presidency, a number of others in the administration had come to share Allen's views. Haig was constantly trying to augment his own authority, and he had upset some of Reagan's closest advisors by raising the unlikely prospect of U.S. military intervention in Latin America and the Caribbean at a time when the administration was working hard to keep the country's focus on its economic message. As for Haig, he wasn't happy either. He felt the Troika—in a recent conversation with Allen, he had called them a "three-headed monster"—went out of its way to interfere with his relationship with the president, making it difficult for him to do his job. Only two months into his tenure, he worried that he wasn't one of Reagan's confidants. He also didn't believe that he was the president's primary foreign policy advisor, which was the role he'd expected to play as secretary of state.

Just a week earlier, Haig's relationship with others in the administration had grown so acrimonious that he'd nearly resigned. What sparked his frustration was a bureaucratic spat with the White House over who would be in charge in the event of a crisis. Word of the battle quickly leaked out, and Haig didn't help his cause when he criticized the administration's policy-making process during a congressional hearing. That same day, the White House issued an official statement declaring that Vice President Bush would play a major role in all crisis planning and would take the lead if a crisis occurred in the president's absence. Afterward, Reagan and Haig smoothed over their differences— the president even issued a public statement declaring his confidence in Haig—and in his diary Reagan recorded the hope that "the Haig issue is behind us."

But Haig remained aggrieved, and now, only days later, he overheard a conversation in the Situation Room that immediately got his back up. Speaking to Allen, Secretary of Defense Weinberger said that he would tell his commanders "to get alerts to the Strategic Air Command and such other units that seem . . . desirable at this point."

"What kind of alert, Cap?" interrupted Haig, sounding incredulous. Any change in the status of U.S. forces might be detected by the Soviets, and Haig was concerned that they would respond by raising their own alert levels. If the alerts spiraled and the escalation became public, tensions and fears would rise worldwide. In Haig's view, the potential consequences of raising the alert level were incalculable.

"It's a standby alert," Weinberger said. "Just a standby alert."

"You're not raising readiness?" Haig asked.

"No, no, no. . . . The alert, they'll probably put themselves on alert, but I just want to be sure."

"Do we have a football here? Do we?" Haig asked.

"Right there," Allen said, smacking the suitcase at his feet.

"Al, don't elevate it," interjected Treasury Secretary Donald Regan. "Be careful!"

"Absolutely," Haig said. "Absolutely. That's why I toned down the message going out," he said, referring to the cable sent to foreign governments.

A moment later, prompted by a question from another official, Weinberger explained that he wanted the military to be ready for potential action but was not planning on taking the more drastic step of raising the country's official alert posture, which was indicated by its defense condition (DEFCON) levels. The U.S. military was currently at DEFCON 5, which signified that the world was at peace. DEFCON 1, on the other hand, would mean that the United States expected an imminent attack. The only time the military had even approached that level was during the Cuban missile crisis. But it soon became clear that Weinberger was confused about DEFCON levels; when asked about whether his proposed alerts would equate to DEFCON 3 or 4, he said, "No, no. It's a matter of being ready for some later call. It's probably DEFCON 2."

Haig was shocked: the defense secretary had referred to one of the highest alert levels instead of one of the lowest. Did he really not even understand DEFCON levels? Weinberger's only previous experience in the military was as an intelligence officer in World War II, and from the start Haig had had doubts about giving someone with so little national security experience such a critical job.

Apparently hoping to put an end to the talk of alerts once and for all, Haig said, "Yeah, I think the important thing, fellows, is that these things always generate a lot of dope stories, and everybody is running around telling everybody everything that they can get out of their gut, and I think it's goddamn important that none of that happens. That the president, uh, as long as he is conscious and can function . . ."

Allen stared at Haig in disbelief—he had told the secretary of state not ten minutes earlier that Reagan was on the operating table.

"Well," Allen said, "just let me point out to you that the president is not now conscious."

"No, of course not," Haig replied.

DOCTORS GIORDANO, GENS, and Price watched saline solution drain from the catheter into a small plastic container. The liquid was crystal clear. The belly tap seemed to confirm that Reagan did not have an abdominal injury, but to be certain they sent the fluid to the laboratory for testing. Now Giordano pulled out the tube, stitched together the various layers of tissue, and allowed Gens to suture the skin. As Gens tied up the small incision with nylon thread, the young doctor was struck—for the first time—by the magnitude of the occasion. He was closing the abdominal incision of the president of the United States.

Gens lifted his head and surveyed the crowded operating room. He'd never seen such a congested OR: it was filled with doctors, nurses, technicians, and at least half a dozen Secret Service agents. Yet except for a cough or two and the beeping of the heart monitor and the *whoosh* of the respirator, it was quiet and still, almost peaceful.

"Does anybody know what's going on out there?" Gens asked.

The medical team was so focused on their patient that no one had thought to find out what was happening outside the hospital—whether other people had been wounded or killed, whether assassins had targeted others in the capital, whether the world was at war. They knew nothing. And if the Secret Service agents knew, they didn't respond to Gens's query.

About half an hour after the belly tap procedure began, Gens sewed up the final bit of skin; then he extracted the chest tube so Aaron and his team could begin their surgery. After pulling out the tube, Gens checked the Pleur-evac container, which had filled with 325 milliliters of fluid in the past hour or so—a significant amount of additional blood and further evidence that the chest tube had not stanched the hemorrhaging. As of 4:30 p.m., the president's total blood loss was 2.6 liters, about 40 percent of his blood volume. Since his arrival in the hospital, doctors had been keeping pace with Reagan's bleeding by pumping donated blood and fluids into his system. So far, the tactic was working and his vital signs were stable. But this compensatory approach couldn't continue forever. They would have to stop the bleeding surgically.

After finishing the belly tap, Giordano and Gens stepped out of the OR to brief the first lady in a small office near the operating rooms. The office was so cramped they sat knee to knee. Giordano explained the significance of the fact that the president's abdomen was clear of blood. The next step, he told Mrs. Reagan, was for Ben Aaron to perform chest surgery and stop the bleeding. The surgery would last a couple of hours, but they expected the president to emerge from it in fine shape.

WHILE HER HUSBAND was in surgery, Nancy Reagan found Sarah Brady sitting quietly in an ER break room. The nurses and social workers had kept the television off to spare Mrs. Brady the trauma of watching the video of her husband getting shot. The room was almost eerily silent, a refuge from the hallways swarming with medical and law enforcement personnel.

The first lady gave the press secretary's wife a gentle hug.

"I'm so scared," Sarah Brady said.

"So am I," Nancy Reagan said.

The first lady then followed George Opfer to a small chapel on the second floor of the hospital. A few minutes earlier, a doctor had mentioned the hospital's chapel to Agent Opfer, thinking that it could provide a refuge. The chapel had plain walls, a wooden altar, and a single piece of stained glass illuminated by artificial light.

At first, Mrs. Reagan and Opfer were alone in the simple and quiet space. The agent held the first lady's hand, and they both kneeled as Opfer said, "All we can do is pray."

A little later, Sarah Brady joined them in the chapel, as did the wife of the wounded Secret Service agent, Tim McCarthy. They were soon followed by Jim Baker, Ed Meese, and Mike Deaver. Baker, a devout Episcopalian, kneeled and prayed.

BAKER AND MEESE left the chapel and found another sanctuary—an out-of-the-way janitor's closet—where they could discuss matters of state. Huddled in the closet, they debated whether to temporarily transfer presidential authority to Vice President Bush under the Twenty-fifth Amendment to the Constitution. It was an option both were loath to take. White House officials had been laboring to reassure the public that the government was functioning normally, and Baker and Meese agreed that transferring power to Bush would send the opposite signal. Moreover, since Bush was on a plane that didn't have secure voice communications, it would be difficult to execute the transfer.

The question of presidential authority also posed personal and political challenges, especially for Baker. Conservatives and Reagan loyalists considered the chief of staff, like the vice president, a moderate, and they therefore viewed him with considerable suspicion. Some thought Baker had too much influence in the White House and was already curtailing Reagan's conservative agenda. Sensitive to these concerns, Baker did not want to be seen as overly eager to hand presidential powers to his close friend.

Baker and Meese understood that even a brief transfer of power would invite further questions about Reagan's age and vigor. Further, they had reason to hope that the president would recover fairly quickly.

After wheeling Reagan into the operating room, doctors had told Baker and Meese that they expected the president to survive the surgery and expressed cautious optimism that Reagan would be able to make decisions by the following day.

Taking all these factors into consideration, Baker and Meese decided that it would be wisest not to transfer presidential authority to Bush, at least not yet. Before leaving the closet, they agreed to closely monitor the president's progress and reassess their decision if he took a turn for the worse.

OTHERS WERE ALSO wrestling with the political and legal implications of Reagan's incapacitation. Before leaving for the Situation Room, Attorney General William French Smith had summoned his top legal advisor, Theodore Olson, to his office at the Justice Department. As they watched television replays of the shooting and received updates from the White House, Smith told Olson that he "better go find out what procedures are necessary if we have to transfer power to the vice president."

Olson, the assistant attorney general in the Office of Legal Counsel, had no idea how the process worked. He only vaguely recalled the Twenty-fifth Amendment, which established the procedure for a transfer of power to the vice president. Walking back to his office, Olson pulled his worn paperback copy of the U.S. Constitution from his jacket pocket and began flipping through the dog-eared pages hunting for the Twenty-fifth Amendment. He couldn't find it, even when he searched the booklet a second time. Then he realized that his copy of the Constitution had apparently been printed before 1967, the year the Twenty-fifth Amendment had been ratified.

Olson summoned his staff to his office. Presidential power had never been transferred from an incapacitated president to a vice president under the amendment. There were no precedents, no legal opinions, no briefing materials. They would have to devise their own directives on the fly.

But at least the amendment gave them a place to start. The framers of the Constitution, by contrast, had provided little guidance about how the government should respond in the event that the president was incapacitated. In the years before the Twenty-fifth Amendment was ratified, there had been several instances when a president was too ill or injured to function. James Garfield, who survived for eighty days after being shot, suffered hallucinations, and his doctors forbade him to work. Even so, his vice president refused to step in. After Woodrow Wilson was incapacitated by a stroke, his wife, his doctor, and his personal secretary essentially ran the country for eight months. And Dwight Eisenhower suffered three major illnesses, including a heart attack and a stroke, during his two terms.

After John F. Kennedy was assassinated, lawmakers realized that it was necessary to create a clear procedure, especially in the age of nuclear weapons. The new constitutional amendment, once written and ratified, declared that the president could temporarily transfer powers to the vice president by submitting letters to the Speaker of the House and the president pro tempore of the Senate. The amendment also stated that the vice president and a "majority of either the principal officers of the executive departments or such other body as Congress may by law provide" could transmit letters to the Speaker and the president pro tempore declaring that the president was unable to discharge the powers of his office. The president could resume office by submitting another letter to the same lawmakers informing them that he was again able to perform his duties.

As THE JUSTICE Department lawyers began drafting a memo for Olson, Fred Fielding, the White House counsel, was already several steps ahead of them. Sitting at the conference table in the Situation Room and smoking cigarette after cigarette, he waited for an aide to bring him a sheaf of papers addressing the procedures required for a transfer of power. Intelligent and soft-spoken, the forty-two-year-old Fielding was widely respected for his careful research of complex legal topics and his keen analysis of ethical quandaries. Within days of Reagan's swearing in, Fielding and his team of lawyers had begun drafting an emergency briefing packet that explained what to do in the event that Reagan was killed or badly injured. Fielding's objective was to create a binder filled with draft letters, memos, and a checklist; even in the absence of White House lawyers, it could be plucked off a shelf and used as a guide to transfer presidential power to Bush. Fielding and his staff hadn't completed the binder, but they had put together much of the needed paperwork.

Even without reviewing the documents, Fielding knew the White House's options were limited. At the moment, Reagan was unconscious, so he couldn't sign a letter transferring power. This meant that if a transfer proved necessary, Bush and a majority of cabinet secretaries would have to sign the required letter and declare the president unable to discharge his duties. Fielding realized that he needed to prepare the men around the table for that possibility.

In a voice only a few decibels above a whisper, Fielding addressed Haig: "A rather technical thing is that the president can pass the baton temporarily under the law and we're preparing that right now."

"That's pass the baton to the vice president?" Haig asked.

"On a temporary basis," Fielding said. "It passes to him in writing from the president until the president rescinds it."

"Has somebody gone into the Eisenhower precedent on this?" Haig asked. "I think we need that from a public relations point of view. The things you want to make note of are first: precisely what happened, the notification of the vice president, the assembly of the key crisis cabinet."

David Gergen approached the table and queried Haig about the president's condition. "Is he under sedation now?" Gergen asked. "Is he conscious?"

"He's on the operating table," Haig replied.

"He's on the operating table?" Gergen said, sounding surprised.

"So the helm is right here," Haig said. "And that means right here in this chair for now, constitutionally, until the vice president gets here."

For a moment, the room grew quiet. Fielding turned to his right and glanced at Richard Allen; catching Allen's eye, Fielding shook his head. Both men wondered the same thing: could it be true that the secretary of state did not understand presidential succession? After all, Haig had held a key position at the White House when Richard Nixon resigned and presidential power was transferred to Gerald Ford; how could he not know that after the vice president the Speaker of the House, not the secretary of state, was next in line to succeed the president? And as for the current hierarchy in the Situation Room, wasn't

Haig simply the point of contact? Nobody actually reported to him, even if technically he was the most senior cabinet official present.

But at this difficult moment, the last thing Allen or Fielding wanted was a confrontation with the combustible secretary of state over his authority. The best course of action, they believed, would be to simply ignore Haig's bluster and try to work around him.

CHAPTER 13

"I AM IN CONTROL HERE"

AT ABOUT 4:30 P.M., NURSES TILTED THE PRESIDENT ONTO HIS right side at a 45-degree angle. After doctors thoroughly scrubbed their patient's chest with antiseptic, it was time for Ben Aaron to begin his part of the surgery.

Assisting Aaron were Kathleen Cheyney, a thoracic surgical fellow, and David Adelberg, a surgical intern. Cheyney had assisted Aaron in scores of procedures, including two demanding heart operations in the last twenty-four hours. Adelberg was no stranger to Aaron's operating room either; he had participated in more than half a dozen of Aaron's recent surgeries. As Aaron washed his hands and arms in the OR's sink before stepping to the operating table, Adelberg boldly asked if he could "lend a hand."

Aaron stared at the young intern for a second. "If you have the time," he replied.

Aaron was determined to conduct the operation as he would any other, and he had discussed the point with Dan Ruge, the White House physician, who fully agreed. Shortly before entering the operating room, Aaron had been approached by one of his friends, an excellent chest surgeon, who asked if he could assist in the operation. Aaron respected the surgeon, but they had never worked together and Aaron worried that adding a new variable to the procedure might lead to VIP syndrome and unexpected problems. Instead, he preferred to work with the two young doctors—Cheyney was thirty-two, Adelberg was thirty-one—who were part of his usual team.

Aaron took his place behind Reagan's elevated back. Adelberg was to his left; Cheyney stood on the other side of the table. From their three vantage points, the surgeons studied the president. All admired his physique: it was hard to believe he had recently turned seventy, because he had the body and muscle tone of a fifty-year-old who lifted weights.

Aaron picked up a No. 10 scalpel and prepared to make a six-inch incision. He started just under the left nipple, slicing the skin in an arc through the chest tube hole and toward the back. He could have made a far longer incision, but a smaller one would require less recovery time and he could always enlarge it if he had to. As Aaron cut through sinew, fat, and skin, Cheyney retracted the tissue, making it easier for Aaron to see what he was doing and to continue slicing deeper into the chest.

Once the incision was deep enough, Aaron used a retractor—a tool also called a rib spreader—to pry apart the president's fifth and sixth ribs, creating a six-inch-wide space. By this point he could see the lung and heart inside the chest cavity; he also noticed that the seventh rib had splintered where it had been struck by the bullet. After cauterizing the blood vessels he had just sliced open, he turned his attention to a large pool of blood and clots deep in the chest cavity. With a gloved hand, he scooped out the gelatinous material and deposited it in a kidney-shaped basin. In combination with the blood collected by the Pleur-evac, this brought Reagan's total blood loss to 3.1 liters, or about half of his total blood volume.

Aaron then lined the chest with sterile surgical sponges to soak up blood so he could inspect organs and tissue. With the help of a powerful light strapped to his head, he began by checking the pericardium, the sac containing the heart. It was uninjured, which meant the heart was fine, too. Next he gently touched and inspected the aorta, which he found free of damage. He looked over the diaphragm; it, too, was intact. Aaron was relieved. If any of these organs or structures had been damaged, the president would be in far more trouble.

Aaron now turned his attention to the track of the bullet. He followed it through the skin, into the chest, and into the lower lobe of the left lung. But the hole puzzled him. The wound on Reagan's skin was a narrow slit no more than half an inch long, suggesting that the president had been hit by a fragment, not an intact round. But the path of injury through the lung looked as if it had been bored by a drill bit the diameter of a dime. Aaron couldn't figure out how that was possible.

As he felt the splintered rib and studied the wound track, Aaron realized that the projectile had ricocheted off the rib and begun to whirl end over end, chewing up tissue as it moved through the body. Aaron was all but certain the bullet had come to rest in the left lung, about an inch from the heart. Now he just had to find it.

WITH HIS BACK to the conference room's table, Al Haig watched the television in horror as it flashed to a live feed of an administration spokesman addressing the media—from the White House press room.

"He's right upstairs here!" Haig said, glaring at the screen.

It was a little after four. No one was supposed to speak to reporters without first consulting the officials in the Situation Room; Haig had made that very clear. But there was Larry Speakes, the deputy White House press secretary, talking to millions of Americans, and he was floundering. Reporters were hurling question after question at him and Speakes didn't have answers.

"Is the president in surgery?" asked Lesley Stahl, an aggressive correspondent for CBS News who was growing increasingly frustrated by the lack of information from the White House.

"I can't say," Speakes answered.

"We have gotten confirmed reports," Stahl fired back. "So have other network news, so have the wires, can't you help us with that, Larry?"

Again Speakes dodged the question: "As soon as we can confirm it, we will."

Unwilling to let Speakes off the hook, Stahl said, "Larry, his brother has been called by the White House and has been told that the president is in surgery right now, that he already has blood transfusions. Is your information going to be that far behind what we are getting from other sources?"

Speakes gave her another nonanswer, and a flood of questions from other reporters followed.

"Could you confirm the surgery report with a phone call or something?"

"Larry, can you give us an understanding of how serious the chest wound is?"

"Do you have any idea? There are reports that it punctured the lung."

To each question, Speakes offered a variation of the same response: I can neither confirm nor deny anything.

He was digging a deeper and deeper hole, not only for himself but for the administration. By now, anyone watching Speakes might well conclude that instead of intentionally holding back information, White House officials actually knew little or nothing about what was really happening. Being secretive was sometimes forgivable; being ignorant or incompetent was not.

Watching this disastrous encounter with the media, Haig became incensed. He wanted to yank Speakes from the podium. The CIA director, William Casey, who had joined the others in the Situation Room within the past hour, thought the spokesman was in "over his head" and his answers were scaring the public. David Gergen, who had struggled during his own attempt to handle the press, was anxious. "What's he doing up there?"

"I don't know," replied Frank Ursomarso. "I thought he was at the hospital."

"Go up there and pull him off," Gergen said.

Ursomarso scribbled a note asking Speakes to leave the podium and raced to the press room.

But even as Ursomarso ran upstairs, the journalists kept pushing Speakes for answers.

"Who's running the government right now?" called out one reporter.

Before Speakes could answer, another asked, "If the president goes into surgery and goes under anesthesia, would Vice President Bush become the acting president at that moment or under what circumstances does he?"

"I cannot answer that question at this time," he replied.

"Larry, who'll be determining the status of the president and whether the vice president should, in fact, become the acting president?"

"Pardon?"

"Who will be determining the status of the president?"

"I don't know the details on that."

For Haig, this was the final straw. He had worked diligently to reassure the country; now, that work was unraveling—and on national television, no less. Leaping from his chair and charging out of the conference room, he declared that he had to "repair" this catastrophe. Passing through the communications area, he spotted Allen, who was just hanging up after taking another call from Meese at the hospital.

"Why don't you come with me," Haig said, grabbing Allen's elbow. "How do you get to the press room?"

"Up here," Allen said, pointing to a set of narrow stairs that led from the basement to the briefing room.

"Yeah," Haig said. "He's just turning this into a goddamn disaster."

"Who has?" Allen asked.

"Speakes."

"Did he walk in up here?"

"He's up there now."

"Christ almighty, why is he doing that?" Allen asked.

Haig jogged up the steps with Allen at his heels. A female staff member saw Haig as he emerged from the stairwell. "They want to know who is running the government," she told him.

"Wait," Allen said, trying to grab the secretary of state before he walked into the room. Gergen and Ursomarso also tried to stop Haig; seeing that he was upset, they wanted to give him a chance to calm down before he stepped into the glare of the television lights.

But Haig would not be denied.

SHORTLY AFTER LARRY Speakes received Frank Ursomarso's note, he made his escape. But before the journalists could even leave the briefing area to call their editors with updates, they heard a female voice yell, "They're coming back, they're coming back. The secretary of state! The secretary of state!"

Haig entered the press room a moment later. Standing in front of a blue backdrop, he gripped the wooden podium with both hands, his West Point ring clacking against it.

Allen joined Haig on stage and stood just off the secretary of state's right shoulder. The national security advisor wore a stern look for the cameras, but he was alarmed about his colleague's physical condition. Haig looked as if he might collapse. His knuckles were white and his knees shook. Sweat popped from his pale forehead and cheeks. He labored for breath.

Standing there, Allen raced through various scenarios and his potential actions. If Haig keeled over, should he hurry to the podium, grab the former general, hand him off to another aide, and then continue the briefing himself? Or should he drag Haig offstage and seek medical attention?

Hunching over the podium and looking down at the throng of journalists in the small press room, the secretary of state said, "I just wanted to touch upon a few matters associated with today's tragedy." Haig was trying to speak in a measured voice but was betrayed by the need to take gulps of air. "First, as you know, we are in close touch with the vice president who is returning to Washington. We have in the Situation Room all of the officials of the cabinet who should be here and ready at this time.

"We have informed our friends abroad of the situation, the president's condition as we know it, stable, now undergoing surgery." Several reporters immediately made a note—for the first time, an administration official had confirmed what the media already knew. "And there are absolutely no alert measures that are necessary at this time we're contemplating."

"The crisis management," a reporter asked. "Is that going to be put into effect when Bush arrives?"

"The crisis management is in effect," Haig said, his tone ominous.

"Who's making the decisions for the government right now?" asked Bill Plante of CBS. "Who's making the decisions?"

"Constitutionally, gentlemen, you have the president, the vice president, and the secretary of state in that order and should the president decide he wants to transfer the helm to the vice president, he will do so. As of now, I am in control here, in the White House, pending return of the vice president and in close touch with him. If something came up, I would check with him, of course."

Allen was stunned. In the Situation Room, he had wondered whether Haig understood presidential succession, and now he knew the answer. How could the secretary of state be confused about this crucial point? Was he simply ignorant or had he gone completely around the bend?

Allen could easily imagine how quickly the media would seize on this latest evidence of Haig's questionable judgment. As he stood stock-still a few feet from the secretary of state, Allen needed every bit of his willpower to prevent the frustration from showing.

As HAIG STEPPED to the podium and began speaking to reporters, Caspar Weinberger watched him on the Situation Room's television. The secretary of defense was baffled. "I wonder why they're running an old tape of Al Haig's," he said.

"That's not a tape," someone replied.

"But I thought he was right there," Weinberger said, looking at Haig's empty seat.

A minute later, when Weinberger and the others watched Haig misrepresent the line of succession, the room erupted.

"That's a mistake!" someone said.

"What's this all about?" Don Regan asked. "Is he mad?"

"He's wrong, he doesn't have such authority," Weinberger said.

Though irritated with Haig, Weinberger was preoccupied by a much more serious concern. The secretary of defense had just gotten off the phone with his top general, who reported that two Soviet submarines were patrolling unusually close to the United States. Already worried that the Soviets might try to take advantage of a perceived leadership vacuum in Washington, Weinberger found it deeply troubling that the submarines were now outside their usual patrol area in the Atlantic Ocean. According to the general, the nearest sub could now drop a missile with a nuclear warhead on Washington in just ten minutes and forty-seven seconds, a span that was about two minutes shorter than usual. During the phone call, Weinberger told the general to increase the readiness of more than two hundred crews of nuclear bombers, which meant ordering them to their planes or ready rooms and thus shaving several minutes off their response times. He also asked the general to ensure that all U.S. troops were prepared for any kind of aggressive action by the Soviet military.

A few minutes later, when Haig and Allen returned to the Situation Room, Weinberger relayed the new information to them. Allen looked across the table at Haig—he wasn't sure the secretary was paying attention. "Al, are you listening?" Allen asked. "Ten minutes, forty-seven seconds—the nearest Soviet sub."

But Haig *was* listening: when Weinberger went on to say more about the submarines and then informed the room that the bomber crews of the U.S. Strategic Air Command were now "moving from alert in their quarters and on the post to their planes," Haig seemed barely able to contain his irritation.

"I said up there, Cap. I'm not a liar. I said there had been no increased alert."

"Well, I didn't know you were going up, Al," Weinberger said. "I think if—"

"I had to," Haig snapped, "because we had the question already started and we were going to be in a big flap."

"Well, I think we could have done a little better if we had concentrated on a specific statement to be handed out," said Weinberger, rebuking Haig for ignoring his own requirement that no official was to address the press without first getting his statements approved by the others in the Situation Room. "When you're up there with questions, why then it's not anything you can control."

Weinberger, a keen lawyer and tough administrator who had

served as California's budget director when Reagan was governor, was not the sort to back away from a fight. Now he and Haig continued their verbal battle about the issue of alerts and DEFCON levels. After several minutes of intense exchanges, Haig again lost patience.

"Let me ask you a question, Cap," Haig said. "Is this submarine approach, is that what's doing this, or is it the fact that the president's under surgery?"

"Well, I'm discussing it from the point of view that at the moment, until the vice president actually arrives here, the command authority is what I have," Weinberger said, reiterating what he had been told by Ed Meese earlier on the phone. "And I have to make sure that it is essential that we do everything that seems proper."

"You'd better read the Constitution," Haig said.

"What?" Weinberger said incredulously.

"You'd better read the Constitution," Haig said. "We can get the vice president any time we want."

Vice President Bush was still a couple of hours away from Washington in Air Force Two. At 3:25, the plane had landed at Austin's Robert Mueller Municipal Airport and pulled to a stop at the far end of the tarmac. Bush and the other dignitaries stayed on the plane, and at one point the vice president slipped unobtrusively into his small cabin for a few minutes of solitude. As he sat in the cabin, he prayed, both for the president and for the country. He also jotted some notes on an in-flight information card, scribbling that it had taken about twenty minutes for the "enormity" of the situation to finally hit him.

The plane's passengers followed reports of the shooting on the fuzzy television set in the conference room. When he returned from his cabin, Bush chatted with his guests, who included Representative Jim Wright, a Texas Democrat who was the powerful House majority leader.

Bush felt awful about what had happened to Reagan, whom he considered a friend. "How could anybody work up a feeling of sufficient personal malice toward Ronald Reagan to want him dead?" he wondered aloud. The vice president also said he felt no special burden, no impending sense of destiny. "He seems so calm," Wright wrote in his diary aboard the plane, "no signs whatever of nervous distress."

The pilots and Secret Service agents hoped to refuel and take off as quickly as possible, but the plane's fuel truck never materialized. Growing uneasy, Bush's military aide and a Secret Service agent ran onto the tarmac in search of fuel. They quickly spotted an Esso truck filling up a Braniff Airways jet and requisitioned it for Air Force Two. By 4:10 the plane was airborne again.

As Air Force Two streaked toward Washington, Ed Pollard and the military aide entered Bush's cabin to lobby the vice president to take a helicopter from Andrews Air Force Base directly to the South Lawn of the White House. Security was paramount, Pollard and the military aide argued, and therefore flying to the White House was the safest thing to do. Besides, there was no time to waste, and it was far more efficient to land on the South Lawn than to fly to the Naval Observatory and then fight rush-hour traffic to the White House.

But Bush wasn't sure. Yes, it would make great television, but he worried that landing on the South Lawn would send the wrong signal to the country and seem disrespectful to the first lady, especially since the helicopter would touch down right outside her bedroom window. Landing at the White House might heighten alarm; it might also suggest that he was usurping power. Bush decided to follow his usual routine and fly to the observatory. "Only the president lands on the South Lawn," he told Pollard and the military aide.

Bush then dictated a secure message for the officials in the Situation Room: "We will touchdown at 1835 local at Andrews. I plan to helicopter to the observatory and motorcade to the White House. Approximate arrival there at 1900. Feel strongly about proper mode of arrival unless situation dictates more immediate route to White House."

THE CROWD OF doctors, nurses, and agents made the normally chilly operating room warm and humid. Aaron's headlamp threw off a good deal of heat as well; a nurse occasionally dabbed his forehead with a towel to prevent sweat from dripping into the president's open chest.

From time to time, Aaron eyed a clock on the wall. He hadn't given himself a deadline, but he didn't want to keep Reagan under anesthesia for any longer than necessary.

As Aaron worked, others on the surgical team continued to transfuse Reagan with red blood cells, as well as with plasma and platelets, blood products that promote clotting and slow bleeding. They pumped several other fluids through the IV lines, including lactated Ringer's, a water solution of calcium, potassium, lactate, and salt that helps rehydrate patients and keep their blood pressure up. They also gave the president an antibiotic to prevent infection, and a diuretic to help him flush all the fluids they had given him. Using blood samples drawn from the arterial line in his left hand, they carefully monitored his oxygen levels. At the start of the operation, the doctors had adjusted the flow of air into Reagan's lungs so that it was 100 percent oxygen; by now, with his readings improved though still far from optimal, they had reduced the flow to a steady 50 percent.

To accommodate Aaron's work, an anesthesiologist carefully worked the respiration bag to inflate and deflate Reagan's lungs. To give Aaron more room to manipulate the left lung as he began searching for the bullet, Cheyney and Adelberg took turns reaching into the six-inch hole in Reagan's chest and cupping the heart and gently nudging it aside. For Adelberg, holding the president's beating heart in his gloved hand was a galvanizing experience; he had never felt so focused in his life.

Massaging the lung with his fingertips, Aaron felt for the piece of metal he knew must be nestled in the spongy tissue. The hemorrhaging was tapering off, likely stanched by the pressure of his fingers and the air flowing from the respirator. But ten minutes of squeezing and probing the lung yielded nothing, and Aaron began to imagine the next day's *New York Post* headline: "Doc Leaves Bullet in President!"

After a few more minutes of fruitless searching, Aaron voiced his doubts. "I think I might call it quits," he said. But speaking the thought aloud only seemed to spur him on—instead, he redoubled his efforts.

At one point, frustrated, Aaron turned to Cheyney and offered her a chance to hunt for the projectile. She pressed the president's lung between her fingers, blindly looking for the metal fragment. She respected Aaron for giving her a chance to find the bullet, and she decided that if she succeeded she would grab Aaron's hand, pull it inside Reagan's chest, and pass him the slug so he would get the credit. But Cheyney had no luck either, and after a minute or two Aaron took over once more.

When Aaron again wondered aloud whether he should halt the surgery without retrieving the bullet, Dutch Lichtman, one of the anesthesiologists, figured it was time to lighten the mood.

"Having a good time, Ben?" he asked.

Some of the doctors and nurses chuckled. Aaron smiled. "I'm having a marvelous time, couldn't be better."

But with each passing minute, his anxiety grew. He had left plenty of bullets in patients when he thought they would do no harm. But this was a special case, and he continued to worry about the medical and political implications of leaving a would-be assassin's bullet in the president's chest. Then, as he kept coming up empty, Aaron was suddenly seized by dread—what if the bullet wasn't in the lung anymore? What if it had slipped into a vein, entered the heart, and then been propelled from the heart into the president's circulatory system? That could be disastrous—if the bullet ended up in the carotid artery, for instance, it could be pumped straight up to the brain.

Aaron asked for another X-ray.

As THE AFTERNOON wore on, the ashtrays scattered around the Situation Room's conference table filled up; plumes of cigarette smoke created a haze under the ceiling's fluorescent lights. Officials sipped Coke, coffee, and Sanka as they worked. Eager for news, they kept an eye on the television and occasionally left the conference room to speak to subordinates by telephone. Aides quietly entered to whisper updates to their bosses. Cabinet secretaries from a number of different departments, including Transportation and Commerce, filtered in and out.

"What's the situation with the Polish strike?" Richard Allen asked an aide. The staff member reported that the labor strike had been put off indefinitely: Solidarity and the Polish government had reached a compromise. Allen was relieved. That was one less international crisis to worry about.

By now, Fred Fielding had obtained the presidential succession documents he and his staff had prepared, and he began reviewing them with Al Haig and Dan Murphy, Bush's chief of staff. One was a letter, to be signed by Reagan, informing congressional leaders of his decision to temporarily transfer power. Fielding also showed Haig and Murphy a second letter, to be signed by the vice president and a majority of cabinet secretaries in the event that the president was unable to sign the first. It declared that Reagan's "present inability to discharge" his duties required the transfer of presidential authority to Bush.

Among the many officials in the conference room at the time was Richard Darman, one of Jim Baker's top advisors. The sight of Fielding, Haig, and Murphy reviewing the succession documents made him uneasy. In Darman's view, many of the president's aides had responded to the crisis far too emotionally. Darman did not think this was the best time or place to discuss a historic transfer of presidential authority.

Darman asked Fielding for the documents, saying that he would hold them until they were needed. Then Darman left the room to call Baker at the hospital. Upon hearing his aide's account of the conversation initiated by Fielding, Baker was annoyed; in his view, Fielding should not have raised the matter without consulting him first. Baker told Darman that he and Meese had already conferred and rejected the notion of transferring power to Bush, at least until they learned more from the doctors. After the phone call, Darman walked to his office and put the papers in his safe.

Just before five p.m., Don Regan, the Treasury secretary, received a note from the Secret Service describing the president's condition. Regan stared at the paper as if he couldn't believe what it said; below the note about the president, someone had jotted two words: "Brady died."

Passing the note to Richard Allen, Regan said sadly, "Jim Brady is dead."

Allen felt as if he'd been punched in the stomach. He stared at the note in disbelief and took a deep breath, exhaling slowly. He couldn't believe that the man he'd come to call his friend had passed away, just like that.

"We just learned Jim Brady has died," Allen told the room.

"We better get a statement ready on that," Regan said.

"We better just have a moment of prayer and silence," Allen replied.

The room went quiet while everyone present mourned the press secretary's death.

The silence lasted for just seven seconds. There was still much work to do.

DR. ARTHUR KOBRINE was by nature an aggressive and confident surgeon, and at the moment he was even more determined than usual: he had made it his mission to save Jim Brady's life. Before beginning the surgery on the press secretary's brain, he gathered his troops in Operating Room 4, one door down from the room where surgeons were trying to find the bullet lodged in Reagan's lung. Hoping to rally his team before a very difficult operation, Kobrine told them, "We are not going to let this fucking guy die."

Brady had been hit above his left eye, and fragments of the bullet had scattered all the way across the right side of his brain. Using a disposable razor, Kobrine shaved the press secretary's head and bathed his scalp in antiseptic. He rested Brady's head on a circular roll of white gauze and drilled several small holes through the skull. After sawing from hole to hole, Kobrine removed a large section of skull. Before he could pluck out any bullet fragments, however, he and Ed Engle, a neurosurgical resident, would have to suction out blood and damaged brain tissue with vacuum tubes so they could see what they were doing. They needed to be extremely careful not to remove any healthy tissue by mistake; since the brain's consistency is that of barely jelled tapioca, even the healthy portions could easily disappear up the tubes.

Just as Kobrine and Engle were about to start vacuuming the debris, a clot in Brady's brain burst, sending a geyser of blood two feet into the air. The eruption proved to be a piece of good luck; not only did it relieve pressure on Brady's brain, it also opened a hole that allowed Kobrine to explore for damage.

While a third member of the surgical team retracted the scalp and rinsed the wound with saline solution, Kobrine and Engle used the vacuum tubes to clear the brain of blood and injured tissue. When Kobrine spotted two bleeding arteries, he clipped them shut. Then he began gently probing the brain with a gloved finger, feeling for bullet fragments. Using forceps, he removed every fragment he could find.

At one point during the surgery, someone ran into the room and said that the radio was reporting that Brady had died. A nurse turned on the room's stereo system so they could listen to the broadcast.

"Those fuckers," Kobrine said. "What do they think we're operating on, a corpse?"

AT 5:25 P.M., a radiology technician finished taking a new X-ray of the president's chest. David Gens trailed the technician to radiology and waited for the cassette to be developed. As soon as it was, he returned to OR 2 and put the film on a backlighted board hanging on one wall.

Ben Aaron studied the image carefully. He was relieved to see that the bullet still appeared to be in the lung; he also noted that it was just a bit lower than where he had been looking. He turned back to the operating table and began hunting again, compressing lung tissue in his fingers, feeling for the small piece of metal. When it didn't turn up right away, he was surprised—after all, now he knew exactly where to look.

Thinking about why the bullet was so elusive, Aaron realized that it must be sliding away every time he squeezed the spongy tissue. He asked for a Robinson catheter, a flexible rubber tube usually used to drain urine, and inserted it into the wound track. Then, using the tube as a barrier to prevent the bullet from slithering away from his fingers, he pressed the lung tissue around the catheter.

After a few minutes, he felt something hard. He wanted to smile but didn't; instead, he asked for a No. 15 blade and then sliced open the lung directly above the bullet. Reaching into the incision with his right thumb and forefinger, he felt for the bit of metal and plucked it out. Smashed but intact, the bullet was clearly too small to be a .38 caliber. Oddly, it had been flattened into a disk about the size of a dime. Its edges were smooth, and one side was silver, the other black.

Over the years, Aaron had retrieved plenty of bullets from patients, and he knew instantly that this one had struck something hard and then ricocheted into the president.

"I've got it," Aaron said, as he held the bullet aloft for everyone to see. Then he dropped it into a paper cup held by a Secret Service agent.

It was 5:40 p.m., a little more than three hours since the president had been shot.

The flattened .22-caliber Devastator bullet extracted from President Reagan's chest.

CHAPTER 14

THE WAITING ROOM

W HILE AWAITING FURTHER WORD ABOUT THE PRESIDENT'S SUR-
gery, Nancy Reagan and several advisors and friends were led to
a large waiting room, where they were buffered from the
bustle of the hospital. Throughout the afternoon, Mrs. Reagan had kept
an eye on the nonstop television coverage of the shooting and its aftermath. The first lady found some small comfort in the networks' steady
stream of words and pictures; she was desperate for any information, and
at least the television offered a semblance of news. Still, most of the
reports were not good, and some of them weren't even accurate. One
network incorrectly stated that Reagan was undergoing open-heart surgery. Then all three major networks reported that Jim Brady had died. A
few minutes later, the ABC News anchor Frank Reynolds corrected his
earlier report and said that the press secretary was in fact alive. Frustrated, he yelled to his producers off camera: "Let's get it nailed down,
somebody!"

At one point, Mrs. Reagan moved to a window in the waiting room
and stared down at the crowd gathered in the streets below. Agent
George Opfer gently took the first lady's arm, drew her into the room,

and closed the blinds. He warned her that standing in front of a window simply wasn't safe, especially since a conspiracy hadn't been ruled out yet.

Waiting with Mrs. Reagan was Mike Deaver, who was unhappy with the way White House officials had responded to the crisis. The performance by Speakes had been dreadful; Haig's appearance in front of the press corps was an utter disaster. Not long after Haig's debacle, Deaver went to find Jim Baker, who had spent much of the afternoon in a temporary command post that had been set up in a hospital conference room. "That thing is out of control over there," Deaver told Baker, urging the chief of staff to return to the White House as soon as possible.

Before leaving the hospital, Baker once again turned to Lyn Nofziger for help. Earlier, Nofziger had proven his ability to set the record straight while providing only a limited amount of information; now, at 5:10 p.m., he stepped to a podium in the main lecture hall at George Washington University School of Medicine, just across the street from the hospital. Speaking in his gruff but authoritative way, Nofziger announced that Reagan was undergoing surgery and confirmed that Jim Brady, though alive, had suffered a serious head wound. He deflected questions about the president's medical condition but said there was no indication that the bullet had nicked his heart.

As he stepped away from the microphones, Nofziger heard a reporter ask one last question.

"Did he say anything?"

Nofziger turned back to the podium, feeling as if God had just sent him an angel.

"Oh, yes," Nofziger replied, barely able to suppress a grin. Pulling out his notes about what the president had said in the emergency room and just before going into surgery, he put on his reading glasses and stared carefully at his scribbled words. Then, gesticulating with his right hand for emphasis, he regaled the journalists with the president's one-liners and quips. He told them about the wink that Reagan had given Baker while heading to the operating room; he read the president's joke about hoping the surgeons were Republicans. And Nofziger made certain to pass on Reagan's first words to his wife: "He told Mrs. Reagan, 'Honey, I forgot to duck.'"

Nofziger's words were enormously reassuring. How could the president be seriously hurt if he was able to crack jokes? For the White House and the nation, Nofziger's comments could not have come at a better moment.

BEN AARON HAD removed the bullet from the president's lung, but his work wasn't done. First he needed to stop all the bleeding in Reagan's chest; when he spotted an artery the diameter of a pencil that had been damaged by the bullet, he stitched it closed, and that problem was finally solved. Next he had to make a decision about the left lung. Should he remove the entire lower lobe, which had suffered the most damage? Aaron wasn't sure the lobe would fully heal. If left in place it might invite dangerous infections. On the other hand, removal would require another hour or two of surgery, and the procedure was hardly simple. Hoping he was making the right choice, Aaron decided to leave the lower lobe in place.

Aaron began the process of sewing up the president just before six p.m. He cleaned the wound thoroughly with saline and then stitched the hole in the lung with chromic catgut, an absorbable and sterile suture derived from beef or sheep intestine. He cleaned the bullet track through the chest and then began sewing up the gaps in the tissues and muscles. After placing two tubes in Reagan's chest to drain more blood—they would remain for several days—he sewed the rib cage shut and asked his two assistants, Doctors Cheyney and Adelberg, to stitch up the president's skin. Turning the final bit of work over to Cheyney and Adelberg was a small deed, but it showed both his confidence in them and his belief that it was important to treat the president as he would any other patient.

A nurse who had been handing Aaron instruments at the operating table began collecting scalpels, sponges, and blades. She and a colleague counted and recounted them to ensure that they didn't leave anything inside the president. Then she turned to a Secret Service agent who had been standing a few feet from her during the entire surgery.

He had watched her every move with an intense, serious stare. Smiling, she raised her middle finger at him. He grinned back, breaking any lingering tension in the operating room.

Aaron and his fellow doctors were optimistic about Reagan's prognosis. His vital signs were solid; he seemed to have weathered both the shooting and the grueling surgery remarkably well. Even so, it had been a rough few hours. Since his arrival at the hospital, the president had lost about 3.5 liters of blood, just over half of his blood volume. He had received eight units of red blood cells and a significant quantity of plasma and platelets. All told, doctors had pumped a total of 5.7 liters of fluids into his veins. His lungs were not working efficiently yet, so he was receiving an air mixture that was about 40 to 50 percent oxygen, in comparison with the 21 percent in ordinary air.

Still, the three-hour operation had been a success. As his surgical team prepared to roll his patient to the recovery room for the night, Aaron was confident that the president's darkest hours were behind him.

SOON AFTER LYN Nofziger's successful news conference, the attention of those in the Situation Room turned to yet another urgent matter—a dairy bill, of all things. The next day, the president had to sign a bill that would halt $147 million in subsidies for the dairy industry; if he didn't, the money would start to flow on April 1, and Reagan's first congressional victory in his assault on federal spending would be lost. For several minutes, the secretaries of state, defense, and Treasury, the attorney general, and several others proposed ways around the problem. Could the president delegate the signing to Bush? Could he give up some of his powers without giving up all of them? Attorney General William French Smith, for one, was dubious. "He either is president or he isn't."

Richard Allen was only half listening to the debate. He thought it was a pointless exercise, especially since the vice president was due to arrive soon. In the end, either Reagan would be well enough to sign the bill or they would need Bush to weigh in and play a key role in any decision about succession.

Allen also knew that Jim Baker would be returning to the White House any minute, and when the chief of staff finally entered the conference room, just before 6:15, he was greatly relieved. "Here's Jim!" Allen said, happy to steer the conversation in a new direction.

At first glance, Baker appeared no worse for wear: his blue-striped tie was carefully knotted, his expensive gray suit was smooth and free of creases, and his hair was still perfectly parted. But the skin under his eyes was puffy and he spoke in a weary, somber tone.

"The president is in good shape," Baker reported. "I don't know whether they have put a statement out over there or not. I assume they haven't. . . . They are probably finishing up in another ten minutes. They found nothing in the abdominal cavity. They opened up his chest and found some bleeding in one lung. They stopped that bleeding. They have removed the bullet, or fragment of the bullet. It looked like it was a ricochet." The prognosis, Baker told the group, "is better than good, but they wouldn't say very good."

Then Baker added, "Jim Brady's condition is not good at all. He is still undergoing surgery." His voice became softer, sadder. "He took a shot right in the brain."

Soon the conversation turned back to the question of how to run the government in the president's absence. Allen told Baker that the group in the Situation Room recommended that Bush take over many of the president's duties the next day; among other things, he should oversee a cabinet meeting and attend a working lunch with the Dutch prime minister in Reagan's place.

"I think that's fine," Baker said. But having heard earlier about the debate concerning the possible transfer of presidential powers, Baker was quick to say that he did not want to get "involved in questions of succession and incapacity and that sort of thing." He also expressed confidence that by the following morning the president would be able to make a decision about whether a transfer was appropriate.

"There is an issue," Allen said. "The issue is a bill, maybe two, that must be signed tomorrow, and that forces our hand."

"That has to be signed tomorrow?" Baker said.

"The dairy bill," Allen said.

"If he says sign it, you can sign it," Haig said, referring to the auto-pen device that signed many documents for the president.

"A machine won't work," Allen said, frustrated by the way the conversation kept going in circles. "They will blow that one up. They will want to know exactly how his hand moved, if his signature was firm, so on and so forth. It's an historic signature."

AT 6:45, REAGAN was wheeled down the hall to the surgical recovery room, a wide-open space with pale yellow walls, a tiled floor, and a central nurses' station. The room could accommodate up to twelve patients, but at the moment it was empty—the hospital had cleared it of others to accommodate the president. Even Agent Tim McCarthy, whose surgery had been quick and relatively simple, made only a brief stop in the recovery room before being transferred.

Reagan was parked feetfirst in the far left corner of the recovery room and his bed was cordoned off with several portable green screens. Normally patients were taken to the intensive care unit soon after a surgery, but doctors planned to leave the president in the recovery room overnight. It had the same equipment as the ICU, and it was close to the operating rooms in case of an emergency.

When a nurse spoke the president's name, Reagan groggily opened his eyes. At about 7:15, as he began emerging from anesthesia, he reached for the breathing tube in his throat and tried to pull it out. His body convulsed and bucked. Respirators and tubes made patients "air hungry": the president undoubtedly felt as if he were suffocating.

As gently as possible, Cathy Edmondson, a recovery room nurse, told the president to relax. "Mr. Reagan," she said, "that is helping you breathe. Don't touch it now. Trust me."

The head of Reagan's bed was raised to reduce pressure on his chest, but both the bullet wound and the surgical wounds caused excruciating pain. At 7:20, on the order of an anesthesiologist, a nurse pumped a fast-acting and powerful narcotic, Fentanyl, into one of Reagan's IV lines; fifteen minutes later, she gave him a second dose.

As Reagan slowly began to return to consciousness, Cathy Edmondson and another nurse, Denise Sullivan, discussed the appropriate way to address their patient. Partly to reduce the stress of caring for the most powerful man in the world, they decided to call him "Mr. Reagan," not "Mr. President." At the moment, Reagan didn't seem very presidential anyway. He was ashen and a machine was breathing for him. A tube snaked into his nostril, down his esophagus, and into his stomach, where it was vacuuming the stomach's contents so he wouldn't vomit. Another catheter was draining and monitoring his urine. He was receiving fluids through three IV lines, two in his left arm and one in his right. And every fifteen minutes or so, a doctor drew blood from an arterial line in his left wrist and sent the sample to the lab.

The president's eyes fluttered open again, then closed. His nurses, who wanted to be able to react to even the slightest change in his condition as quickly as possible, decided to treat Reagan as if he were recovering from open-heart surgery. Such patients require two nurses to constantly monitor blood pressure, drainage tubes, and breathing.

During the president's first forty-five minutes in the recovery room, his nurses spent most of their time ensuring that he didn't rip out his breathing tube, since he couldn't survive without it. When he pulled at the tube, Edmondson or Sullivan would push down his arm. At one point, Sullivan told him, "I'm going to ask you not to touch the tube, Mr. Reagan. If you are not able to leave it alone, I'm going to tie your hands to the bed."

THE FIRST OF Reagan's four children to arrive in Washington was his youngest, Ron Reagan, who had landed at National Airport while his father was in surgery. The others—Michael and Maureen Reagan, and Patti Davis—were still in southern California, scheduled to board a late-evening flight to Washington on a military cargo plane.

Ron, a twenty-two-year-old dancer, had started the day in Lincoln, Nebraska, where he was touring with the Joffrey II Dancers. He and his wife were eating lunch in the restaurant of the Hilton hotel there when his Secret Service agent hurried into the room. "A serious incident has taken place," said the agent. "Someone fired shots at your father. We don't think he was hit."

Ron ran to his room, where he turned on the television and watched news accounts of the shooting. He called the White House and learned that in fact his father had been shot and that his mother was at the hospital. He wanted desperately to get to Washington to comfort his parents; fortunately, although there were no commercial flights from Lincoln to the nation's capital, someone arranged a private jet to take him. As he flew to Washington, he thought about the past twenty years of political assassinations and grappled with the horrifying possibility that he might soon be attending his father's presidential funeral.

A Secret Service car picked him up at the airport and took him straight to the hospital, where he found his mother in a waiting room, staring at a television. She remained composed, but he could see that she was distraught. "I'm so frightened," she said.

"Don't worry, Mom," Ron said. "He is going to be all right. He is strong. He is going to pull through."

The first lady and her son were allowed to visit Reagan after he had been awake for about twenty-five minutes. Doctors escorted them into the recovery room and then stepped back as they slipped between the portable screens that cloaked Reagan's bed.

Mrs. Reagan clasped her husband's arm. "I love you," she said. "Everything is going to be fine."

Ron was shocked by his father's appearance: his face was stone gray and he was struggling for breath. Reagan requested a pencil and paper; a nurse handed him a blank hospital record, a clipboard, and a pen.

"I can't breathe . . . at all."

"He can't breathe!" Mrs. Reagan shouted as the president tried to sit up.

"He has to get used to it," a doctor replied. "The respirator is breathing for him. It's all right."

Ron tried to reassure his father. "Dad, it's okay," he said. "You're going to be fine. It's just like scuba diving. You have to let the machine breathe for you."

Ron had no idea why that analogy popped into his head; he knew his father had never been scuba diving. "Just relax," he added.

As he tried to soothe his father, Ron saw the fear and confusion in his eyes. At that moment, he understood: his father had almost died.

AT ABOUT 6:20, Richard Allen received word that the vice president would be landing at Andrews Air Force Base within minutes. While they waited for Bush in the Situation Room, Allen and the others were keeping abreast of the recent movements of Soviet military forces. Allen was particularly concerned about a new intelligence assessment from the CIA delivered to him just minutes earlier, stating that "photography of Soviet forces near Poland provides the initial indications of troop mobilizations." But the photos mentioned in the assessment were a day old, and now that the Polish strike had been averted, Allen was less worried about the possibility that the Russians would take advantage of a perceived power vacuum in Washington to move aggressively on their western neighbor. Even so, he made sure that the assessment would be passed to Bush when he arrived at the White House.

At seven p.m., the vice president finally strode into the Situation Room. Even before taking a seat at the head of the conference table, Bush asked, "What's the latest?"

Baker told him the doctors would hold a press conference in ten minutes to inform the country about Reagan's condition.

Allen then raised the issue they'd been debating earlier. "There are questions of shift of authority that is required," he said, mentioning the dairy bill that had to be signed the next day.

"My view on that is we ought to wait," Bush said calmly. "These reports are so encouraging. . . . The best thing would be to wait to see, tomorrow, how the president feels."

Weinberger briefed the vice president about his decision to increase the readiness of bomber crews in the hours after the assassination attempt and told Bush that military intelligence had received no indications of a pending attack. The secretary of defense began to describe the location of the Russian submarines when Baker interrupted him.

"Excuse me? Would it be appropriate to ask about clearances?" Baker said, clearly worried that classified information might be passed inadvertently to those not approved to receive it. "It might be appropriate to make sure."

"Let's get it straightened out," Bush said.

"I think we need to make sure we don't break the law right here in the Situation Room," Baker said.

Before Weinberger continued, a number of officials without the proper security clearances streamed out of the room.

THE FBI AGENTS leading the investigation of John Hinckley were still struggling to get a better understanding of their suspect. By now, they knew that several months ago Hinckley had been arrested at the Nashville airport with three handguns on the same day that Jimmy Carter was visiting the city. They also knew that Hinckley had arrived in Washington after a cross-country bus trip just a day earlier, which suggested a certain level of sophistication in his planning if his goal had been to shoot Reagan outside the Hilton. Meanwhile, Hinckley remained remarkably placid and was one of the politest suspects they had ever questioned; he even answered their questions with "Yes, sir" and "No, sir." Whether he was a loner or part of a plot, the man they had in custody was unlike any gunman or assailant they had ever encountered.

Since arriving at the FBI's Washington field office an hour and a half earlier, Hinckley spent most of the time sitting in a small white interview room containing a few chairs and a plain desk. Hinckley had been read his rights by the D.C. police, but FBI agents decided to read them to him again. Hinckley now agreed to talk, on condition that he could first speak to his parents. Agents made call after call in a fruitless attempt to get them on the phone.

Though unable to reach the Hinckleys at their home in Colorado, the FBI decided just before seven p.m. to make another attempt to get the suspect to open up.

The first agent to sit with Hinckley in the interview room was George Chmiel, who was among the field office's most aggressive and thorough agents. Chmiel had been concerned all afternoon about possible accomplices, and he had been reluctant to agree with other investigators who believed that Hinckley was a troubled loner.

Pulling a chair close to the small desk and taking a seat, Chmiel brought his face to within six inches of Hinckley's. "John," he said, speaking softly, "I really need to know something. Were you acting alone or were others involved?"

Hinckley remained quiet for a few seconds. "No," he said finally. "No one else was involved."

Chmiel believed him.

After Chmiel left the room to brief his supervisors about his conversation with Hinckley, it was Agent Henry Ragle's turn. Ragle, a dogged investigator who liked to wear tailored suits and starched shirts, recalled that, earlier, Hinckley had seemed curious about the Secret Service; as he was being taken into custody at police headquarters, Hinckley asked Ragle why the FBI and not the Secret Service was arresting him. Ragle explained that the Secret Service was charged with protection, but the FBI handled investigations into actual incidents. Now, thinking about how he might get his suspect to talk, Ragle decided that having a Secret Service agent in the interview room might encourage Hinckley to loosen up. Ragle asked Stephen Colo, the agent who was serving as liaison between the two federal agencies, to participate in the session. Colo was happy to oblige.

Ragle and Colo entered the interview room. The FBI agent began by telling Hinckley that the bureau still hadn't been able to reach his parents; for now, Ragle said, he merely wanted to ask some background questions. When Hinckley didn't object, Ragle launched a string of terse queries, most of them calling only for a yes or no.

Within minutes, Colo could see that the interview was going nowhere. Hinckley was defensive, perhaps because Ragle—who was more accustomed to questioning bank robbers—seemed to be grilling him. Colo took Ragle aside in a corner of the room and suggested that since he, Colo, had plenty of experience with disturbed people outside the White House, he might be able to get somewhere with Hinckley. Ragle agreed to let him try.

Colo took a seat directly across from Hinckley, who'd been brought a fast-food hamburger and a Coca-Cola. With Ragle sitting next to him, Colo used a personal history form as a guide and began asking a series of questions that delved into Hinckley's background. Hinckley seemed to like the new approach and began to provide more complete answers. He wasn't married, he said, but he had a brother and a sister, and his sister had two small children. He had studied at Texas Tech but dropped out because of medical problems; he had also attended writing school at Yale University. (The two agents heard this as "riding school.") His parents had recently given him an ultimatum to "clean up his act" or move out and be cut off financially. He described his last year of travels to the District of Columbia, Denver, New York, New Haven, and Los Angeles, and he mentioned that he'd sold stock in his father's company to finance his trips. He even provided the exact price of his cross-country bus ticket.

Colo asked whether he had ever seen a doctor. Hinckley told him that his parents had urged him to seek psychiatric help the previous year and that since then he'd been seeing a psychiatrist regularly.

"What was wrong?" Colo asked.

"I have no direction in life," Hinckley said simply.

After about twenty-five minutes of questioning, Hinckley went quiet for a moment and then told Colo that he didn't want to say any more until he consulted a lawyer.

Ragle left the interview room to tell others in the office what they had learned; as he did, George Chmiel returned.

"Is this on television?" Hinckley asked him.

"No, this isn't being taped," replied Chmiel.

"I didn't mean that. Is this on television?"

Now Chmiel understood that Hinckley meant the assassination attempt. "Yes," he said, "it is on national television."

"Will this affect other people?" Hinckley asked. "Will they be pulled into it?"

Something about Hinckley's question caught Colo's attention. Earlier, watching as FBI agents inventoried the contents of Hinckley's wallet, Colo spotted a note with a phone number scribbled on it—the kind of note a man jots down after meeting a woman in a bar. The number had a Connecticut area code, and Colo recalled that Hinckley had said that he'd visited New Haven several times and attended Yale's "riding school." Colo also remembered that the wallet's plastic sleeve contained several photographs of a pretty girl. Investigators had initially assumed these were just filler photos of the kind that often come with a new wallet, but now Colo wondered whether they were pictures of a real woman in Hinckley's life, perhaps a girlfriend.

"Yes, others will be pulled into it," Colo replied. "Are you talking about your parents and your friends?"

"And others," Hinckley said.

"I know about the telephone number in your wallet, the one that goes to Connecticut," Colo said, bluffing.

"Well," Hinckley shot back, his face tightening, "if you know about that, you know everything." Then he slumped his shoulders and took a deep breath.

It was the first time Colo had seen his suspect show any emotion. Hinckley seemed relieved, as if he could finally let go of a long-held secret.

Silence filled the room.

"Yes," Colo said, "but I have to hear about it in your own words."

"That goes to a dorm at Yale University," he said. "The girl is Jodie Foster, the actress."

"Is she your girlfriend?" Colo asked.

"It's really a one-sided relationship."

"Does she know you?"

"She probably knows my name," Hinckley said, adding that he had spoken to her two or three times on the phone. Then he told Colo that he had tape-recorded the conversations, and that the tapes were stashed in a suitcase in his hotel room.

"She was very courteous," Hinckley added.

At last Colo understood. The assassination attempt wasn't about politics or the presidency or even Ronald Reagan. It was about impressing a movie star.

Colo was flabbergasted. What kind of crazy motive was that? But now he was sure that Hinckley had been acting alone—no conspiracy would ever revolve around a fantasy of attracting the attention of an actress. He ran to find Ragle and an FBI supervisor. As they pieced together Hinckley's story, Jodie Foster could prove to be a critical witness, but they had to get to her before the media did.

CHAPTER 15

"WHAT DOES THE FUTURE HOLD?"

N A CORNER OF THE RECOVERY ROOM, BEHIND PORTABLE SCREENS, Ronald Reagan drifted in and out of consciousness. Nurses worked constantly at his bedside, checking his blood pressure, monitoring his respirator, offering words of reassurance. When the president seemed uncomfortable, doctors increased his pain medication; when the level of oxygen in his blood was still too low, they raised his air intake to 80 percent oxygen. Doctors who had examined him could hear blood clots and mucus rattling in both lungs, but they detected no breath sounds at the base of either one. The left lung, of course, had been badly damaged by the bullet and the surgery, but blood and other debris had now worked their way into the right lung, so it too was not performing well. Reagan's most recent X-ray was also somewhat troubling: in addition to showing the effects of the secretions in both lungs, it confirmed that the lower lobe of the left one remained collapsed.

Ben Aaron, who was keeping a close eye on Reagan, considered how he might clear out the lungs and help improve his patient's breathing. The best approach, he thought, would be to perform a fiber-optic bronchoscopy—a procedure that would involve inserting a probe with a camera lens down the president's breathing tube—to examine the lungs and the material collecting in them. Through the probe, Aaron could also inject saline into the lungs to loosen mucus and clots, then use the same device to remove the debris.

As one of Aaron's assistants sterilized the bronchoscope, doctors increased Reagan's air intake to 100 percent oxygen. Another physician, Jack Zimmerman, a specialist in treating critically ill patients after surgery, took his place at the head of the president's bed, where he would operate the two-liter respiration bag to ensure that his patient got enough air during the procedure. Like many others that day, Zimmerman was struck by Reagan's naturally dark hair.

Aaron lubricated the probe and inserted it into the president's breathing tube. The probe got stuck about eight inches down; despite the pain medications, Reagan stirred and became agitated. Zimmerman assured him that everything would be okay.

The surgeon tried again but still couldn't maneuver the probe past a kink in the tube. They now had two options. They could swap out the breathing tube for a new one—a laborious and somewhat risky maneuver—or try a more conservative procedure, recommended by Zimmerman, that involved hyperinflating the lungs with a respirator bag, infusing them with a small amount of sterile saline, and then using a separate catheter to vacuum out the clots and secretions. Aaron told Zimmerman to give it a try, but then he was called out of the recovery room to operate for a second time on his patient from the night before; the man was once again bleeding badly.

Under Zimmerman's direction, the two nurses attending the president in the recovery room—Denise Sullivan and Cathy Edmondson—inflated Reagan's lungs, injected the solution, and sucked out debris. As Sullivan and Edmondson worked, Zimmerman explained the procedure to the president and told him to relax. But Reagan continued to tug at the uncomfortable tube. Edmondson had to admonish him several times. "Don't pull at it now," she said. "You are going to have to let me breathe for you."

As time went on, the president's blood tests steadily improved. Zimmerman adjusted the respirator to deliver 60 percent oxygen, then 50 percent. Soon Reagan felt well enough to ask for a pencil and a piece of paper. Lying on his back, he began jotting notes on white and pink hospital records attached to a clipboard. His handwriting was shaky—he was still groggy from the anesthesia and the painkillers—but it impressed the nurses that he could write at all.

"All in all, I'd rather be in Phil.," he scratched, a near quotation of a famous crack by the comedian W. C. Fields.

Everyone around the bed chuckled. *Okay,* thought Denise Sullivan. *He's going to make it.*

In another note, this one somewhat garbled, Reagan wrote, "I am aren't alive aren't I?" The nurses assured him that he was.

He also asked about the shooting. "What happened to the guy with the gun? Was anyone else hurt?"

Sullivan thought hard about how to respond. She had been told to say nothing to the president about the other victims, particularly Jim Brady. "Two other people were shot," Sullivan replied, apparently unaware that three others had been wounded, "but they are okay, don't worry about them. And yes, they got the guy with the gun."

A flurry of notes followed. Some were serious; more than once, the president asked why he couldn't breathe. But many were lighthearted and alluded to Hollywood and acting. At one point, on the same piece of paper he'd used to ask about the gunman, he scribbled: "Could we rewrite this scene beginning about the time I left the hotel?"

AFTER LYN NOFZIGER'S second appearance in front of the media, he went looking for a doctor at the hospital who could speak to the press after the president came out of surgery. Nofziger ruled out Dan Ruge, the White House physician, because reporters might suspect him of downplaying the seriousness of the president's condition. He also didn't want to turn to the surgeons who had operated on Reagan: they might be too tired and too emotional to handle the harsh media spotlight.

Several doctors at GW told Nofziger that Dr. Dennis O'Leary, a hospital administrator, had some experience with the press.

Nofziger found O'Leary in his office and introduced himself. "So," Nofziger said, "who is going to do this, going to brief the press? There is a lot of media over there and somebody has got to talk to them." Nofziger let his words hang for a moment as he stared at O'Leary.

"Who, me?" O'Leary asked. "You mean there is nobody else?"

"There's nobody else."

After persuading O'Leary that he was up to the job, Nofziger told him, "You have to be prepared to answer every stupid question these guys can dream up. And, by the way, be yourself."

O'Leary, in fact, knew quite a bit about reporters. His father had been a correspondent for *Sports Illustrated,* and in his current job as dean of clinical affairs at GW Medical Center—an assignment that put him in charge of all patient-related issues at the center's hospital and medical school—O'Leary dealt with journalists fairly frequently. Confident and poised, he didn't back down from arguments and often deployed his dry wit as a weapon.

Before the press conference, O'Leary was briefed by the surgeons who had operated on the president. Then he asked Nofziger if there was anything he should be careful about mentioning.

"Just tell the truth," Nofziger said.

During the five-minute walk from the hospital to the medical school, O'Leary sketched out his opening statement in his mind. It would be short and to the point, a straightforward description of Reagan's current condition.

At 7:30 p.m., after a brief introduction by Nofziger, O'Leary stepped to the podium in Room 101 of Ross Hall, where he usually taught a class on hematology. But instead of respectful medical students, he faced scores of reporters, photographers, and television cameramen. The television lights nearly blinded him, but he could see that the noisy crowd was so big it barely squeezed into the spacious classroom. He felt as though he'd landed on Mars.

"The president is in the recovery room," O'Leary began. "He is in stable condition and he is awake."

The rest of the brief statement was accurate except in one instance. O'Leary said that the president "was at no time in any serious danger," which was clearly incorrect. If Jerry Parr hadn't decided to redirect the limousine from the White House to the hospital, Reagan would likely have died; if Reagan had arrived in GW's emergency room even five or ten minutes later, his chances of survival would have been slim. But in O'Leary's defense, he had not been told what had transpired during Reagan's most perilous moments in the ER.

When responding to questions from reporters, however, O'Leary's answers were sometimes wrong. To a shouted query about transfusions given to the president, O'Leary understated the amount of blood Reagan received by three units, an important difference. Then he understated the amount of blood loss by about 1.5 liters. If medical experts had heard the truth about how much blood Reagan had lost and how much had been replaced, they might have raised serious questions about the severity of the president's injuries.

In response to another question, O'Leary said the bullet "was really not very close to any vital structure," and added that it was "several inches" from the president's heart. In fact, the bullet had mangled Reagan's lung and come to rest just an inch from his heart.

O'Leary was also asked about the president's arrival at the hospital, but he failed to mention that Reagan had collapsed upon entering the emergency room. "He got out of the car and stood up and walked in on his own," O'Leary said. "As I say, he was alert and awake all the time."

When asked whether he found it "extraordinary that a 70-year-old man could be shot in the lung and then brought to the hospital and walk in under his own power," O'Leary paused and replied: "I think it speaks well for the physiologic health of the president. We do have elderly people—much more elderly than the president is—who do undergo chest surgery, but he certainly sailed through it."

"Do you find that medically extraordinary?" someone asked.

"Maybe not medically extraordinary," O'Leary responded, "but just short of that, okay?"

SITTING AROUND THE conference table in the Situation Room, George Bush and the administration's top officials watched O'Leary's performance and felt enormous relief. "This guy is good," said the vice president.

When the press conference was over, Bush led a discussion about whether he should give a statement. "I think I could," Bush said. "And just say we are very pleased. I don't think we need questions, either."

The meeting adjourned at eight p.m., at which point the vice president and several officials moved upstairs to Bush's small office, down the hall from Reagan's. Baker, Meese, and the others clustered around Bush's desk and talked through a range of issues, from national security to the vice president's schedule. Just outside the office, one of Bush's aides attempted to draft a statement for the media. Frazzled, he couldn't find the words. Ken Khachigian, the president's chief speechwriter, put a piece of paper in a secretary's typewriter and quickly produced a brief and confident statement that papered over the day's trials and problems.

A few minutes later, Bush entered the White House press room and stepped up to the podium.

"I am deeply heartened by Dr. O'Leary's report on the president's condition, that he has emerged from this experience with flying colors and with the most optimistic prospects for a complete recovery," the vice president said. "I can reassure this nation and the watching world that the American government is functioning fully and effectively. We've had full and complete communication throughout the day and the officers of the federal government have been fulfilling their obligations with skill and with care."

Then, having taken no questions, Bush was gone.

BEFORE HEADING HOME that evening, Joe Giordano, the head of the trauma team, stopped by Reagan's bedside to check on his patient. He was pleased to see that the president was improving and didn't seem to have suffered any adverse effects from the surgery or the anesthesia. During the operation, Giordano had thought about how much the outcome mattered—for every doctor in the room, for the hospital, and for the nation. As he stood at the president's bedside and looked through his chart, Giordano was relieved to reach an unambiguous conclusion: the surgery had gone perfectly.

A little after nine, David Gens—who had spent the past hour and a half removing a patient's ruptured appendix—sat down next to Reagan. As he had once before, Gens wondered whether anyone had told the president what had happened that day.

"Mr. President, do you remember me from the ER?" Gens asked.

The president nodded.

"Do you know what happened?"

Reagan shook his head.

"Your lung had been torn by the bullet," Gens said. "And we repaired that. We took out the bullet. But everything is going to be all right."

Reagan nodded again.

"Mrs. Reagan did fine throughout all the excitement," Gens said with a grin.

Reagan smiled. Gens could see that the president was doing much better. Even as doctors continued to reduce the proportion of oxygen in his air supply, his color and his blood oxygen levels were improving. Gens left the recovery room and tried to catch a nap in a comfortable chair in the dialysis unit. But the day's adrenaline hadn't worn off and he couldn't sleep.

DENISE SULLIVAN AND Cathy Edmondson were impressed by how compliant the president was—he was so unlike most VIP and celebrity patients. Despite his pain and his weakened condition, he followed instructions and showed remarkably good cheer. He even seemed apologetic about causing them undue stress.

But Reagan had long felt a great respect for nurses, especially since a near-death experience more than three decades earlier. After a movie premiere in 1947, he had suddenly become very ill. He was taken to a hospital where he was diagnosed with a dangerous strain of viral pneumonia. He burned with fever, then froze with chills. Medications seemed to have no effect. One night, Humphrey Bogart appeared in his dreams, and together they acted out a scene under a streetlamp on a dark and lonely patch of sidewalk.

The attending nurses wrapped Reagan in blankets and fed him hot tea through a glass tube. Each breath hurt so much that he reached a point where he wanted to die. But one nurse in particular wouldn't let him. She gripped his hand and urged him to inhale and exhale. "Come on now, breathe in once more," she said, leaning over him. "Now, let it out." Reagan followed the nurse's gentle instruction. He breathed and he survived.

Now here he was again, this time putting his trust in two nurses who refused to leave his side. They, too, held his hand and coaxed him to relax. They told him that they would stay right there with him and that everything would be fine. He just needed to let the machine breathe for him.

"Don't fight it," they said over and over again.

"I keep on breathing?" he wrote.

Yes, they said. And so he did.

AFTER JERRY PARR left the hospital that evening, he grabbed a bite to eat at the White House mess, where he also sipped a glass of vodka, straight up. He felt at once excited and devastated. He could feel the adrenaline still coursing through his system, and he kept trying to sort out what had gone both right and wrong. He knew he had saved the president's life, but he also understood that the Secret Service had failed by allowing the gunman to get so close to the president. He was head of the presidential detail; this was his error to bear.

As he replayed the shooting in his head, Parr realized that he and his agents had been lulled into complacency by the routine nature of trips to the Hilton and other sites like it in Washington. If the president had given a speech in Baltimore or Philadelphia or New York, everyone would have been more alert—the agents, the police, even the spectators—because of the less familiar settings. Nursing his drink, Parr wondered whether he and the other agents would be portrayed as goats or heroes. When he finally got home, Parr hugged his wife and crawled into bed. He was exhausted, but sleep wouldn't come.

Back at the White House, George Opfer sat in the command post below the Oval Office; folded uncomfortably in a chair, he tried to catch some sleep. Though agency supervisors had told him to go home, he'd refused. If something went wrong in the recovery room, he wanted to be the agent who brought the first lady to the hospital.

Upstairs, in the residence, Nancy Reagan was curled up in a ball on her husband's side of their bed, fast asleep. She clutched one of the president's white T-shirts in her hands.

THAT NIGHT, GW's doctors gave Jim Brady only a 50 percent chance of survival. Arthur Kobrine had done everything possible to save the press secretary's life. He and the other surgeons plucked out all the shrapnel they could reach and removed the dead and damaged brain tissue. They irrigated and cleaned the wound with particular care.

As he finished up the surgery, Kobrine faced a dilemma: should he reattach the bone flap, the section of Brady's skull he had removed to gain access to the brain? Leaving the flap off was the safer course. Although it had been soaking in a pool of antiseptic, it had inevitably collected germs and replacing it could lead to a serious infection. Besides, Brady could live without it, though his head would be misshapen until the gap could be covered with a ceramic plate. Then, not uncharacteristically, Kobrine had a macabre thought: if he didn't replace the bone flap and Brady later died, the press secretary's head would be so disfigured that his casket would have to be closed at his funeral.

Kobrine weighed his options and then made his decision. He replaced the bone flap and stitched up Brady's head. After a brief stop in the recovery room, the press secretary was sent to the intensive care unit on the hospital's fourth floor.

Sarah Brady stayed at her husband's side all through the night. Several visitors came by, including Richard Allen, Brady's friend and fellow commuter. Allen, whose wife, Pat, joined him at the hospital, was devastated by the press secretary's condition. Blood seeped through the bandages on Brady's head, which had swollen to the size of a basketball. The left side of his friend's body twitched uncontrollably. Allen and his wife both hugged Sarah Brady, who then leaned over her husband and, calling him by his nickname, whispered in his ear, "Bear! Bear! It's Dick and Pat—they're here, Bear!"

Allen took Brady's right hand in his own. He was stunned when the wounded press secretary squeezed back so hard it hurt. Emotion swept over him; for the first time that day, tears streamed down Allen's face.

HOUR BY HOUR, the president's condition improved. As if to keep his small audience entertained, he continued writing notes. In a barely legible chicken scratch, he quoted Winston Churchill's famous line about how there was "nothing more exhilarating than to be shot at without result." And in his innocent, movie-star way, he flirted with the nurses. A little after 11:30, he wrote to Denise Sullivan, "Does Nancy know about us?" Sullivan, a hazel-eyed thirty-four-year-old, laughed. She tried to put the note in her pocket, but a gruff Secret Service agent snatched it from her hands.

When the night shift began, two new nurses, Marisa Mize and Joanne Bell, took over the president's care. While Bell monitored Reagan's vital signs and updated his chart, Mize sat at the right side of his bed and held his hand. A few minutes after taking her seat, she saw that phlegm had become stuck in the president's throat. Anxious and uncomfortable, he clutched at his breathing tube. After Mize patted his head and told him it was okay to be scared, she persuaded him to let go of the tube. Just as the other nurses did, she told him to let the machine breathe for him. And she, too, promised to stay with him.

"I'm going to hold your hand and not leave you," she said.

Reagan gripped her right hand and didn't let go. He wouldn't take his eyes off her. His lids would droop and then shut, only to snap open again a moment later.

"Go to sleep," Mize told him again and again. "I'm right here. I haven't left."

After finishing his latest surgery, Ben Aaron returned, still wearing his blood-tinged scrubs. He reviewed Reagan's chart, talked for a moment with a nurse and another doctor, and then said something the president couldn't quite make out.

Suddenly Reagan seemed frantic. "What did he mean 'this is it'?" he wrote to Mize. "Will I like it?"

Mize could see that the president was frightened by whatever he thought Aaron had said. She guessed that Reagan believed that "this is it" meant that something terrible was about to happen.

"No, no, you are fine," Mize said. "They are going to remove your breathing tube soon."

Aaron told Zimmerman he was going to take a nap; he lay down on a nearby cot and fell instantly asleep. Zimmerman, too anxious to sleep, guzzled his sixth cup of coffee.

A few minutes later, Reagan struggled with the tube again. Calmly, Mize took his hand. "You have to let this machine breathe for you," she reminded him.

Hoping to distract the president, Mize began talking a bit about herself. She told Reagan that she was from southern California and had gone to college in San Francisco, where she'd studied music before getting into nursing.

The mention of his home state seemed to perk up the president. Once again he reached for the clipboard and wrote, "Send me to L.A. where I can see the air I'm breathing."

A seemingly endless series of doctors and nurses came by the president's bed. Soon Reagan wrote another note to Mize: "If I had this much attention in Hollywood I'd have stayed there."

A bit later, he wrote that he felt "like I've done a remake of *Lost Weekend*," referring to the Oscar-winning film about an alcoholic who goes on a bender and loses all sense of time.

Mize chuckled. She was surprised that Reagan was able to joke with her so soon after his surgery; still, he sometimes seemed confused.

"Do you know where you are?" she asked him.

He shook his head.

"You are in the GW recovery room," she said, adding that it was early in the morning of March 31.

"I thought it was still afternoon," he wrote back.

A little after two a.m., Mize noticed a perturbed look on Reagan's face. Suspecting that he was feeling anxious about something, she tried to lighten the mood. "What, do you think your wife is holding dinner or something?"

"No," he wrote, "I'm not really hungry for some reason."

Then, on the same sheet of paper, he wrote: "What does the future hold?"

Mize wasn't quite sure what he meant, nor did she know how to answer. As she thought about how to respond, Reagan scribbled, "Will I be able to do ranch work, ride, etc.?"

"Sure," Mize told him. "Give yourself three months and you'll be able to do those things again."

"How long in the hospital?" he wrote a minute or two later.

"Three weeks," Mize said.

By this point, Reagan's oxygen levels were acceptable and his lungs were working more efficiently. Mize and the other nurses thought he could breathe on his own; so did the doctors who were monitoring his care. At three a.m., they removed the breathing tube. Then, as Reagan caught his breath, they waited by his bedside—they all wanted to hear the president's first words.

When Reagan finally cleared his throat and spoke in a hoarse voice, he was characteristically jaunty. "What was that guy's beef?" he quipped.

For the next forty minutes, the president held court, telling stories and jokes. Everyone was amused by his performance and amazed at his stamina.

After his audience filtered away, it was just Reagan, Mize, and Joanne Bell, who continued to monitor Reagan's vital signs and make notes on his chart. The president and Mize chatted back and forth for a while, talking about everything from his work schedule to his advisors. As they spoke, Mize realized that Reagan didn't seem to hear everything she was saying; he also seemed to be trying to read her lips. When she asked whether he was hard of hearing, Reagan said he was, in his right ear. "But I'm too vain to wear a hearing aid," he told her.

At one point, referring to the White House, the president asked who was "running the show."

Mize intuitively understood that she should avoid mentioning the controversy about Alexander Haig's news conference, which was already getting a lot of attention. Instead, she answered, "The vice president caught a plane back to Washington." She felt foolish for making it sound as if Bush had hopped on an American Airlines flight; then, feeling even sillier, she said, "In situations like this the vice president is in charge."

But the question led Mize to wonder whether Reagan's many duties as president were on his mind. Gently, she said, "I bet you are pretty anxious with everything you have to do."

No, not really, Reagan said. He told her he had a great routine: he walked to the office before nine and was home in the residence by five or five-thirty. He ate dinner and often watched a movie with his wife, then went to bed. "I have three guys who mostly run things for me," he said modestly.

As the hour passed four a.m., Joanne Bell became increasingly frustrated. She knew the president needed to rest, and she wanted him to stop talking to Marisa Mize and everyone else. Finally, deciding it was time for decisive action, she placed a moist washcloth over Reagan's eyes.

"Now, Mr. President," Bell said, "you need to get some sleep. In the most polite way I know how, I'm putting this cover over your eyes, and I want you to shut up and go to sleep."

For the first time in almost twenty-four hours, the world around the president came to a stop. Someone turned off the overhead lights. Nurses read charts by flashlight; doctors quietly finished their reports. Around the recovery room, Secret Service agents stood sentry. Only one sound could be heard—the *beep-beep-beep* of the machine monitoring the president's steadily beating heart.

EPILOGUE

FTER A FITFUL HOUR OF SLEEP AND A SPONGE BATH, RONALD REA-
gan was wheeled from the recovery room into an elevator for the
ride to the hospital's intensive care unit on the fourth floor. There,
as Secret Service agents and police officers stood at attention, he was
rolled down a hallway until he reached room 4025-N, one of the larg-
est in the ward. The plain white room had been scrubbed clean for the
president, and his bed was placed headfirst against a wall. To his right,
sunlight from a bright new day seeped around the edges of the stuffy
room's thick window shade.

The door closed, and now the president was alone with two nurses
and a Secret Service agent who stood guard behind a drawn green curtain. For the rest of Reagan's stay in the hospital, an agent was always
stationed in his room.

Nurse Maureen McCann, wearing a yellow scrub dress, introduced herself. Though he was still weak and in pain, Reagan smiled
and said, "I have a daughter named Maureen."

McCann and the second nurse, Carolyn Ramos, then conducted a
basic medical assessment, checking the president's blood pressure, his

pulse, his temperature, the position of his chest tubes and dressings, and his IV lines. Everything was fine. Ramos asked Reagan a series of questions to test his mental acuity. After querying him about the year and whether he knew his whereabouts, she paused and said, "I was going to ask you who is president, but I don't think that is necessary."

Reagan laughed, and Ramos went on to say that when she had asked the same question of a patient a few weeks earlier, the patient replied, "It's that actor fellow—Jimmy Stewart." Again Reagan was amused, and he responded with one of his favorite yarns about being mistaken on a New York City street for his fellow movie actor Ray Milland. Not wanting to disappoint the fan, Reagan had signed an autograph in Milland's name.

The nurses were impressed that Reagan could joke after his ordeal, but the laughter stopped when they began performing respiratory therapy, which involved pounding on the president's back with cupped hands and then forcing him to cough up debris from his lungs. The therapy was so vigorous that it could be heard by anyone in the vicinity; later, when Nancy Reagan spent time in a nearby room while the therapy was administered, she described it as sounding like someone was "slapping a side of beef."

The therapy session exhausted the president and made him sweat; to help him cool down and to quench his thirst, McCann gave him some ice chips to chew on. Then, knowing that he would soon have visitors, she asked whether she could brush his tangled hair to make him look a bit more presentable. "I meant to have it cut," Reagan said, adding that he hadn't washed it in a couple of days. She gently combed and parted the president's hair.

Ramos offered to brush Reagan's teeth for him. Looking puzzled, the president said, "But they're mine." Ramos was embarrassed—most ICU patients around Reagan's age had dentures. She gave him what he needed to brush his own teeth.

At 7:15, the president's official day began. Jim Baker, Ed Meese, and Mike Deaver filed into the room. "I should have known I wasn't going to avoid a staff meeting," Reagan quipped, drawing laughter from his top advisors. Someone handed the president the dairy bill to sign. Borrowing a pen, Reagan scrawled his signature in the proper place and the bill became law. The men discussed the shooting briefly, and one of the members of the Troika told the president that the gunman was "a kid from a good family in Colorado who just happened to be crazy."

This was the first Reagan had been told anything about his assailant, and he reflected on the news for a moment. "I had hoped it was a KGB agent," the president said, referring to the Soviet spy agency. "On second thought," he added, "he wouldn't have missed then."

For most of the rest of the day, the president napped, read the newspapers, and visited with Mrs. Reagan and the children, all four of whom were now in Washington. At one point, joking with his son Michael, Reagan said, "If you ever get shot, make sure you're not wearing a new suit." But that afternoon, the one-liners and the stories came to an abrupt halt when Dan Ruge, the White House physician, stopped by and broke the sad news about the shooting of Jim Brady, who was still fighting for his life just around the corner.

"Oh, damn," Reagan said, his eyes welling up with tears.

THE FIRST SEVERAL days of Reagan's recovery went better than the doctors could have hoped. The president regained his color and grew steadily stronger. He successfully spat up dark blood, a sign that his body was working to clear his lungs. To ensure that he got plenty of rest, his White House staff strictly limited the number of visitors. Not until April 6 was anyone outside the president's closest circle permitted to see him; that afternoon, Tip O'Neill, the Democratic Speaker of the House, came by to pay his regards. O'Neill—Reagan's political nemesis— entered the room and walked straight to the bed, where he grabbed the president's hand and kissed his head. Then the Speaker knelt and together they recited the Twenty-third Psalm—"The lord is my shepherd; I shall not want." Speaking through tears, O'Neill said, "God bless you, Mr. President. We're all praying for you."

A temporary setback—a high fever of mysterious origin—puzzled and worried Reagan's medical team, but it eventually dissipated. On April 11, his thirteenth day in the hospital, the president was released from GW. Doctors, citing hospital protocol, tried to insist that Reagan be taken by wheelchair to his waiting limousine. But Reagan refused. "I walked in," the president said. "I'm walking out."

As he shuffled stiffly out the hospital's doors at 10:43 a.m. that day, Reagan smiled, masking his obvious pain as he slipped into the limousine. At the South Lawn of the White House, he was greeted by a cheering crowd of several hundred people. Wearing a bright red sweater over a white shirt, the president waved to the spectators and turned to walk into the White House, resembling, as an aide later put it, a "championship golfer strolling toward the eighteenth green."

For the next two weeks, Reagan rested and worked a few hours each day from the White House residence; he returned to the Oval Office for the first time on April 24. Though a number of his aides were stunned by how weak he seemed, he continued to gain strength. On April 28, he traveled to Capitol Hill to give his first public address since the shooting, a speech advocating the passage of his economic package. Favoring his left arm and appearing thinner, the president walked into the House chamber to what one reporter described as a three-minute "rafter-shaking ovation."

When the applause finally died down, Reagan began by thanking everyone for their prayers and messages of support in the wake of the assassination attempt. Then, speaking about "those others who fell beside me," the president said:

> Sick societies don't produce young men like Secret Service agent Tim McCarthy, who placed his body between mine and the man with the gun simply because he felt that's what his duty called for him to do. Sick societies don't produce dedicated police officers like Tom Delahanty or able and devoted public servants like James Brady. Sick societies don't make people like us so proud to be Americans and so very proud of our fellow citizens.

Applause broke out each time he named one of the wounded men. In all, his twenty-minute address was interrupted twelve times by applause.

With his behavior immediately after the shooting and his speech that day, Reagan turned a near tragedy into a political triumph, helping to ensure passage of his ambitious economic program several months later. As one top Democrat wrote in his journal the night of the president's address, "We've been outflanked and outgunned."

REAGAN WAS NOT one to dwell on the negative and, unless asked, he rarely spoke about the assassination attempt. He slept fine; he ate fine; he didn't startle when he heard a bang. He wasn't afraid to travel or to leave the White House grounds, although for the rest of his two terms security tightened significantly, keeping him farther from reporters and the public.

Reagan kept a diary throughout his presidency. On April 11, 1981, his first day back in the White House, he described the shooting. His prose was typically spare:

> Left the hotel at the usual side entrance and headed for the car—suddenly there was a burst of gunfire from the left. S.S. Agent pushed me onto the floor & jumped on top. I felt a blow to my upper back that was unbelievably painful. I was sure that he had broken my rib. . . . Getting shot hurts. Still my fear was growing because no matter how hard I tried to breathe it seemed I was getting less & less air.

By then, almost two weeks after the attempt, he had been told that the bullet that struck him—John Hinckley's sixth and last shot—had ricocheted off the right rear quarter panel of the armored limousine and flown through the small gap between the car's door and its frame. Because the bullet hit the car at an angle, it was flattened and its Devastator charge was eliminated; the shape of the bullet as it struck Reagan also explains why the bullet's track through his body was a dime-sized channel even though the wound in his chest was merely a slit.

In the hours after the shooting, while being worked on by doctors and nurses at the hospital, the president prayed for his life. He also prayed for his assailant, realizing that he couldn't ask for God's grace while feeling hatred in his heart for the man who had shot him.

The president concluded his entry about the shooting by writing: "Whatever happens now I owe my life to God and will try to serve him in every way I can." Over the next few years, aides and friends recalled Reagan telling them the same thing. "He felt like he had been spared for a purpose," James Baker recalled.

Never one to presume that he understood God's intentions, Reagan later speculated that he'd been granted his wish to live so that he could help mitigate the risk of Armageddon. "Perhaps having come so close to death made me feel I should do whatever I could in the years God had given me to reduce the threat of nuclear war," he wrote. "Perhaps that is the reason I was spared."

Soon after his discharge from the hospital, Reagan retreated to the White House solarium and handwrote a personal appeal to Leonid Brezhnev. Reagan stated that he hoped to create "the circumstances which will lead to meaningful and constructive dialogue which will assist us in fulfilling our joint obligation to find lasting peace." Though neither Brezhnev nor his immediate successors proved particularly responsive, Reagan continued to pursue an end to the Cold War. Even as he spoke harshly of the Soviets, increased the nation's defense budget, and launched the expensive antimissile program popularly known as Star Wars, he hoped to engage with a Soviet leader who would commit himself to serious negotiations. That leader appeared in 1985, when Mikhail Gorbachev became the general secretary of the Communist Party of the Soviet Union. Reagan and Gorbachev held four summits and in 1987 achieved a historic accord that substantially reduced nuclear weapons. In 1989, ten months after Reagan left office, German citizens tore down the Berlin Wall. Two years later, a decade after Reagan's appeal to Brezhnev, the Soviet Union collapsed, ending the Cold War.

THE PRESIDENT'S PERFORMANCE on the day of his near assassination reassured the nation; in particular, his ability to entertain his doctors and nurses with stories and jokes caused much astonishment. Not surprised was his son Ron Reagan. "He was a performer, basically, and that was what his background was," the younger Reagan said three decades later. "It's hard to turn that off. He also probably wanted to put everyone else in the room at ease." In fact, the president himself commented on the reflexive impulse that drove him to tell jokes and jot notes late into the night. "There was a crowd standing around," he told an interviewer in 1985. "Somebody ought to entertain them some way."

Even under the most harrowing of circumstances, Reagan's prodigious memory held a ready supply of one-liners; relying on his years of training as an entertainer, he used his quick wit to defuse the tension in both the emergency room and the recovery room. Ironically, Reagan's two most famous roles as a Hollywood actor involved dramatic hospital or medical scenes. In 1940, he played George Gipp, the famed Notre Dame football player, in *Knute Rockne All American*. In the movie, Gipp's coach, Rockne, visits him at his bedside as the star player lies dying. "I haven't got a complaint in the world, Rock, I'm not afraid," Gipp says, fighting to keep his eyes open. "What's tough about this? Rock, some day, when the team is up against it, the breaks are beating the boys, ask them to go in there with all they got, win just one for the Gipper. I don't know where I'll be then. But I'll know about it. I'll be happy."

In 1942, Reagan gave what is generally regarded as his best performance in *Kings Row*, a film in which he plays Drake McHugh, a playboy who suffers hard times and is badly injured in a train accident. In the film, a doctor unnecessarily amputates McHugh's legs. When he awakens from his delirium, McHugh looks down at the bed and screams in terror, "Where's the rest of me?"

It seems fitting, then, that Reagan delivered his best line of the day—"I hope you are all Republicans"—right before he was put to sleep on the operating table.

That line and others, as well as the president's extraordinary courage and poise, had a powerful effect on Reagan's tenure. Immediately after the assassination attempt, Reagan's popularity improved dramatically: his approval rating went from 59 percent in mid-March to 73 percent within days of the shooting. In late May, it was still standing at 68 percent. David Broder, one of the country's most respected political journalists, wrote just two days after the assassination attempt that "what happened to Reagan on Monday is the stuff of which legends are made." Broder went on: "As long as people remember the hospitalized president joshing his doctors and nurses—and they will remember—no critic will be able to portray Reagan as a cruel or callous or heartless man." Three decades later, Broder stood by that assessment. "He was politically untouchable from that point on," Broder said in an interview. "He became a mythic figure."

Lou Cannon, Reagan's most esteemed biographer, came to a similar conclusion. In a recent interview, Cannon said that Reagan's actions after the assassination attempt "cemented a bond with the American people that never dissolved. And that's because they saw a genuine person that day. They began to feel for him the way they would feel for a friend or someone close to them, not just some politician."

Of course, Reagan's popularity fluctuated throughout his eight years in office, rising and falling in response to his actions and to events beyond his control. He and his policies were roundly criticized by liberals and moderates, and he often frustrated even his most loyal supporters by compromising on core issues. He preached the importance of balancing the budget but left behind massive deficits. He railed against the evils of taxes but supported substantial tax increases to save Social Security and prevent the budget deficit from spiraling further out of control. He pledged to rid the government of waste, fraud, and abuse but stood by passively as many of his closest aides became ensnared in ethics probes and criminal investigations.

Reagan clearly enjoyed the role of president, but he was disparaged for sometimes seeming less than engaged with his presidential duties and for providing minimal supervision of his staff. That hands-off approach paid dividends in his first term, when he succeeded in his effort to avoid becoming mired in the details of governing. But it contributed to near catastrophe in his second, when the most difficult crisis of his presidency—the Iran-contra scandal—severely tested his reputation for integrity. Even then, Reagan never faced a serious threat of removal from office. The American public would not have stood for it: most people had come to genuinely like the man, even if they didn't always support his decisions or policies.

By the time he left office in January 1989, Reagan had the highest approval rating of any departing president since Harry Truman. In November 1988, his vice president, George H. W. Bush, was elected president, a clear sign that the country wanted to keep the Reagan legacy alive.

History has come to regard Ronald Reagan fondly. A survey by C-SPAN of historians that was released in 2009 ranked Reagan as the tenth most successful president out of the forty-two men who had held the office to that point. He was rated the eighth most successful president in international relations and the seventh most successful in "performance within the context of the times." And Reagan is widely credited with reinvigorating the conservative movement at a particularly perilous moment in its history; many of today's most prominent Republicans consider him their party's most inspiring and transformational figure of the past several decades.

NOT ALL OF the president's advisors fared as well. Mike Deaver, who did more to shape the public's perception of Reagan than any other aide, left the White House in 1985 and was later convicted of lying to Congress and to a grand jury investigating his lobbying practices. Ultimately, Deaver became involved in several philanthropic organizations and regained his stature as a powerful Washington insider; he died in 2007. Ed Meese remained presidential counselor until 1985, when he became attorney general. Several months before the end of Reagan's second term, however, Meese resigned after a lengthy but inconclusive investigation by an independent counsel (he was never charged with a crime). Meese has since become one of the country's most influential advocates for conservative causes. Jim Baker, widely admired as an excellent chief of staff, became secretary of the Treasury during Reagan's second term. He then served as secretary of state in the presidential administration of his good friend George H. W. Bush.

Within months of the assassination attempt, National Security Advisor Richard Allen became ensnared in an investigation into whether he improperly accepted a $1,000 honorarium from a Japanese journalist who interviewed Nancy Reagan shortly after the inauguration. In fact, Allen had simply intercepted the payment, turned it over to a secretary to forward to White House lawyers, and forgotten about it. (The cash was rediscovered later in a White House safe, prompting an FBI investigation.) Although cleared of wrongdoing by the White House and Justice Department, Allen resigned anyway, saying that his relationship with Reagan had been sabotaged by other White House aides for unrelated reasons. Allen, who had used a personal tape recorder to document what happened in the Situation Room that day, turned his tapes over to the Ronald Reagan Presidential Library in 2010.

Alexander Haig's tenure in the Reagan administration remained stormy; after a number of other clashes with White House aides, he left the administration in June 1982. In 1988, he ran unsuccessfully for the Republican presidential nomination. For the rest of his life—he died in February 2010—he was most often remembered as the official who, on the day of the assassination attempt, asserted on national television that he was "in control" and then provided a mangled version of presidential succession.

PRESS SECRETARY JAMES Brady survived his terrible wound, but he never fully recovered. He spent 239 days at George Washington University Hospital; during that time, he underwent three additional operations to prevent blood clots from reaching his lungs and heart and to stop leakage of spinal fluid. He suffered from pneumonia, fevers, and other infections. Partially paralyzed, he endured hundreds of hours of excruciating physical therapy so he could learn to walk again; nevertheless, he was largely confined to a wheelchair for the next three decades. Despite the damage to his brain, however, he never lost his trademark wit. "When life gives you lemons, you make lemonade," he told a reporter in 2006. "I have several stands around here."

In the wake of the shooting—and after spotting her five-year-old son holding a loaded handgun at a friend's house four years after the assassination attempt—Sarah Brady became a major proponent of stiffer gun-control laws. After Reagan left office, Jim Brady joined his wife in that effort, which culminated in the passage of the Brady Law in 1993. The law requires background checks of anyone buying a firearm from a licensed dealer.

Officer Thomas K. Delahanty, an eighteen-year veteran of the Washington police force, retired on full disability in November 1981; the bullet that struck him in the back caused nerve damage too severe to allow him to return to duty. Though doctors had at first decided not to operate because the round lay so close to his spine, they changed their minds after learning that the bullet was a Devastator: it retained the potential to explode or leach toxins within the officer's body even after the shooting. Surgeons wearing bulletproof vests successfully removed the bullet three days after the assassination attempt. FBI agents would later determine that only one of the Devastator rounds actually exploded. That one struck Jim Brady.

Secret Service agent Tim McCarthy was the first of the wounded men to be discharged from the hospital. Before leaving GW on April 7, he paid a visit to the president, who had asked to see him so that he could thank the agent for saving his life. "Hey, Tim," Reagan said, his eyes twinkling. "You know—Brady, Delahanty, McCarthy, and Reagan. What did this guy have against the Irish?" McCarthy laughed, and later realized that the joke was really a lesson: if the president could put the shooting behind him, he could, too.

The first lady, however, had a difficult time in the aftermath of the assassination. A natural worrier, Nancy Reagan found herself sobbing uncontrollably at times. She lost weight and became panicky whenever her husband left the White House gates. She finally gained solace from an unconventional quarter: an astrologer who claimed that she could have warned Reagan not to leave the White House on March 30. In her autobiography, the former first lady wrote that she came to rely on the astrologer as much for her "personal concern and support" as for her interpretation of the stars. To this day, friends say, Mrs. Reagan has trouble discussing the shooting and chokes up when she is forced to relive those first terrible moments at the hospital when she didn't know whether her husband would live or die.

AFTER THE ASSASSINATION attempt, Jerry Parr was indeed hailed as a hero. As law enforcement officials reviewed the tapes of the shooting, it became clear that the agent's quick actions saved the president's life. If Parr had been a split second slower, Reagan would have been struck in the head by the ricocheting bullet; if Parr had frozen, even for a second, Hinckley would have been presented with a stationary target standing well within his effective shooting range.

In 1985, after twenty-three years on the job, Jerry Parr retired from the Secret Service. Before leaving, he paid a final visit to Reagan in the Oval Office. When the president saw him, he said, "You're not going to throw me over the couch, are you?"

Parr had decided to travel to the Hilton hotel that day in March 1981 so that he could build a better bond with Reagan. In that he succeeded, but the shooting also changed him. After leaving the Secret Service, Parr came to believe that God had directed his life so that he could one day save the president's. He ultimately obtained a master's degree in pastoral counseling and became the copastor of the Festival Church, a member of a network of ecumenical churches in Washington.

Now eighty, Parr doesn't want anyone to forget what happened— not because he considers himself a hero, but because he worries that security agents and officers may become complacent again. In March 2010, he visited the Federal Law Enforcement Training Center (FLETC) in Glynco, Georgia, to speak to two dozen young agents with the Naval Criminal Investigative Service who are often assigned to protect dignitaries and high-ranking navy officials all over the world. Parr was no longer the husky fifty-year-old agent who protected the president on that day in 1981. His hair and eyebrows were gray and bushy, and his once-confident strut had been replaced by a shuffle. But the young investigators—many of whom had not been born when the assassination attempt occurred—listened in rapt attention as Parr described how he pushed Reagan into the armored limousine and moments later decided to drive to the hospital instead of the White House. The president ultimately survived, Parr said, thanks to "human flesh, training, technology, and courage."

IN THE DAYS following the assassination attempt, several congressional panels promised investigations into the shooting, but none ever took place. The Treasury Department issued its own report on the attempt in August 1981. While it lauded the efforts of Jerry Parr and Tim McCarthy, it noted that there were often conflicts between the White House and the Secret Service over security arrangements. It urged the service and the White House to determine "the balance that is to be struck among the security, scheduling and public exposure requirements of the president." The report also noted the dramatic and dangerous difference between the elaborate security precautions taken to screen those attending the president's speech and the lax security provided outside the hotel, where "members of the general public, without any Secret Service pre-screening whatever, could walk to a rope barricade and stand within 15 feet of the president."

The Secret Service tried to deflect blame for the shooting onto the FBI by saying that the bureau never told them about Hinckley's arrest in Nashville. In an internal report, the service offered an unpersuasive defense of its procedures that day. Among other dubious points, it took credit for locating the president's limousine so that it could "effect instantaneous evacuation following the shooting." Nowhere does this report—or any public statement by the Secret Service—admit that the service made a colossal mistake by allowing a crowd of unscreened spectators to stand so close to the president's path to the limousine.

After the shooting the Secret Service did change a number of procedures for the better. It required that everyone entering a presidential event pass through a metal detector. It installed magnetometers at the White House (and discovered that a surprising number of guns were being toted in the purses of elderly ladies taking the official tour). And since March 30, 1981, presidents have rarely, if ever, walked in public without elaborate security arrangements. The revised procedures—which are regularly reviewed—have significantly increased the president's safety. Still, no security perimeter is impenetrable, as demonstrated by the two socialites who in 2009 sneaked through the White House gates, attended a state dinner, and shook President Barack Obama's hand.

Over the years, the Secret Service has steadily grown. In 2010, it had 3,500 agents—double the number in Jerry Parr's day—and its budget was nearly $1.5 billion. Training has become ever more important. In the early 1960s, Parr received six weeks of training at Secret Service school; agents entering in 1981 received eight weeks of training at FLETC and eight weeks at a Secret Service school in the Washington area. Today, new hires spend twelve weeks at FLETC and nineteen weeks at Secret Service school before they become full-fledged agents. The training of the presidential protective detail is especially intense. These agents spend two weeks out of every eight at the agency's sprawling training center in Beltsville, Maryland.

RONALD AND NANCY Reagan were forever grateful to the doctors and nurses who saved the president's life. A decade after the shooting, the Reagans attended a gathering at George Washington University Hospital to commemorate the event and to announce the renaming of the emergency department: it became the Ronald Reagan Institute of Emergency Medicine. The speakers told a number of jokes, and everyone particularly enjoyed recalling the note Reagan wrote to Denise Sullivan: "Does Nancy know about us?" A few days later, Sullivan received a handwritten note from the president. Chagrined that he might have embarrassed her, Reagan apologized for his "ill-timed joke 10 years ago" but went on to write that "your hand clasp was one of the most comforting things done for me during all of my hospital stay."

Dr. Joseph Giordano, who retired in 2010 as chairman of surgery for the George Washington University Medical Center, also received occasional notes from Reagan. In 1984, when Giordano was supporting Walter Mondale, a Democrat, for president, he wrote an op-ed piece that attacked the president's position on government assistance. Within days, Giordano received a letter from the president. "There has been a steady drumbeat of political demagoguery duly reported in the press that we have slashed away at essential social programs in our cost-cutting efforts," Reagan wrote. "The truth is we have done no such thing. . . . I owe you too much to let you go on believing the current propaganda." A decade after the shooting, the Reagans dropped Giordano a kind note when they heard about the death of his father.

A year after the assassination attempt, Dr. Benjamin Aaron, Dr. David Gens, and Dr. Paul Colombani paid a house call to see how the president was doing, and a film crew making a documentary on behalf of the hospital tagged along. Reagan said he appreciated the doctors' efforts to save his life, but he also told them he had a question. "I understand that you really kind of loaded me up with other people's blood, about a whole full charge, and now am I back on my own blood now, and if so where did all of the other blood go?" Aaron explained that the donated blood broke down quickly and was replaced by new blood produced by the president's body. Satisfied with the answer, Reagan chatted with them for a few more minutes and then thanked them again.

Ben Aaron retired from GW in 1996, but not before performing surgery on several other prominent patients, including future vice president Dick Cheney. (Aaron performed heart bypass surgery on Cheney in 1988, just before Cheney became defense secretary in George H. W. Bush's administration.) Currently, David Gens is a senior attending surgeon at the University of Maryland's R Adams Cowley Shock Trauma Center, and Paul Colombani is the chief of pediatric surgery at the Johns Hopkins Hospital.

The George Washington University Hospital building where Reagan was treated was demolished in 2003, a year after a new facility was erected across the street at a cost of $96 million. But the emergency department still bears the president's name, and the hospital remains classified by the city government as a Level 1 trauma center. In the years after Reagan was shot, trauma care in the United States has steadily improved, despite the elimination of a federal program that oversaw the development of trauma centers and emergency response systems around the country. In 1981, there were 145 Level 1 and Level 2 trauma centers in the nation. Today, there are more than 470 such centers, as well as 392

Level 3 centers; about 80 percent of the country's population is within an hour of a trauma center.

In June 1982, John W. Hinckley Jr. was found not guilty by reason of insanity of attempting to assassinate the president; the jury reached the same verdict on twelve other charges related to the shooting. The eight-week trial focused heavily on the testimony of psychiatrists who had examined Hinckley. It also featured videotaped testimony from Jodie Foster, who, though scarred by her brush with the would-be assassin, completed her education at Yale and then continued her film career.

Since his trial, Hinckley has been confined to St. Elizabeths Hospital for the mentally ill. The terms of his confinement require that he remain there until a federal judge determines that it is safe to free him.

Both St. Elizabeths' doctors and Hinckley's lawyers have in recent years argued that Hinckley's depression and his unspecified psychotic disorder have been in remission for years and that his narcissistic personality disorder has receded. Accordingly, they have petitioned a federal judge to grant Hinckley—who turned fifty-five in May 2010—more freedom in preparation for the day when he is eventually released. Often over the objections of prosecutors, U.S. District Judge Paul L. Friedman has granted Hinckley frequent and lengthy unsupervised visits with his mother at her home in Williamsburg, Virginia. (Hinckley's father died in 2008.) In 2009, Friedman also ruled that Hinckley could obtain a driver's license. Hinckley still spends his time much as he did in the months before shooting President Reagan—composing music and playing his guitar. Though his boyish looks have faded, his hair remains sandy blond and his face displays the same emotionless affect that so puzzled detectives and investigators thirty years ago.

In January 1989, Ronald Reagan rode quietly into retirement. One of his first acts was to visit his tailor and replace the suit that had been cut to shreds in the GW emergency room. Over the next few years, he dedicated much of his time to writing his memoirs, giving speeches, and cutting wood on his sprawling ranch.

A decade before his death in 2004, Reagan was diagnosed with Alzheimer's disease. But he refused to allow the devastating affliction to darken his outlook on life. When he performed his final act as a public man in November 1994, Reagan once again displayed the optimism that had always been so central to his character.

"I now begin the journey that will lead me into the sunset of my life," he wrote in his own hand. "I know that for America there will always be a bright dawn ahead."

NOTES

A Note on Sources

Writing a detailed history about a single day three decades ago is a substantial challenge. Fortunately, I was able to unearth a wealth of documentary evidence in the form of hundreds of pages of Secret Service and FBI reports, confidential court records, long-forgotten trial transcripts, closely held audiotapes, and the contemporaneous notes and diaries of a number of people who participated in the drama that unfolded on March 30, 1981. I supplemented that record with interviews of more than 125 people, many of whom played a part in what happened that day. In deciding whether to trust memories of such distant events, I used the standard of a person's "best recollection," as long as it squared with the official record or the memories of other participants. On occasion, I relied on newspaper and magazine articles published soon after the assassination attempt. Sometimes, of course, I had to make a judgment call about whether to use a detail, a line of dialogue, or a sequence of events recalled by someone who was present at some point during the day re-created in this book. In every instance, my objective was to provide a scrupulously accurate record of what actually occurred, and my fervent hope is that I did not fail those who took so much time to tell me their stories in the expectation that I would get them right.

In constructing these notes, I chose not to provide a citation for every fact in the text. Instead, I cited the facts that seemed most important to this account, as well as those that might help readers better understand the story and my thought process in telling it. The comments I have included with a number of citations also allowed me to spare a few nuggets of information from what Leon Trotsky—and later Ronald Reagan—called "the ash heap of history."

In describing the response by the Secret Service and the FBI to the assassination attempt, I relied heavily on interviews with former agents, as well as a review of trial testimony and extensive—and, until recently, confidential—Secret Service and FBI reports that I obtained under the Freedom of Information Act. I also benefited from a lengthy Treasury Department report that provided a detailed description of the actions of Secret Service agents during the attack and in the days leading up to it.

To provide an account of the medical care given to Ronald Reagan and the other wounded men, I relied on interviews with more than thirty doctors and nurses, medical records that I obtained from various sources, and extensive unpublished recollections and journal entries written by several participants. Further, I read many news stories about Reagan's treatment in the hospital, including articles in both medical journals and the popular press. One of the most comprehensive reports—an article by journalist John Pekkanen—appeared in the August 1981 issue of *Washingtonian* magazine.

Fortunately, I also obtained a copy of a thirty-minute documentary produced by George Washington University Hospital about the events of that day. Called *The Saving of the President*, it featured all of the principal doctors and nurses reenacting their own roles, thus providing an accurate record of what occurred in the hours following the president's arrival in GW's emergency room. This documentary—which aired once on national television and once on Washington-area television in 1982—was particularly helpful when describing locations in the hospital, which was torn down in 2003.

In telling John Hinckley's story, I relied extensively on transcripts from his eight-week trial, which are housed at the U.S. District Court for the District of Columbia. I obtained a 638-page confidential psychiatric assessment of Hinckley that was produced by prosecution psychiatrists. This document—which has never been made public—delved into every aspect of Hinckley's life, from birth until his arrest, and featured interviews with the suspect, his family, his associates, and police and federal agents who confronted him on the day of the shooting. I also benefited from Secret Service and FBI reports that were attached to an appeals court filing and apparently forgotten. Hinckley did not respond to several letters seeking an interview; his attorney, Barry Wm. Levine, said Hinckley and his family members declined to comment for this book.

In writing about Ronald Reagan and his White House, I was fortunate to interview James A. Baker III, Edwin Meese III, and others who worked for the president in that time period. Richard V. Allen was especially helpful; besides providing extensive notes and making himself available for many interviews, he gave me access to the audiotapes he recorded in the Situation Room during that day's most difficult hours. Unless noted otherwise, every line of dialogue used in the scenes set in the Situation Room comes from Allen's tapes. I also benefited from a transcript of an interview conducted with Michael Deaver by another White House official the day after the shooting. This transcript provides the most detailed and illuminating account of the assassination attempt from any White House official who followed Reagan to the hospital. In telling the story of Air Force Two, I relied on Chase Untermeyer's recollection and his diary entry for the day, as well as a transcript of an interview he conducted with Vice President Bush as they flew back to Washington.

The Ronald Reagan Presidential Library has a trove of records—documents, photographs, and audiotapes—that helped me construct this narrative. Among those records were memos produced by key administration figures that described their actions that day. In writing Reagan's story, I referred to the diaries he kept while president and to his two autobiographies, *Where's the Rest of Me?* and *An American Life.* Also useful was a detailed account of the events of March 30, 1981, provided by Nancy Reagan in her memoir, *My Turn.* Finally, I benefited from reading hundreds of newspaper and magazine articles about the Reagan administration; biographies of the former president by, among others, Lou Cannon and Garry Wills; and a history of the administration's first few years by Laurence I. Barrett.

In the interests of clarity, all times in this book are Eastern Standard Time.

Guide to Abbreviations and Shorthand in Notes

Secret Service reports: After the shooting, the Secret Service interviewed dozens of agents, police officers, and witnesses after the shooting. In citing information from these reports, I use the name of the agent or person who was interviewed. For example, Secret Service inspectors interviewed Jerry Parr, the chief of the White House detail. If I relied on information supplied to inspectors in that report, I cited it as Parr Secret Service report. Sometimes, the agent's name was redacted in the record, but I have determined his or her identity through interviews. In that case, for example, I cite it as Green Secret Service report (redacted).

FBI reports: I obtained hundreds of pages of FBI reports, including the never previously released summary of agents' interview of Ronald Reagan in the days after the shooting. These documents are cited the same way as the Secret Service reports.

Richard Allen's tape recordings of the Situation Room: Allen tapes.

Memos by White House officials and cabinet secretaries: cited using the last name of the memo's author (for example, Weinberger memo).

Unpublished material: I name the person who wrote it and provide a brief description of the record. For example, Dr. Benjamin Aaron wrote a sixteen-page personal reflection in the weeks after the shooting. In the notes, it appears as Aaron reflection. I have included most of these reflections and notes in my bibliography.

The Management Review on the Performance of the U.S. Department of Treasury in Connection with the March 30, 1981, Assassination Attempt on Ronald Reagan: Treasury report.

"Psychiatric Report in the Case of United States vs. John W. Hinckley, Jr.": government psychiatric report.

Trial testimony: unless otherwise noted, all references to testimony refer to the trial of John W. Hinckley Jr. in 1982.

Author interviews: unless otherwise noted, all interviews were conducted by the author in 2009 and 2010.

Ronald Reagan, *The Reagan Diaries*: Reagan Diaries. All citations in the notes section are from volume 1.

Daily Diary of President Ronald Reagan: DDPRR. Unless otherwise noted, this refers to the diary of March 30, 1981, and was obtained from the Ronald Reagan Presidential Library.

Ronald Reagan Presidential Library: RRPL

George Bush Presidential Library: GBPL

White House Communications Agency: WHCA

Miller Center for Public Affairs at the University of Virginia: Miller Center

United States Attorney's Office for the District of Columbia: USAO

Associated Press: AP

United Press International: UPI

Los Angeles Times: LAT

Washington Post: WP

New York Times: NYT

Prologue

1   *Ronald Reagan walked*: Photos, RRPL; DDPRR, March 29, 1981; "Reagans Attend Church, Enjoy Spring Stroll," AP, March 29, 1981; Dean Reynolds, UPI, April 4, 1981.

1   *had not been able*: Review of Reagan's diary and the DDPRR for each Sunday since the inauguration.

1   *didn't want to impose*: Ronald Reagan, *An American Life*, p. 396. Reagan wrote that he also stopped going to church because authorities warned him about terrorist hit squads attacking him during services. This alert most likely occurred four or five

months after the assassination attempt. Michael Reagan told me that his father was not happy about missing church. On an Air Force One flight in April 1988, Reagan told his son that he was counting the months until he could return to services. "He shared with me that in nine months he could once again start going to church and how much he was looking forward to it," Michael Reagan said. Reagan's other son, Ron, also said his father was a regular churchgoer before and after his presidency.

1   *St. John's Church*: History provided by Hayden Bryan, executive director of operations for St. John's Church, and the church's website.

2   *the Reverend Harper delivered*: John C. Harper, "The Son of the Man," sermon delivered at St. John's Church, Lafayette Square, Washington, March 29, 1981.

2   *They ate lunch*: *Reagan Diaries*, p. 30; DDPRR, March 29, 1981.

2   *The only event of note*: "The President's Schedule, March 30, 1981," RRPL.

3   *By mid-March*: "Reagan Approval Rating Trails Earlier Presidents," *WP*, March 18, 1981, p. A3.

4   *White House officials and pollsters*: There were numerous press accounts detailing this, including a column that ran on March 30, 1981, in newspapers across the country. It was by the influential Robert Novak and Rowland Evans. "The Reagan honeymoon is truly over," they declared in discussing the anticipated fight ahead over the administration's plans to slash federal spending.

4   *The news of the shooting stunned the country*: Many newspapers and wire services published stories describing local reaction to the assassination attempt. Among those I relied on were articles in: *Des Moines Register, Chicago Tribune, Quad-City Times, Baltimore Sun, Boston Globe, State Journal-Register* (Springfield, Illinois), *Peoria Journal Star, WP, Kansas City Star*, AP, and UPI.

4   *never broke protocol*: Secret Service agents, who reviewed the audiotapes of their radio broadcasts of that day, assured me that they never uttered Reagan's name on the air, nor used the word "president" to describe him. I requested a copy of this tape from the Secret Service. As this book went to print, I had not yet been granted access to it. However, the Secret Service did provide me with a transcript of the radio calls, which confirms that agents never violated procedure.

5   *Every modern president*: Former president George W. Bush was Trailblazer; President Obama is Renegade.

5   *It was first given*: Interview with Pete Peterson. Peterson and Pete Hannaford, a close Reagan advisor in the 1970s, told me that the Secret Service bestowed the code name in 1976. In a copy of a long-defunct magazine, I found a reference to Rawhide being his code name during that year's campaign (Richard Reeves, "Brown, Reagan, and Self-Destruction," *New West*, June 7, 1976, p. 12).

5   *By all accounts*: Several friends, advisors, and Secret Service agents reported this. "The Reagans were amused by and rather liked Rawhide and Rainbow," Hannaford said. In 1984, while on a break at his ranch, Reagan was rooting around at the base of trees. This greatly concerned Secret Service agent Robert DeProspero,

then head of Reagan's detail, because venomous rattlesnakes were a common sight on the ranch. "Mr. President, you make me really nervous," DeProspero said. "I really don't want you getting bitten by a rattlesnake." Reagan looked up with a big smile. "Well," he said, "you can't be afraid with a name like 'Rawhide.'"

5 *years later, describing*: Ronald Reagan, *An American Life*, p. 104.

6 *Reagan viewed the presidency*: Many biographers have made this point, none better than Lou Cannon in *President Reagan: The Role of a Lifetime*.

1: Rendezvous with Destiny

8 *When President Ronald Reagan awoke*: Several people, including agents and White House staffers, remembered the dreary weather this day, but I also relied on an aviation meteorological report from www.weatherunderground.com to chart the weather hour by hour. In describing Reagan's attire, I utilized FBI inventories of what he wore that day; I also relied on official photographs, RRPL, and an interview with Gary Walters to depict the White House residence and grounds. Michael K. Deaver described Reagan using Brylcreem in *A Different Drummer*, p. 14; the president made a point of informing several nurses that he did not dye his hair and did not wash it that morning. He told at least one that he used Brylcreem. Deaver described the president's routine that morning in *Nancy: A Portrait of My Years with Nancy Reagan*, p. 121; Reagan's suit, crafted by his personal tailor Albert Mariani, is on display at the Ronald Reagan Presidential Library and Museum in Simi Valley, California.

8 *nicest watch on*: Ronald Reagan, *An American Life*, p. 259. Before going to the Hilton, Reagan swapped this watch for a cheaper one that he used on his ranch.

8 *Reagan's clothes draped*: Several of the president's friends, former advisors, and former Secret Service agents described Reagan's ranch work, his workouts, and his pride in his physique. Richard Williamson, for example, said he once saw Reagan jokingly pose in such a way to show off a biceps muscle for an official photograph.

9 *fifty-three movies*: Thomas, *The Films of Ronald Reagan*, and the official White House biography of Reagan.

9 *captain sounded more dashing*: Interview with Edwin Meese III. Reagan later wrote in *Where's the Rest of Me?* (p. 117) that he turned down the promotion because he had not served in combat. "Who was I to be a major for serving in California," he wrote, "without ever hearing a shot fired in anger?"

10 *despite widespread skepticism*: This is another example of how Reagan was underestimated. His opponent in the 1966 California governor's race, the incumbent Democrat Edmond G. Brown, did not take the former actor seriously—to his own detriment. During the campaign, Brown derided Reagan's experience as an actor and often mentioned that he starred in the movie *Bedtime for Bonzo*. As the race heated up, Brown famously told a classroom of young schoolchildren: "I'm run-

ning against an actor, and you know who shot Lincoln, don't you?" Reagan crushed Brown by nearly one million votes.

10 *most populous*: California officially became the most populated state just before Reagan won the 1966 gubernatorial election; "California Takes Population Lead," NYT, September 1, 1964, p. 37.

10 *hundreds of radio*: Ronald Reagan, *Reagan, in His Own Hand*.

10 *Tough and demanding*: This was echoed by nearly every former White House official I interviewed, and is a common thread in many Reagan biographies and newspaper stories of the era.

11 *the couple had celebrated*: Helen Thomas, UPI, March 5.

11 *"As Pres. of the U.S."*: Nancy Reagan, *I Love You, Ronnie: The Letters of Ronald Reagan to Nancy Reagan*, p. 140.

11 *A much more elaborate celebration*: Photographs of festivities, RRPL; DDPRR, February 6 and 7, 1981; *Reagan Diaries*, p. 17; stories published in WP, NYT, AP, UPI about the events.

12 *did not retire until after midnight*: DDPRR, February 7, RRPL.

12 *Now, a little more than seven weeks*: Deaver, *Nancy: A Portrait of My Years with Nancy Reagan*, p. 121. "The President's Schedule, Monday, March 30, 1981," RRPL; the call with the German chancellor was not on the official schedule, but there is no doubt that Reagan was told about it at least a day earlier.

12 *Reagan's first task*: "The President's Schedule, Monday, March 30, 1981," RRPL; interviews with David Fischer and Jose Muratti; photographs of event and meet-and-greet, RRPL; audiotape of Reagan's speech by WHCA, RRPL.

14 *Reagan made it clear that the Oval Office*: Author review of DDPRR for first two months in office.

14 *go horseback riding*: Reagan went horseback riding with Fischer and James A. Baker III, his chief of staff, on March 25, according to the DDPRR and other scheduling records, RRPL. An official White House photograph shows Reagan and Baker chatting on the marine helicopter as it flew back to the White House. Reagan was wearing his brown riding breeches and boots; Baker had a pack of Red Man chewing tobacco poking out of his left breast pocket.

15 *But Reagan, a perpetual optimist*: Interviews with Meese, Frederick Ryan, Baker, and Fischer; Reagan's autobiographies.

15 *in a commencement address*: Kengor, *God and Ronald Reagan*, p. 95.

15 *At 8:50, shadowed by*: DDPRR; photograph of Reagan walking to the Oval Office, RRPL.

16 *Earlier that morning*: Interviews with former Secret Service agents Jerry Parr, Johnny Guy, and James E. Le Gette, as well as Parr's wife, Carolyn.

18 *Hollywood's version of an agent's*: Reagan thought the film was terrible, writing in a later memoir that the studio agreed not to release it in Hollywood to protect its actors' reputations. "Never has an egg of such dimensions been laid," he

wrote in *Where's the Rest of Me?* (p. 83). After the assassination attempt, Reagan also told Parr that the movie was the worst he had ever made.

19 *He often told friends that devising*: Interview with Parr; Zach Nauth, "Fan Who Saved Life of President to Get His Reward Today," *LAT*, February 15, 1985, p. 5.

20 *As morning light*: Government psychiatric report; Hinckley's whirlwind of travel in the months leading up to the assassination attempt were documented in a trial stipulation. His belongings were cataloged in trial testimony, trial stipulations, witness testimony, and FBI reports.

20 *drab hotel room*: Photographs of room introduced at trial, USAO.

21 *But returning to Evergreen*: Government psychiatric report; testimony of psychiatrists at Hinckley's trial, as well as the testimony of his parents, Jo Ann and Jack Hinckley.

21 *As he stepped from the car*: Hinckley and Hinckley, *Breaking Points*, p. 138; testimony of Jo Ann Hinckley.

22 *he pondered suicide*: Dr. William T. Carpenter, a psychiatrist who examined Hinckley for his defense, testified that the gunman was thinking about these things on the morning of March 26. "He decided, then, to go to the East Coast, his final destination being New Haven, where he planned to end it all [with] either suicide or the homicide-suicide plan being foremost in his mind." In the weeks before he took a bus to Washington, Hinckley often pondered a dramatic conclusion to his life. "He had to do something to end it," testified Dr. Thomas G. Goldman, another defense psychiatrist who examined Hinckley. "He could not live. He made some motions towards looking for a job. Basically, he was selling his property to raise enough money to make another trip to the East where he thought he would do something, kill himself, kill Miss Foster, possibly kill both of them."

22 *On Thursday, March 26*: Stipulations entered at Hinckley's trial, as well as the government psychiatric report and testimony by government and defense psychiatrists.

22 *The four-day trip*: Government psychiatric report.

22 *A minister who boarded*: Reverend Richard Parke, the minister traveling with Hinckley, was interviewed by government psychiatrists and his comments were included in their report. Parke confirmed the report's details in phone and e-mail interviews.

23 *He didn't even tell the minister*: Parke learned Hinckley's last name by seeing it on a luggage tag, according to the government psychiatric report.

23 *he barely had enough energy*: Government psychiatric report; testimony of various defense and prosecution psychiatrists.

23 *the jumbled detritus*: FBI reports and trial testimony.

23 *Just after nine a.m.*: Government psychiatric report.

24 *On his walk back to the hotel*: Government psychiatric report. "He noticed the president would be at the Hilton," the report states. "He noticed the schedule without excitement, put down the paper and took a shower."

2: The Man

25 *When President Reagan*: DDPRR.

25 *the space looked much as*: Photographs of Oval Office, RRPL; photographs of Oval Office displayed at www.whitehousemuseum.org.

25 *the* Resolute *desk*: Interview with Fischer; White House Historical Association website.

26 *resigned himself to a bit of discomfort*: The desk was raised two inches by adding a wooden base at some point between October 1981 and August 1982, according to Monica McKiernan, curatorial assistant in the White House Office of the Curator.

26 *miniature bronzed saddles*: *Reagan Diaries*, p. 25. Reagan received these statues from Walter Annenberg, one of his wealthy California friends, on March 12. According to *Time* magazine, "Six Shots at the Nation's Heart," on April 13, 1981, Reagan and his wife put these saddles on display in the Oval Office the day before the shooting.

26 *his three top advisors*: DDPRR; biographical sketches of Baker, Meese, and Deaver were derived from their autobiographies, stories in *WP, NYT, Newsweek*, and *Time*. Laurence I. Barrett provided detailed character studies in *Gambling with History*.

27 *Meesecase*: Interview with Richard Allen; Robert L. Pfaltzgraff and Jacquelyn K. Davis, *National Security Decisions: The Participants Speak*, p. 74.

28 *Their efforts had already earned*: On March 19, 1981, the *Christian Science Monitor* ran a story about the three aides under the headline "Reagan's Troika: Setting the Pace." A *Newsweek* piece on February 2, 1981, also referred to the men as the Troika. The nickname became more widely known after the assassination attempt.

28 *Nearly every morning*: Interviews with Baker and Meese. Details about that morning's meeting came from two memos prepared for Baker: "Senior Staff Meeting Action Items (3/30/81)" and "Meese/Deaver Breakfast and Senior Staff Meeting." They were provided by the Seeley G. Mudd Manuscript Library at Princeton University.

29 *The Troika entered*: DDPR; interviews with Baker, Meese, and Fischer.

29 *Jerry Parr found*: Details about Parr's career were supplied by Parr; Guy described the preview of the inaugural address. During the transition, Guy also got into a discussion with Reagan about the military and U.S.-Soviet relations. A few months later, Reagan mentioned Guy's thoughts on the subjects in a meeting with cabinet officials, and within minutes the agent received a stern call from a supervisor: He was never to discuss foreign relations with the president again. "Oh," the supervisor added, "you might also want to avoid Jim Baker for awhile. He's pretty steamed."

30 *"Do you mind timing me?"*: Reagan's inaugural address lasted twenty minutes.

31 *Richard V. Allen arrived*: Interview with Allen; DDPRR; Allen's oral history (May 28, 2002) with the Miller Center. Allen's career was also heavily chronicled in the press. The most helpful stories in charting his life and career appeared in the *Washington Post*: Stephen S. Rosenfeld, "The Return of Richard V. Allen," April

18, 1980, p. A2; Spencer Rich, "Reagan's Foreign Affairs a Pro on Policy, Trade," August 24, 1980, p. A2; and Elizabeth Bumiller, "The Powers and the Puzzles of Richard Allen: The Disappearing 'Disappearing Act' of the National Security Advisor," June 28, 1981, p. H1. Bumiller, in particular, wrote many illuminating character sketches of key players in the Reagan administration.

34　*"we have to find a way to knock"*: Interview with Allen; Reagan echoed these words later during one of his most famous speeches at the foot of the Berlin Wall in 1987 when he urged the Soviet leader Mikhail Gorbachev to "tear down this wall." I encourage anyone interested in this speech to read Romesh Ratnesar's *Tear Down This Wall.*

　　In another revealing episode from the European trip, Reagan had some fun with the German language. Shortly after arriving in West Germany, Reagan was sitting in the back of their sedan as they roared down the autobahn. He kept jerking his head to read road signs.

　　"Everything okay, Governor?" Allen asked from the front passenger seat.

　　Reagan replied that he wanted to know when they got to a place he pronounced as "Owls Fart."

　　"No, Governor, that isn't a place," Allen said, realizing that Reagan was reading German road signs with a German word in all capital letters on them. "It's Ausfahrt," Allen said. "It means exit."

　　"No, there is no place like that," Reagan said. "You just can't have a word like that."

　　Allen, fluent in German, rattled off a stream of words derived from *fahrt*: *wassenfahrt* (trip on water), *himmelfahrt* (Ascension of Christ), *einfahrt* (entrance), *rundfahrt* (tour).

　　"Can you write them down for me?"

　　Allen jotted a few dozen German words on a sheet of paper and gave it to Reagan. That afternoon, at a meeting with high-ranking German officials, the future president pulled out the list and chuckled.

34　*at the president's first news briefing*: Transcript of the president's news conference, January 29, 1981, RRPL; interview with Allen.

35　*While taking a shower*: Government psychiatric report; testimony from psychiatrists at Hinckley's trial.

35　*Instead, he found himself thinking*: The government psychiatric report delves into this moment, as did several psychiatrists at Hinckley's trial. Dr. Sally A. Johnson, a psychiatrist at a federal prison where Hinckley was held in 1981, testified that the idea to assassinate Reagan "resurfaced" after Hinckley saw the schedule in the paper. "He denies really thinking about doing this prior to seeing the schedule, I mean as I have described he thought about doing it in the past, but he denied having any specific plan when he first got up that morning," Johnson testified. "He said it was not until he read the schedule in the paper that the idea resurfaced. He said that at that point in time he showered and while in the shower thought about the idea and then when he came out of the shower he said that, using his words, his mind 'was starting to turn,' and he took some Valium to calm himself down."

In the government psychiatric report, the assailant was quoted as saying: "I guess it was in the shower or getting toweled off that I debated whether to 'detour to the Hilton' or to 'go up to New Haven.' I was thinking should I go over to the Hilton and take my little pistol, and see how close I could—well, see what the scene was like. . . . Maybe I can get close enough that I could end this madness."

36 *Born in 1955*: Government psychiatric report; trial testimony; FBI reports.

36 *Hinckleys moved to Dallas in 1958*: Hinckley and Hinckley, *Breaking Points*, p. 44.

36 *But in junior high school*: Government psychiatric report and testimony from various psychiatrists at trial.

36 *Later, his mother*: Government psychiatric report.

36 *"College isn't all that important for a musician"*: Hinckley and Hinckley, *Breaking Points*, p. 51.

36 *enrolled at Texas Tech*: Hinckley's college transcripts were introduced at trial; government psychiatric report; trial testimony; Hinckley and Hinckley, *Breaking Points*, p. 53.

36 *After completing his freshman year*: Hinckley's college transcripts.

36 *His new roommate was black*: Undated autobiographical essay by Hinckley seized by the FBI.

37 *In the fall semester*: The government psychiatric report and various newspaper stories described Hinckley's college life. Carpenter testified that Hinckley "lived off campus in an apartment that he rented and at that point was not attending classes with any regularity and not having any relationship, acquaintanceship with other college students, so that he was spending this time, virtually, entirely alone with the exception of those occasions when he would go to classes, and he had no social network that he built up." Johnson also testified that Hinckley lived alone in apartments.

37 *The following spring*: Government psychiatric report; trial testimony; Hinckley and Hinckley, *Breaking Points*, pp. 66–83.

37 *One film in particular*: There was extensive trial testimony about Hinckley's interest in *Taxi Driver*.

37 *Travis Bickle, an angry*: *Taxi Driver*, and its screenplay by Paul Schrader. The movie's most memorable scene comes as De Niro stands in front of a mirror—armed with a gun that slides out from his left sleeve—and imagines a conversation with another man: "You talkin' to me? You talkin' to me? You talkin' to me? Then who the hell else are you talking—You talking to me? Well, I'm the only one here. Who the fuck do you think you're talking to?"

37 *Directed by Martin Scorsese*: Newspaper critics lauded the movie, especially the performance by De Niro and the directing of Scorsese. One reviewer described the movie as "a vivid, galvanizing portrait of a character so particular that you

may be astonished that he makes consistent dramatic sense" (Vincent Canby, "Flamboyant Taxi Driver by Scorsese," *NYT*, February 9, 1976, p. 35).

37   *one reason the movie rang true*: Gregg Kilday, "'Taxi Driver'—Up from the Dark Side of Schrader's L.A.," *LAT*, May 14, 1976, p. V32; Alethia Knight and Neil Henry, "Love Letter Offers Clue to Motive in Shooting," *WP*, April 1, 1981, p. A1.

37   *Hinckley was all but hypnotized*: Government psychiatric report. Hinckley told government psychiatrists that he "identified totally" with Bickle. The government report also said that Hinckley felt "he was hypnotized by the music and he identified with Travis because Travis was living alone the way he had been living and Travis was also trying to accomplish something. He said that Travis was totally alienated and hated New York City and all of society."

3: Without Fail

39   *His feet planted shoulder width*: Interview with Parr; the former agent described going to the range that morning for target practice and provided a detailed description of the range and the shooting test; interview with Paul Kelly, who was an instructor at the Secret Service's training center at the time.

40   *Originally formed*: Excerpts from the History of the United States Secret Service 1865–1975, U.S. Government Printing Office, 1978.

40   *By the time*: Testimony of Secret Service officials on March 7, 1962, before the Senate Appropriations Subcommittee on Treasury and Post Office Departments and Executive Office Appropriations. At the hearing, Secret Service chief James J. Rowley requested more agents because the agency was stretched thin. "We have 325 agents devoted to investigative and protective activities, but this is simply not enough to meet our responsibilities," Rowley said, six months before Parr joined the service. "With the advent of President Eisenhower the mode of presidential transportation was stepped up from Constellation to jets and to helicopters. President Kennedy has continued in this pattern and we find today that we require more agents. When I was on the detail years ago, I could hedgehop, as it were, in a DC-3 and keep ahead of the president across the country. Today, with the use of the jet, we cannot hedgehop. We have to put two or three men at another stop, so that in all you may have 20 men out there in advance, whereas I only took five men in those days." After Kennedy's death, the agency swelled—to 575 agents in 1968, another watershed year in the service's history. By 1973, there were 1,238 agents, according to congressional testimony.

42   *During Parr's nearly two decades*: Treasury report; Secret Service testimony before the Appropriations Subcommittee of Treasury, Postal Service and General Government, April 2, 1981; "The U.S. Secret Service: An Examination and Analysis of Its Evolving Mission," Congressional Research Service, January 23, 2009.

42   *But one fundamental aspect*: Interviews with more than a dozen Secret Service agents.

42 *recent assassinations*: Of these three men, only President Kennedy had Secret Service protection.

42 *Better training might have*: Many Secret Service agents expressed this sentiment in interviews. Vincent Bugliosi meticulously documented Kennedy's slaying in his tome *Reclaiming History: The Assassination of John F. Kennedy* (Kindle location 2068–2094 is an especially helpful reconstruction of what transpired in Dallas); William Manchester, who also chronicled the assassination, criticized the service's lackluster training. When Kennedy was shot, the driver of his limousine, Bill Greer, and another agent in the car, Roy Kellerman, froze, according to Manchester. "Even more tragic was the perplexity of Roy Kellerman, the ranking agent in Dallas, and Bill Greer, who was under Kellerman's supervision. Kellerman and Greer were in a position to take swift evasive action, and for five terrible seconds they were immobilized," Manchester wrote in *The Death of a President*, pp. 155–56. Manchester blames the Secret Service hierarchy for the agents' failures. "It was the responsibility of James J. Rowley, Chief of the Secret Service, and Jerry Behn, Head of the White House Detail, to see that their agents were trained to cope with precisely this sort of emergency. They were supposed to be picked men, honed to a matchless edge," he wrote.

42 *Nearly a decade later*: The description of the Wallace shooting comes from transcripts of the trial of Arthur Bremer and a lengthy interview with former Secret Service agent Larry Dominguez, who was guarding Wallace when the politician was nearly assassinated on May 15, 1972. Because he was never properly trained on what to do when someone opened fire in a crowd with a pistol, Dominguez thought he was hearing a "string of firecrackers" when Bremer started shooting, and he hesitated before taking any action. In later years, Dominguez went through stepped-up training. Assigned to protect Reagan at the Hilton on March 30, 1981, the agent reacted instantly when he heard Hinckley's first shot and raced to subdue the gunman. Dominguez made Secret Service history that day, becoming the first and only agent to be present at two assassination attempts.

43 *The agency began by revamping*: Interviews with Fran Uteg, Robert Powis, John Simpson, Le Gette, Kelly, Parr, and other former agents. Former agent Ernest Kun described the "Attack on Principal" drills he helped create in Los Angeles. The Secret Service provided me with a course outline of "Ten Minute Medicine" from 1975, as well as a 1981 internal newsletter that briefly described the agency's "AOP" training.

44 *At 9:15*: DDPRR; details of the phone conversation between Schmidt and Reagan come from Allen's extensive notes and my interviews with Allen, as well as a transcript of a press briefing that morning by James Brady, RRPL.

44 *laborers in the Solidarity movement*: News accounts and U.S. intelligence reports.

44 *"possible turning point"*: CIA memo entitled "Poland: Possible Turning Point," March 25, 1981. "Solidarity and the government are on another collision course

and will have greater difficulty than ever before in avoiding violence," the report said. "The chances have increased markedly that the regime will impose martial law even though doing so risks provoking widespread disorder and a military intervention by the Soviets."

45   *the two leaders agreed*: At his press briefing, Brady said, "The situation in Poland was discussed and both the president and the chancellor feel on behalf of their own countries, that in the event suppression be applied either externally or internally in Poland . . . it would be impossible to render further economic assistance."

45   *The president spent the next hour*: DDPRR; Allen's notes of briefing.

45   *This event, like every other*: "The President's Schedule, Monday, March 30, 1981," RRPL; DDPRR; photos, as well as audio and video recordings of meeting by WHCA, RRPL.

46   *Reagan thanked the men*: Tape recording of meeting by WHCA, RRPL.

46   *At 11:30 p.m., after all*: Transcript and tape recording by WHCA of Reagan's remarks at Gridiron Dinner, RRPL.

46   *During a long stint*: For eight years, starting in 1954, Reagan hosted a weekly television show sponsored by General Electric. He also served as a company spokesman, touring GE plants and delivering speeches to its employees, managers, and civic and business groups. The long weeks on the road and rail—Reagan did not get over a fear of flying until he ran for governor—refined his speech-making skills and honed his political philosophy.

46   *Reagan told the ballplayers a favorite*: Transcript of luncheon, RRPL.

47   *It was a great story*: "I was broadcasting the Cubs when the only mathematical possibility, and Billy Herman will remember this very well, that the Cubs had of winning the pennant was to win the last 21 games of the season," Reagan said. "And they did." The streak was an accomplishment for the Cubs. They clinched the pennant after their twenty-first straight victory, this one over the St. Louis Cardinals, on September 27, 1935. The Cubs won their next game, but then lost their final two to St. Louis. When the Cubs started the streak, the team was just 2½ games behind the Cardinals and 2 games back of the New York Giants. The Cubs lost the World Series to the Detroit Tigers.

47   *That same morning*: Interview with Chase Untermeyer, as well as Untermeyer's diary. In describing the trip on Air Force Two, I also relied on Bush's autobiography, *Looking Forward*, and notes and a transcript of an interview of Bush by Untermeyer on the plane. Bush's biographical details came from his memoirs, the White House website, www.whitehouse.gov, various newspaper stories, and the Naval Historical Center. Tension between Reagan and Bush during the 1980 campaign was drawn from newspaper accounts, as well as Craig Shirley's exhaustive history of the 1980 campaign, *Rendezvous with Destiny*.

50   *Shortly before eleven a.m.*: Nancy Reagan's monthly schedule, RRPL; Carla Hall, "The First Lady and Barbara Bush Meet the Arts Volunteers," WP, March 31,

1981, p. D2; photos of event, RRPL. In describing the outfits of the first lady and Barbara Bush, I relied on descriptions provided by Cheryl Tan, a former fashion writer for the *Wall Street Journal*.

50 *A number of commentators*: Nancy Reagan's struggles are well documented, and I relied on various books, newspaper stories, and magazine accounts to describe her first few weeks in the White House. Particularly helpful were: "First Lady Has Gotten Rid of Gun," AP, March 5, 1981; Melinda Beck, "Nancy: Searching for a Role," *Newsweek*, February 2, 1981; and "A Chat with Nancy Reagan," *Newsweek*, March 9, 1981.

51 *Still, she was where she wanted*: Details of the Reagans' courtship were drawn from *Where's the Rest of Me?* and *My Turn*.

51 *Much later, it was revealed*: The *San Jose Mercury News*, which obtained Reagan's FBI file under the Freedom of Information Act, documented Reagan's role as an informant in an August 25, 1985, story by Scott Herhold.

52 *Now she was first lady*: Hall, "First Lady and Barbara Bush Meet the Arts Volunteers."

4: "I'm Not Dangerous"

54 *John Hinckley pulled*: Trial testimony; government psychiatric report; photos of note, USAO.

54 *"Dear Jodie"*: Photocopy of letter introduced at Hinckley's trial, as well as photos of letter, USAO.

55 *Foster seemed so*: Government psychiatric report.

55 *He told his parents*: Trial testimony; government psychiatric report; Hinckley and Hinckley, *Breaking Points*, pp. 102–6.

55 *left her a dozen*: Transcript of testimony by Jodie Foster; Johnson testified that Hinckley told her that he had left Foster his best poems and letters.

55 *In a series of halting conversations*: Transcript of calls introduced at Hinckley's trial.

56 *Hinckley was devastated*: Carpenter and other psychiatrists described Hinckley's response to Foster's rejection. "And his reaction at the end of that effort was that he had been a total failure, had no ability—I mean he was there, had an opportunity to do this, had blown it, was unable to establish it," Carpenter testified, adding that Hinckley "was totally incompetent in making contact. So his reaction was one of despair and depression and fury with himself."

56 *By late October*: After being rejected by Foster, Hinckley traveled across the country. Among the cities he visited during this monthlong period: Washington, D.C.; Dayton, Ohio; Lincoln, Nebraska; and finally Nashville. He purchased two handguns in Texas on September 26 and two more on October 13 from a Texas pawnshop. He finally returned home late in October. He was stalking President Carter during this time frame.

56   *a doctor had diagnosed him*: Government psychiatric report; testimony of Dr. Baruch Rosen.

56   *his writing had grown increasingly dark*: I read many of Hinckley's letters, essays, poems, and short stories, most of which were introduced at trial. Federal prosecutors contended the writings were simply fantasies. "They are fiction," prosecutor Roger Adelman told jurors. "If you tried to diagnose somebody based on writings, you would fill the mental institutions in our country with some of our best writers." Hinckley's attorneys countered that the writings provided insights into his troubled mind. "I think it's an insult to our intelligence to suggest that all poetry is fiction," Vincent Fuller, a defense lawyer, said at trial. "For some it may be. For others it's a way of expressing their innermost thoughts and that is the case of this defendant."

56   *Hinckley made a halfhearted attempt*: Hinckley tried to overdose on twenty to twenty-five antidepressants, according to trial testimony. Though he succeeded in making himself sick to his stomach, it was enough to spur his parents to send him to a Denver-area psychiatrist.

57   *In late November*: Carpenter testimony; copy of threatening note introduced at trial.

57   *"Your prodigal son"*: Hinckley and Hinckley, *Breaking Points*, p. 131.

57   *His approaches to Foster*: Copies of notes introduced at trial, USAO.

58   *With that, he neatly folded the letter into thirds*: Photographs of the letter and the envelope, USAO. In describing from which bag Hinckley pulled various items— including the gun and ammunition—I relied on FBI reports documenting where the ammo and gun boxes were recovered by agents after the assassination attempt.

58   *The speech was printed in all capital letters*: Copy of speech on heavy bond paper, RRPL; interviews with Ken Khachigian and Mari Maseng.

58   *had spent part of his Saturday editing*: Reagan Diaries, p. 29.

58   *It was now a little after eleven*: Interviews with Khachigian and Maseng; according to the DDPRR, Reagan was in the Oval Office between 10:54 a.m. and 11:24 a.m. Maseng and Khachigian remember meeting with Reagan alone in the Oval Office at about this time. The president's schedule for the day listed two and a half hours of speech preparation time starting at 11:00 a.m.

58   *But White House officials*: Interview with Raymond Donovan; copy of a memorandum, dated February 17, by a White House official recommending acceptance of the union's invitation to speak. "This is biggest possible breakthrough group in the AFL-CIO," the memo reads. "*Very Strongly* recommend this event" (emphasis in original), RRPL.

58   *On election day*: Owen Ullmann, "Labor Leaders See GOP Senate as Nightmare," AP, November 6, 1981.

58   *already being dubbed*: The first reference to "Reagan Democrats" that I could find appears in a UPI story on March 12, 1981. In a story on March 24, 1981, the

Christian Science Monitor refers to a group of conservative Democratic lawmakers as "Reagan Democrats."

59   *But the speech mattered*: Reagan wrote at length in *Where's the Rest of Me?* about his time as president of the Screen Actors Guild; he was known to regale advisors and friends with stories about his time negotiating contracts with the major Hollywood studios.

59   *The text of Reagan's talk*: Interview with Maseng, first draft of speech, RRPL.

59   *Reagan read the text*: Copy of Reagan's rewrite of speech, as well as his editing marks on the rest of the draft, RRPL.

60   *Now, as he reviewed the final draft of the speech*: Reagan summoned Maseng and Khachigian to his office to point out errors in the quote from Gompers as it appeared on his speech cards, according to Maseng. Maseng does not recall the nature of the error, but believes the president indeed found a mistake that had been introduced by someone else. In truth, Reagan most likely made the mistake. The Gompers quote is included on his stack of index cards of quotations, but Reagan's version has the two errors that were later corrected by a researcher in the speech-writing office, according to various drafts of the address (RRPL). Joanne Drake, chief of staff of the Ronald Reagan Presidential Foundation, provided me with the quote as it appears on Reagan's cards. The full and correct Gompers quote (I will note Reagan's errors in parentheses): "Doing for People what they can and ought to do for themselves is a dangerous experiment. In the last analysis the welfare of the workers depends upon (Reagan used 'on' instead of 'upon') their own initiative. Whatever is done under the guise of philanthropy or social morality, which in any way lessens initiative, is the greatest crime that can be committed against the toilers. Let social busybodies and professional public (Reagan left out 'public') morals experts in their fads reflect upon the perils they rashly invite under the pretense of social welfare." Darryl Borgquist, the researcher who discovered Reagan's errors in the draft, eventually obtained a photocopy of the president's quotation cards, greatly aiding his fact-checking efforts. Still, Borgquist said, he often struggled to verify quotations inserted into addresses by the president, especially those attributed to authors. Then the researcher realized that the president was culling the language from movie scripts, not books or magazine articles. Invariably, a call to Warner Bros. would reveal that an author had also submitted a screenplay to the studio, and Reagan had likely read it. The future president had committed it to memory.

60   *One of the city's prime venues*: The history of the Hilton was culled from various stories in the archives of the *Washington Post*, and an interview with Frank Passanante, a Hilton regional vice president of sales and marketing.

61   *At eleven that Monday morning*: Interview with Bill Green; Green Secret Service report (redacted).

61   *Green had been working on the visit since Wednesday*: Treasury report; Green
      Secret Service report (redacted); interview with Green.

61   *Green read a standard security survey*: Green Secret Service report (redacted);
      interview with Green.

61   *On Friday, he went to the Hilton*: Interviews with Rick Ahearn, Al Fury, and
      Green; Ahearn Secret Service report (redacted), Green Secret Service report
      (redacted), Fury Secret Service report (redacted); Treasury report.

61   *But union officials did not*: Interview with Ahearn; Ahearn Secret Service report
      (redacted).

62   *Green, Ahearn, and the others*: Interviews with Green and Ahearn; their Secret
      Service reports (redacted).

62   *they agreed to place a rope line*: Treasury report; Green and Ahearn Secret Ser-
      vice reports (redacted); interviews with Green and Ahearn.

62   *This was the rope line's usual location*: In their interviews with Secret Service
      inspectors, agents said the rope was positioned where it had usually been placed
      during past presidential visits.

62   *about thirty-five to forty feet*: Treasury report.

62   *On at least one previous visit*: An unidentified agent told inspectors this, accord-
      ing to a Secret Service report. "It was done on that occasion due to the size of the
      crowd," the report said. The agent believed the dignitary was from China, accord-
      ing to the report.

62   *On Saturday, Green visited*: Interview with Green; Green Secret Service report
      (redacted).

62   *This news pleased him*: Green Secret Service report (redacted).

62   *Later, he would be disappointed*: Green Secret Service report (redacted).

62   *A little before eleven*: Green Secret Service report (redacted).

63   *giving his most experienced agents*: Green Secret Service report (redacted).

5: The Rope Line

64   *By 1:10 p.m.*: Interview with Mary Ann Gordon; Gordon Secret Service report.

64   *The 21½-foot car, code-named Stagecoach*: Interviews with Parr, Ray Shaddick,
      and other agents, as well as two Ford Motor Co. press releases provided by the
      Secret Service. Derek Moore, a conservation specialist at the Henry Ford
      museum, which now has the limousine on display, said the Lincoln was recently
      weighed and it topped out at 10,400 pounds. The museum's records indicate
      that the limousine weighed 13,000 pounds before it was delivered in 1992.
      Moore could not explain the discrepancy. More than likely, the Secret Service
      removed something before the limousine was delivered to the museum or the
      limousine's weight dropped after a refurbishment in the years following the
      shooting.

65   *He was quickly assigned*: "Reagan Gets Secret Service Protection," *LAT*, June 22,

1968, p. 13; Tom Goff, "Reagan Blames Bomb Attempt on Hoodlums," *LAT*, July 11, 1968, p. 3.

65 *At his seventieth birthday party*: David Broder, "Outsider Quietly Moves to Inside Lane," *WP*, March 30, 1981, p. A1.

65 *A month and a half later*: *Reagan Diaries*, p. 28; Ronald Reagan, *An American Life*, p. 262; Joseph McLellan, "Stars and Austerity at Ford's Theater Gala," *WP*, March 23, 1981, p. C1.

65 *Now, at 1:45*: DDPRR; Treasury report; various Secret Service reports.

65 *Riding next to Reagan in the passenger*: Interview with Donovan; Treasury report.

65 *got a chilly reception*: Interview with Donovan.

66 *Reagan and Donovan chatted briefly*: Interview with Donovan; Tom Matthews, "Reagan's Close Call," *Newsweek*, April 13, 1981, p. 31.

66 *Riding in the front passenger*: Interviews with Parr and Drew Unrue; Parr Secret Service report and Unrue Secret Service report (redacted).

66 *Directly ahead of Stagecoach*: Interviews with Secret Service agents; Secret Service reports.

66 *riding in the passenger seat of a marked cruiser*: Interview with Gordon; Gordon Secret Service report.

66 *she'd chauffeured Jimmy Carter*: Interview with Gordon; "Carter Feels 'Safe' with Woman at Wheel," AP, September 4, 1980.

67 *Gordon had driven*: Gordon Secret Service report.

67 *wielded handguns*: Interview with Shaddick.

67 *In the front passenger seat*: Interviews with Shaddick, Tim McCarthy, Jim Varey, and Joe Trainor. Trainor won the coin toss with McCarthy and Dalton McIntosh. Trainor stayed behind at the Secret Service command post, called W-16, under the Oval Office.

67 *Behind Halfback*: Interviews with Fischer and Muratti; Deaver, *Behind the Scenes*, p. 16; in later books and interviews, Deaver said he rode in the limousine with Donovan and the president to the hotel. The Treasury report identified only Donovan and Reagan as passengers in the limousine.

67 *made up the "escape package"*: Interview with Parr.

67 *staff car ferrying*: Interview with Maseng, who rode with Brady to the speech in the staff car. The motorcade assignments were also specified in the president's daily schedule, RRPL.

68 *As the scheduled departure*: Larry Speakes, *Speaking Out*, p. 7; Mollie Dickenson details Brady's life and work at the White House and describes his day on March 30, 1981, in her thorough book, *Thumbs Up*.

68 *The string of limousines*: Tim McCarthy testimony.

68 *The ride had covered 1.3 miles in about four minutes*: Treasury report.

68 *A few minutes before the president's arrival*: Interview with Herbert Granger; Granger Secret Service report (redacted); Thomas Delahanty FBI report.

68 *seven reporters and ten spectators*: Green Secret Service report (redacted).

68 *At seven that morning*: Interview with Granger; Granger's Secret Service report; Delahanty FBI report. Few others were wearing bulletproof vests that day. Tim McCarthy wasn't wearing one, nor was Parr. Reagan was not wearing one, either. Before the attempt on his life, the president rarely donned one, according to agents. After the shooting, at the request of the Secret Service, Reagan wore a bulletproof vest or bulletproof clothing more often.

68 *Hell . . . it's just the Hilton*: Interview with Granger.

69 *but his dog, Kirk*: Mailed response by Delahanty to questions by the author; Alfred E. Lewis, "In Recuperation, Delahanty Recalls Reagan Shooting," WP, May 11, 1981, p. A10.

69 *About forty-five minutes*: Granger Secret Service report (redacted); interview with Granger; Treasury report; interview with D.C. police officer Richard Hardesty, who was deployed above the VIP entrance.

69 *"They're coming"*: Delahanty FBI report.

69 *Granger, a former*: Interview with Granger.

69 *Looking back at the police sergeant*: Government psychiatric report; testimony of psychiatrists who interviewed Hinckley.

69 *His RG 14 revolver*: The FBI allowed me to hold the gun. It has a very heavy trigger pull. An FBI agent testified to this same fact at Hinckley's trial.

70 *He removed the six Devastator*: Hinckley described these bullets as "stingers," and FBI agent Gerald Wilkes testified that these bullets were more deadly than others in the would-be assassin's possession because they explode on contact. "Upon detonation, the bullet is fragmented, producing a shrapnel-type effect," Wilkes testified. "This vastly increases the area of contact of that bullet with the medium through which it is passing. Also a new kinetic energy is produced by the explosion of the explosive agent. Not only that, the intensely high temperature produced by the detonation of [the bullet] can produce damage to the local areas where it" exploded. Wilkes testified that only one bullet exploded on impact—the one that struck Brady. The others most likely did not explode because they did not reach high enough speeds, hit soft targets, or struck objects at an angle, reducing the force of impact required to set off the explosion, according to John Finor, a firearms examiner for a police force in Pennsylvania and president of the Association of Firearm and Tool Mark Examiners. Finor said such bullets have since gone out of favor; they are less likely to inflict mortal wounds because they fragment and disperse much of their energy at impact and do not penetrate as far as conventional bullets, he said.

70 *This was also not the first time*: Testimony at Hinckley's trial; government psychiatric report. I could find no public record of how many guns Hinckley brought with him to Dayton. Just a few days later—without ever stopping at home—he was arrested at a Nashville airport, where authorities seized three revolvers from

his luggage. It's safe to surmise that he had those same three guns with him in Dayton.

70 *The rally was a test run*: Carpenter and Johnson testimony: "He felt clearly that if he would have had a gun he could have succeeded in shooting President Carter," Johnson testified. "He said at one point that he was only about a foot away. And he was very surprised at how easy it was to get in a position to do this."

70 *Five days later*: Hinckley flew from Columbus, Ohio, to New York City on October 2. On October 6, he flew from New York City to Lincoln, Nebraska. Carpenter testified that Hinckley traveled to Lincoln to "make contact with the person he describes as one of the leading [ideologues] of the Nazi Party and hopes to have some shared recognition with them of the importance of what he is doing in his life. . . . If I can just say what he in fact had was a post office box address in Lincoln, so that he sort of showed up in Lincoln and didn't know where to find this person, what to look for. He spent the day in Lincoln but did not make contact." On October 7, he flew from Lincoln to Nashville.

70 *A security officer noticed what she*: Testimony of Officer John A. Lynch, who arrested Hinckley at the airport.

71 *Hinckley felt especially lucky*: Government psychiatric report.

71 *In November, Hinckley turned*: Hinckley was home in Evergreen, Colorado, with his parents on election night. When it was clear that Ronald Reagan was a big winner, Hinckley was pleased. "Maybe there is hope for the country yet," he told his father (Hinckley and Hinckley, *Breaking Points*, p. 119).

71 *He flew to Washington*: Photographs introduced at trial; government psychiatric report; testimony of Johnson. NBC News reported in 1982 that Hinckley had stalked Reagan during the inauguration.

71 *With a gun in his pocket*: Johnson testimony.

71 *On December 8, while standing outside Blair House*: Government psychiatric report.

71 *He bought a postcard*: Postcard introduced at trial.

71 *After loading the gun in his hotel room*: Government psychiatric report.

72 *On the way, he thought about:* Johnson testimony.

72 *Once the cab pulled to a stop near the hotel*: Government psychiatric report.

72 *He didn't think*: Johnson testimony.

72 *Hinckley felt as if the president were staring right at him*: Government psychiatric report.

72 *Jerry Parr hovered by Reagan's*: Interviews with Parr, Fury, Tim McCarthy, other agents, and a review of numerous Secret Service reports, as well as videos of Reagan's arrival at the hotel.

72 *At two p.m., Reagan walked down the short*: DDPRR.

73 *Reagan popped out one of his contact lenses*: Reagan always gave speeches this way, according to Fischer and Ryan; Deaver, *A Different Drummer*, pp. 73–74.

73   *At the sound of "Hail to the Chief"*: Videotape and audio recordings of speech, RRPL.

73   *about a young baseball player*: In an interview, Danny Villanueva said he met Reagan as the former actor was gearing up for a gubernatorial run in the mid-1960s. Reagan was courting Hispanic voters, and Villanueva was placekicking for the Los Angeles Rams, a professional football team. At their first lunch, the pair hit it off, and soon Villanueva was introducing Reagan at speeches across the state. At one event, Reagan overheard Villanueva tell a humorous story about an up-and-coming minor leaguer whose wife gave him a hard time for refusing to change their baby's diaper. Reagan appropriated the joke and inserted Villanueva into it for good measure.

74   *Outside the Hilton*: Interview with Unrue; Unrue Secret Service report (redacted); Treasury report; interviews with Parr, Gordon, and other agents.

74   *fifteen to twenty feet*: Treasury report.

74   *peculiar design of the Hilton*: Treasury report; interviews with Unrue, Gordon, Parr, and Shaddick; multiple Secret Service reports.

75   *Herbert Granger decided*: Treasury report; interview with Granger; Granger Secret Service report (redacted).

75   *would still be about fifteen feet*: Granger testified at trial that the gunman was between ten and fifteen feet from Reagan when he started shooting.

75   *Unrue, having parked*: Interviews with Unrue and Dennis Fabel, who was driving the follow-up car, as well as their Secret Service reports, FBI reports, and Treasury report.

75   *A heckler had caused*: Interview with Fury; Fury testimony; Secret Service reports. In this photograph, you can clearly make out Hinckley's face in the back of the crowd, as if he is standing on his tiptoes to see over the heads of those in front of him.

75   *they allowed the Hilton's*: Hilton security officer Secret Service report.

75   *As departure time neared*: Interviews with Unrue, Gordon, and Fabel; those agents' Secret Service and FBI reports; Treasury report.

75   *to about twenty-five people*: Interview with Granger; an unnamed D.C. police officer estimated the crowd size at twenty-five, according to a Secret Service report.

6: 2:27 P.M.

77   *Agent Jerry Parr stood backstage*: Interview with Parr.

77   *the four thousand union members*: Treasury report.

77   *The crowd rose to its feet*: Audio and video of event, RRPL.

77   *Parr moved to the edge*: Interview with Parr; video of event, RRPL.

78   *They took the stairs up from the ground*: Interviews with various Secret Service agents.

78   *One agent aimed for the rope line*: Dennis McCarthy Secret Service report.

78   *another trotted along*: Green Secret Service report (redacted).

78   *a third angled for the limousine's right front fender*: Varey Secret Service report; interview with Varey.

78   *A fifth, carrying an Uzi*: Bob Wanko Secret Service report.

78   *A sixth, Tim McCarthy*: Interview with Tim McCarthy; Tim McCarthy Secret Service report.

78   *Jerry Parr's wife, Carolyn*: Interview with Carolyn Parr.

78   *The crowd outside the VIP*: Interview with Granger; government psychiatric report; Treasury report; various Secret Service reports.

78   *The reporters and cameramen who*: Interviews with Sam Donaldson, Lou Cannon, and Ron Edmonds; Lou Cannon, "The Shooting: The Shooting Scene," *WP*, March 31, 1981, p. A1; Michael Putzel, "The Presidential Smile Disappears," AP, March 31, 1981; Gilbert Lewthewaite, "A Reporter Who Witnessed the Attack Recalls the 'Bloody Seconds,' the Chaos," *Baltimore Sun*, March 31, 1981, p. 1; wire services, "'You Shot at My President, I'll Kill You,'" *Miami Herald*, April 2, 1981, p. A21; Fred Barnes, "Routineness of President's Visit to Hotel May Have Abetted Gunman," *Baltimore Sun*, March 31, 1981, p. A6; Tom Collins, "They Were There When Bullets Flew," *Quad-City Times*, March 31, 1981, p. 3.

79   *"Press, press, let us through!"*: Government psychiatric report.

79   *"No, we were here first!" screamed*: Government psychiatric report.

79   *"They think they can do anything they want!"*: AP radio reporter Secret Service report.

79   *Seconds behind him, David Fischer*: Interview with Ahearn.

79   *Mike Deaver and Jim Brady*: Deaver, *Behind the Scenes*, p. 16; Dickenson, *Thumbs Up*, p. 63.

79   *Reagan saw the same reporters*: Reagan FBI report.

80   *did plan to make one dramatic gesture*: Reagan FBI report.

80   *Jerry Parr slid a step behind*: Interview with Parr; Parr Secret Service report; Parr FBI report (redacted).

80   *carried a bulletproof steel slab*: Interview with Shaddick.

80   *eighteen inches behind*: Parr FBI report (redacted).

80   *If an attack had occurred*: Interview with Parr.

80   *his plan changed*: Interview with Parr.

80   *Tim McCarthy, Parr's point man*: Tim McCarthy Secret Service report; Tim McCarthy FBI report; video of shooting, various television networks.

81   *Instantly, Parr's left hand*: Interview with Parr; slow-motion video of shooting, USAO.

81   *the corner of his eye*: Interview with Parr.

81   *Parr's mind raced*: Interview with Parr.

81   *John Hinckley couldn't believe his luck*: Government psychiatric report; Johnson testimony.

81 *felt exceedingly calm*: Government psychiatric report.

81 *even now he wondered*: Johnson testimony. Johnson testified that Hinckley thought, "Should I, should I pull out the gun and start firing?"

82 *he saw himself dying*: Government psychiatric report.

82 *then he crouched*: Interview with Granger; Granger testimony.

82 Goodbye, *he thought*: Government psychiatric report.

82 *Blue flame spat from the gun*: FBI interview of witness standing next to Hinckley.

82 *The first person hit*: Adelman laid out the order of shots during the trial.

82 *Instinctively, he pivoted*: Delahanty FBI report.

82 *"I am hit!"*: Delahanty FBI report.

82 *The sight line between Hinckley and the president*: Opening statement by Adelman. The third shot sailed high and hit a building across the street.

82 *1.7 seconds*: FBI reports.

82 *Sitting at the Lincoln's wheel*: Interviews with Unrue and Parr; Unrue Secret Service report (redacted). The limousine was so heavily armored that Unrue would not have heard the gunfire if the door had been closed.

83 *Agent Dennis McCarthy*: Dennis McCarthy trial testimony; Dennis McCarthy Secret Service report; Dennis McCarthy, *Protecting the President*, pp. 65–84.

83 *Herbert Granger was facing*: Interview with Granger; Granger testimony. Granger and Delahanty were facing the wrong direction when Hinckley started shooting because they had momentarily turned from the crowd to orient themselves to the president. Later, Delahanty said he felt terrible about this, according to Hardesty, who spoke to the wounded officer in the hospital. In an internal report, the Secret Service defended the officers, saying "a study of tapes showed that the police officers were facing the crowd; however, in glancing around, providing 360 degrees of coverage, or checking on the exact position of the president gave the impression of watching the president." Others, however, see a valuable lesson in the officers' actions. In the conference room of her office in police headquarters, D.C. police chief Cathy Lanier displays a large photo of both officers looking at Reagan, not the crowd, in the seconds before the assassination attempt. It's a reminder, she says, to always remain vigilant and focused on the crowd, not the president.

84 *with such force that*: Interview with Granger.

84 We have to keep him alive: Dennis McCarthy, *Protecting the President*, p. 76.

84 *Another agent scrambled inside*: Rick Tobin Secret Service report.

84 *"Let's move him to another car"*: Dennis McCarthy, *Protecting the President*, p. 77.

84 *thinking about Oswald*: Interview with Danny Spriggs.

85 *McCarthy exploded*: Dennis McCarthy testimony during a pretrial evidence suppression hearing.

85   *Agent Jim Varey watched*: Interviews with Varey and Ahearn, as well as their FBI and Secret Service reports.

85   *leaped from the front passenger seat*: Interview with Gordon; Gordon Secret Service report.

86   *"Let's go!"*: Robert Weakley Secret Service report (redacted). Weakley was a Secret Service protective support technician and the driver of the spare limousine.

86   *Dan Ruge, who was standing*: Dan Ruge FBI report; interview with Tom Ruge, son of Dr. Ruge.

86   *"Doctor, get in that car!"*: Interview with Tom Ruge.

86   *as Mary Ann Gordon climbed*: Ruge FBI report.

86   *his first impulse was to jump*: Interview with Shaddick; Shaddick Secret Service report.

86   *"We've had shots fired"*: Treasury report.

86   *One climbed through the open right rear door*: Interview with Russell Miller; Miller Secret Service report.

86   *The other agent*: Dalton McIntosh Secret Service report.

87   *it was still 2:27 p.m.*: Trainor, manning the Secret Service command post, checked a clock when he heard the reports of the shooting and noted it was 2:27 p.m., according to his Secret Service report. The Treasury report also notes the time of the shooting as 2:27. The FBI report put the shooting at about 2:25. I relied on the times in the Treasury report because it is the most exhaustive government account of the shooting and the actions of Secret Service agents.

87   *people were frightened and upset*: Various FBI reports and newspaper accounts.

87   *Seeing an agent*: Interview with Carolyn Parr.

87   *"He's with the Man"*: News coverage of the shooting; Wanko is the agent with the Uzi.

7: "I Can't Breathe"

88   *As the president's limousine*: Interview with Parr; Parr Secret Service report and Parr FBI report (redacted).

88   *Reagan sat slumped*: Interview with Parr.

88   *he looked like an exhausted basketball*: Interview with Parr.

88   *"Were you hit?" . . . Reagan said*: Unrue Secret Service report (redacted); Parr FBI report (redacted).

89   *Parr fumbled for the radio*: Interview with Parr.

89   *"Give me the radio"*: Interviews with Parr and Unrue.

89   *"Rawhide is okay"*: Treasury report; transcript of radio calls provided by the Secret Service. All radio dialogue in this section comes from the Treasury report, Secret Service reports, or the transcript of the radio calls.

89   *A few seconds later*: Treasury report.

89   *the president looked as if*: Interview with Parr.

89   *"I think you hurt my rib"*: Interview with Parr; Parr FBI report (redacted); Reagan FBI report.

89   *"Is it your heart?" Parr asked*: Unrue Secret Service report (redacted).

89   *it was coated in blood*: Interview with Parr.

89   *"I think I cut the inside"*: Parr FBI report (redacted).

89   *Half kneeling, half sitting*: Interview with Parr.

89   *Hunched forward in the driver's seat*: Interview with Unrue; Unrue Secret Service report (redacted); Unrue FBI report.

90   *Unrue saw two agents, their Uzis drawn*: Unrue Secret Service report (redacted).

90   *About a mile from the Hilton*: Weakley Secret Service report (redacted).

90   *D.C. police officers were not far behind*: D.C. police officers' FBI reports.

90   *Jerry Parr examined the president*: Interview with Parr.

91   *was now pressing his handkerchief to his lips*: Interview with Parr.

91   *"I think we should go to the hospital"*: Unrue FBI report (redacted).

91   *"Get us to George Washington as fast as you can"*: Unrue Secret Service report (redacted).

91   *"We want to go to the emergency room of George Washington"*: Treasury report.

91   *"Go to George Washington fast"*: Treasury report; Secret Service transcripts.

91   *"Get an ambulance, I mean, get a stretcher out there," Parr said*: Treasury report; Secret Service transcripts.

91   *streaked across L Street*: Gordon Secret Service report.

91   *Mary Ann Gordon tried to reach*: Gordon Secret Service report.

92   *she received no reply*: Interview with Gordon.

92   *"We have to get in front of the limo"*: Gordon Secret Service report.

92   *The spare limousine made the sharp right*: Gordon Secret Service report.

92   *It was the so-called route car*: Timothy Burns Secret Service report; Secret Service report of unidentified driver of route car. Burns was a passenger in the route car.

92   *Only Jerry Parr knew*: Interviews with various agents and police officers; review of Secret Service reports.

92   *Deaver had scrambled*: Deaver, *Behind the Scenes*, p. 17; interview with Fischer.

93   *Fischer reached over*: Interview with Fischer.

93   *Holding back tears, he started to pray*: Interview with Fischer.

93   *A few blocks away*: Interview with Trainor; Trainor Secret Service report; interview with Guy; Guy Secret Service report; Treasury report.

94   *Drew Unrue asked Jerry Parr*: Interviews with Unrue and Parr.

94   *The two agents with Uzis*: McIntosh Secret Service report; interview with Miller; Frederick White Secret Service report; interview with White.

94   *I guess he wants to*: Interview with Parr.

94   *He steadied himself and hitched*: Interview with Fischer; Deaver, *A Different Drummer*, p. 135.

94   *So far, so good*: Deaver, *A Different Drummer*, p. 135.

94   *Fischer felt less*: Interview with Fischer.

95   *It was 2:30 p.m.*: Shaddick radioed Trainor at the command post that they had arrived, and Trainor checked the clock to mark the time, according to Trainor's Secret Service report.

95   *a 512-bed medical center*: "Excitement, Inconvenience; Reagan Stay Has Its Effect on GW Hospital," *WP*, April 2, 1981, p. A6.

95   *a dozen or so patients*: White Secret Service report. He estimated that there were twelve to fifteen patients in the area of the emergency room.

95   *In Trauma Bay 5*: Interviews with Dr. Joyce Mitchell, Kathy Paul, and Bob Hernandez; contemporaneous notes taken by Kathy Paul; *The Saving of the President*.

95   *"I'm tired of my buddies getting shot down!"*: Paul notes; interview with Paul.

95   *Mitchell knew that anyone*: *The Saving of the President*.

96   *was wheeled to a nearby room*: Interviews with Paul and Mitchell.

96   *A moment later, a small white telephone began*: Interviews with Wendy Koenig and Mitchell.

96   *A busy clerk at the nurses' station*: Interview with Koenig.

96   *a gruff male voice*: Interview with Koenig.

96   *"That means the president is coming here"*: Interview with Koenig.

96   *"I have to cancel," she told*: Interview with Judith Whinerey.

96   *Whinerey told a clerk*: *The Saving of the President*.

97   *"We have three gunshot"*: John Pekkanen, "The Saving of the President," *Washingtonian*, August 1981.

97   *Wendy Koenig hurried*: Interviews with Whinerey, Mitchell, Paul, and Koenig.

97   *Near the nurses' station*: Interview with White; White Secret Service report. White, a civilian Secret Service employee, was in the hospital helping the daughter of a friend who had broken her ankle.

97   *Kathy Paul watched as*: Interview with Paul.

97   *"This is the president, let's"*: Parr FBI report (redacted).

97   *"I feel like I can't breathe"*: Interview with Paul; Paul notes.

98   *felt suddenly overwhelmed*: Interview with Mitchell.

98   *"Was he shot?" she asked*: Interview with Mitchell.

98   *"No, we think he got an elbow in the ribs"*: Interview with Mitchell.

98   *"Maybe broke a rib"*: Interview with Parr.

98   *Seeing the president*: The description of Reagan collapsing in the emergency room and being taken to the trauma bay was derived from interviews with Hernandez, Parr, Shaddick, Paul, and Mitchell, as well as several others at the scene; I also relied on a number of Secret Service and FBI reports, including those from Hernandez and his partner.

98   *196 pounds of*: Reagan's GW physical examination form listed his weight as 196 pounds.

98 *Paul was dizzy*: Interview with Paul.

98 *having a heart attack right here*: Paul notes; interview with Paul.

99 *Please don't die*: Interview with Paul.

99 *Hernandez, the paramedic, was convinced*: Interview with Hernandez.

99 *"We're going to cut your clothes off"*: The Saving of the President.

99 *"I feel so bad," Reagan said*: Interviews with Paul, Mitchell, Parr, and Hernandez.

99 *Paul loosened the president's tie*: Paul notes; interview with Paul.

99 *"I've got a line!"*: Interviews with Hines and Paul. Hines said these words.

99 *At first the technician*: Interview with Cyndi Hines, the technician, as well as interviews with Hernandez, Paul, and Koenig.

99 *But his trousers wouldn't budge*: Interview with Hernandez.

100 *Wendy Koenig had helped cut away*: Interview with Koenig.

100 *"I can't get a systolic pressure"*: Interview with Koenig.

100 *"Oh, shit, try it again!"*: Interview with Mitchell.

100 *"Set up a perimeter"*: Parr FBI and Secret Service reports.

101 *Watching the nurses struggle*: Interview with Parr; Parr, "One Moment in Time," *Guideposts*, March 1992.

8: The Trauma Bay

102 *Agent George Opfer*: Interview with George Opfer.

102 *The first lady immediately*: Nancy Reagan, *My Turn*, p. 3; interview with Sheila Patton.

102 *The first lady's next major*: Nancy Reagan's monthly schedule, RRPL.

103 *who sometimes received fan mail*: Interview with Opfer.

103 *had led a team assigned*: Interview with John Simpson.

103 *the supervisor told Opfer*: Guy Secret Service report.

104 *as she walked toward him*: Interview with Opfer.

104 *"There was a shooting"*: The dialogue and action in this section are derived from Nancy Reagan, *My Turn*, and an interview with Opfer.

105 *With Opfer leading*: Interview with Opfer.

105 *Opfer took his*: Interview with Opfer.

106 *pulse was steady*: Pekkanen, "The Saving of the President"; interview with Tom Ruge.

106 *to prevent anything "foolish"*: Abrams, *The President Has Been Shot*, pp. 232–33.

106 *Ruge was determined*: Several doctors, including Joseph Giordano, Benjamin Aaron, and David Gens, commented on Ruge's efforts to ensure that Reagan was treated like any other patient. Ruge also told his son, Tom, that one of the first things he told doctors and nurses was that he wanted Reagan to be treated like any other patient. "My dad was very clear that a big part of his job was to make sure that everything moved according to normal procedures," Tom Ruge said. "He told me that when he went into the emergency room, he asked the staff,

'If this was anyone else coming in with a gunshot wound, what is the first thing you'd do?' They replied, and he said, 'Then, that is what we are going to do.'"

107 *Seeing Ruge, Deaver*: Transcript of interview of Deaver by Richard Darman, a top aide to James Baker (hereafter "Deaver transcript"). This interview was conducted the day after the shooting and is a detailed reconstruction of events from Deaver's perspective. The presidential aide forgot he had this record in his possession until shortly before he died, according to Jeff Surrell, one of Deaver's colleagues at Edelman, a public relations firm, and a collaborator on two of his books. Surrell and Amanda Deaver, the advisor's daughter, provided me with this key record. Deaver told Surrell that Darman also interviewed Baker and Meese. However, none of these interview transcripts are at the Ronald Reagan Presidential Library. Barrett excerpted a small portion of Deaver's transcript in *Gambling with History*.

107 *Deaver recalled*: Lou Cannon, "The Day of the Jackal in Washington," WP, April 5, 1981, p. 1.

107 *Realizing that providing*: Deaver transcript.

107 *An assistant picked up*: Deaver transcript; the assistant is Margaret Tutwiler; interview with Tutwiler.

107 *"Find Jim," Deaver said*: Deaver transcript.

107 *"Do you know the name"*: Deaver, *Behind the Scenes*, p. 19.

108 *Reagan's systolic blood pressure*: Interview with Koenig.

108 *indicated that he was in shock*: There is some debate about whether Reagan was in shock or near shock. Dr. David Gens and Dr. Joseph Giordano, who treated Reagan, believe he was in shock. So do several outside experts whom I interviewed, including Dr. Donald Trunkey and Dr. Howard Champion, two of the country's most respected trauma surgeons.

108 *Only five or six minutes*: Interviews with doctors, nurses, and Secret Service agents.

108 *Joyce Mitchell, the ER doctor*: Interview with Mitchell.

108 *"O positive," Parr replied*: Interview with Parr.

108 *One of the first to arrive*: Interview with Dr. William O'Neill.

110 *"Who's the patient?" Price asked*: Interview with Dr. G. Wesley Price; Kim Darden, "Highpoint Native First to Examine Reagan," *Highpoint Enterprise*, April 6, p. 1A.

110 *As he entered the room*: Interview with Price; *The Saving of the President*.

110 *"I can't breathe," the president*: G. Wesley Price, "An Eyewitness Account by the First Doctor to Get to the President," *Washingtonian*, August 1981.

111 *"I don't hear very good"*: *The Saving of the President*.

111 *Price noticed*: Interview with Price.

111 *about five inches*: Interview with Gens.

111 *As he did, Drew Scheele*: Interview with Dr. Drew Scheele.

111 *Price nodded*: Interview with Price.

111 *"Everything is going to be okay"*: Pekkanen, "The Saving of the President."

111 *Price had treated*: Interview with Price.

112 *Ed Meese had been*: Craig Fuller memo; Richard Williamson memo; Deaver transcript; interviews with Baker, Tutwiler, and Williamson.

112 *"He's taken a shot in the back"*: Deaver transcript.

112 *"Shit," said Baker*: Interview with Baker.

112 *Baker jotted "P hit/fighting"*: Interview with Baker; Barrett, *Gambling with History*, p. 113.

112 *Lyn Nofziger, one of Reagan's*: Interview with Williamson.

112 *"It looks quite serious," Baker added*: Haig, *Caveat*, p. 151.

113 *"I'll be in touch with"*: Transcript of Baker's press conference, March 31, 1981, RRPL. Once at the hospital, Baker and Haig spoke by phone and agreed that the secretary of state would be "the point of contact" for information flowing between the White House and the hospital. There are many conflicting accounts of when and how top White House officials learned about the shooting, and even when Baker and his team left the White House. Some press accounts reported that Haig arrived at the White House before Baker left for the hospital. However, this is impossible. Allen witnessed Meese and Baker leaving for the hospital; he then saw Haig arrive. According to his memoirs, Haig left the State Department at 2:59 p.m.—about the same time that Baker would have seen Reagan being wheeled into surgery.

113 *"You want four units"*: Interview with Gens. According to medical records, this was actually four units of "packed red blood cells," a component of blood. A unit of packed red blood cells is about 320 milliliters. Doctors commonly refer to packed red blood cells as blood.

113 *second shooting victim*: This patient is James Brady. In the interest of narrative clarity, I describe his arrival at the hospital in the next chapter.

114 *Approximately seven minutes*: Interview with Gens; chronology provided to the author by Dr. Benjamin Aaron, who reviewed Reagan's entire medical file at my request. The chest tube was put in at about 2:40 p.m., according to Aaron's time line. Dr. Joseph Giordano believes he was in the ER for about three minutes before inserting the tube. At this moment, Giordano is about to arrive in the ER.

9: STAT to the ER

115 *Dr. Joseph Giordano leaned*: Interview with Joseph Giordano.

116 *a backwater by the medical establishment*: I relied on interviews with Dr. Donald Trunkey and Dr. David Boyd, as well as numerous articles in medical journals, in describing the history and evolution of trauma care; "Accidental Death and Disability: The Neglected Disease of Modern Society," National Academy of Sciences, September 1966.

116 *As Giordano discovered*, GW: Interviews with Giordano and Craig DeAtley.

117 *R Adams Cowley, an innovative surgeon*: In describing Shock Trauma, I relied on interviews with doctors who worked there, as well as stories in the *Baltimore Sun*, the *Baltimore Evening Sun*, and Jon Franklin and Alan Doelp's *Shocktrauma*.

118 *by having maintenance*: Interview with DeAtley.

118 *Within two years*: Interviews with various doctors and nurses at GW.

118 *In 1979 the District of Columbia's*: B. D. Colen, "City Names Adult Trauma Unit for Patients Lifted by Copter," WP, September 1, 1979, p. C2.

119 *Just after 2:35 p.m.*: Interviews with Giordano and Gens.

119 *"How are you doing"*: Interview with Giordano.

119 *Giordano felt*: Interview with Giordano; Giordano narrative; Giordano, "Doctor's Story: A Delay Could Have Been Fatal," *LAT*, April 4, 1981, p. 1.

120 *Without hesitating*: Interviews with Gens, Giordano, and Price.

120 *The space was slightly too small*: Interviews with Scheele and Dr. Theodore N. Tsangaris, the son of Dr. Neofytos Tsangaris, the hospital's acting chief of surgery. Tsangaris told his son that Giordano appeared nervous about inserting the tube—not because he was treating the president but because he hadn't performed this procedure in several years. Neofytos Tsangaris died in 2009.

120 *"Everything is going to be okay," he said*: The Saving of the President.

120 *Looking up from the gurney*: Interview with Parr, who said Reagan tried this joke several times in the ER. Koenig also heard him use this line in the trauma bay.

120 *One nurse monitoring*: Interview with Koenig.

121 *"I don't mean to trouble you"*: Interview with Mitchell.

121 *When Nancy Reagan*: Interview with Opfer; Nancy Reagan, *My Turn*, p. 4.

121 *As she approached the ER*: Interview with Dr. Arthur Kobrine.

121 *At least one journalist*: Interview with Ahearn; another journalist slipped into the hospital when Brady's wife arrived, according to Tom Shales's column "TV's Day of Trauma & Instant Replay," WP, March 31, 1981, p. C1.

121 *One of Mrs. Reagan's friends*: Nancy Reagan, *My Turn*, p. 5; interviews with Simpson and Opfer.

122 *As Jacobson stepped away*: In describing Brady's treatment, I relied on interviews with Dr. Jeff Jacobson, Dr. Judith Johnson, and Dr. Paul Colombani, as well as Colombani's detailed notes and Dickenson, *Thumbs Up*, pp. 76–84.

123 *was reviewing X-rays*: Interview with Kobrine.

123 *"I hope you are not"*: Interview with Kobrine.

124 *Shortly after Brady arrived*: Giordano narrative.

124 *Pett grabbed an orderly*: Interview with Dr. Stephen Pett.

124 *Pett and another doctor*: Interview with Pett; Colombani's notes and interview with Colombani.

124 *"What happened?"*: Interview with Colombani.

125 *The bullet was nestled*: Interview with Dr. Michael W. Dennis.

125 *Doctors gave Delahanty*: Interview with Dennis.

125 *Within fifteen minutes*: Testimony of Eddie Myers at an evidence suppression hearing before Hinckley's trial.

125 *McCarthy had his gun*: Dennis McCarthy Secret Service report.

125 *Once in the cell block*: Dennis McCarthy, *Protecting the President*, p. 79.

125 *Spriggs patted*: Spriggs testimony. Spriggs's previous employment provided one of the few lighthearted moments in Hinckley's trial. Before joining the Secret Service, Spriggs was a defensive back for the Dallas Cowboys professional football team from 1972 to 1974. This fact was elicited by a prosecutor when he asked whether Spriggs had ever been exposed to stressful situations before his career in law enforcement (Spriggs served as a police officer in New Mexico before joining the service in 1976). Vincent Fuller, Hinckley's lawyer, snapped to attention. "What years did you play for the Dallas Cowboys?" Fuller asked.

"1972 through 1974," Spriggs said.

"Did you beat the Redskins?"

"Now just a second," said the judge as the courtroom filled with laughter. Anyone who has lived in Washington will understand the town's obsession with the Redskins and will appreciate Fuller's tongue-in-cheek effort to impeach the witness.

125 *Spriggs retreated to a small*: Interview with Spriggs.

126 *homicide office was eerily empty*: Interview with Myers.

126 *his silver badge clipped to the lapel*: FBI photo provided by Myers.

126 *"Watch out for my wrist"*: Myers testimony. Hinckley's wrists were not injured in the arrest.

127 *"I'm not sure"*: In writing this section about Hinckley's questioning by Myers, I relied on interviews with the former detective, his trial testimony, and his extensive testimony at an evidence suppression hearing, as well as an interview of Myers by the prosecution's psychiatrists that was included in the government psychiatric report.

128 *Myers was floored*: Interview with Myers.

10: "My God. The President Was Hit?"

129 *Hospital personnel continued*: Interviews with doctors and nurses; review of Secret Service reports. Agents tried—sometimes in vain—to keep away medical students and other onlookers. They grew increasingly aggressive at screening people and once even momentarily prevented Michael Deaver from entering the trauma area, according to a Secret Service report.

129 *blood pressure had risen*: Gens tape-recorded narrative; Gens diary.

129 *more than half a liter*: Gens diary; Giordano narrative.

129 *Joe Giordano and David Gens*: Interviews with Giordano and Gens; Gens diary.

130 *"We better get a chest X-ray"*: The Saving of the President.

130 *over a liter of blood*: narratives and diaries of various doctors.

130 *more than 15 percent*: The average person contains about 5 liters of blood. Blood is about 7 percent of body weight. Reagan weighed 196 pounds, which is 89.1 kg, so his blood volume was about 6.2 liters. Most journalists have used the 5-liter average, falsely inflating Reagan's estimated blood loss. I used the more precise "7 percent" estimate after speaking to trauma surgeons and reviewing emergency room textbooks and literature. I also consulted with outside experts to arrive at this figure. Adam Myers, a professor of physiology and biophysics at the Georgetown University Medical School, was particularly helpful.

130 *Giordano was running out*: Interview with Giordano.

130 *Speaking as much to*: *The Saving of the President.*

130 *Not wanting to stoke panic*: Interview with Woody Goldberg.

130 *and he'd long suspected*: Interview with Goldberg.

131 *Upon their arrival*: Interviews with Goldberg, Allen, and Tutwiler.

131 *His square jaw clenched*: Interviews with Tutwiler and Allen.

131 *"How do we do that?"*: Interview with Goldberg.

131 *When the White House*: Interviews with Goldberg, Allen, and Tutwiler. This conversation has been drawn from Bush's memoirs and Haig's memoirs, as well as Ken Khachigian's detailed handwritten notes of Haig's end of the conversation, RRPL.

131 *set could potentially listen*: In fact, this occurred. Two University of Alabama graduate students—Stewart Stogel and Carl Kappresser—spent the afternoon listening to conversations between Air Force Two and the White House on a shortwave radio set. They even taped the conversations. After a search in 2010, Stogel said he was unable to locate these tapes.

131 *Until now, the vice president's*: Vice President Bush's briefing book for the trip.

132 *"Are you continuing to"*: Interview with Stetson Orchard.

132 *Secret Service agent was getting*: Interview with John Magaw, the agent who heard this report over his radio earpiece.

132 *Ed Pollard, who unclipped*: Interview with Ed Pollard.

132 *"Oh, no," said Bush*: Interview with Pollard.

132 *"Mr. Vice President"*: Haig, *Caveat*, p. 152. I filed a Freedom of Information Act request for this record from the George Bush Presidential Library. Although it was published in the former secretary of state's memoir and a subsequent message from Bush to the White House was released by the Ronald Reagan Presidential Library, the National Archives considers this message to be classified.

132 *His first concern, of course*: Transcript of interview of Bush aboard Air Force Two by Chase Untermeyer. This record was provided by Untermeyer but is held at the GBPL.

133 *three congressmen*: Untermeyer diary entry; trip briefing book. The three members of Congress were Jim Wright, the Democratic House majority leader, and two Texas Republicans, William R. Archer Jr. and James M. Collins.

133 *on a couch and crowded around*: Photos from flight, GBPL.

133 *whenever the pilots*: Interview with Untermeyer.

133 *"Mr. Reagan was not hit"*: ABC News broadcast.

134 *Dr. Benjamin Aaron, head*: Interview with Aaron; Aaron reflection; *The Saving of the President*.

134 *Except for a short nap*: Aaron reflection; interviews with Aaron and Dr. Kathleen Cheyney, who assisted Aaron in the earlier surgeries.

134 *Aaron didn't look*: Interview with Aaron; Aaron reflection.

135 *Aaron could see that*: Interviews with Giordano and Aaron.

135 *"He's responding"*: The Saving of the President.

135 *1.2 liters*: Aaron reflection.

135 *As Aaron surveyed the situation*: Interview with Aaron; Aaron reflection; *The Saving of the President*.

136 *He looked up and exchanged*: Interview with Gens.

136 *That meant it*: Interview with Aaron.

136 *Since the president was*: Interview with Aaron.

136 *Gens asked him what had*: Interview with Gens; Gens diary.

136 *Again Gens leaned close*: Tape-recorded interview of Gens by John Pekkanen in 1981, which was provided to the author by Gens.

136 *Once the gurney had*: Gens diary; interview with Gens; interview with Dr. Bradley Bennett.

137 *X-ray image of Reagan's*: Interviews with Aaron and Dr. David Rockoff; Aaron and Rockoff, "The Shooting of President Reagan: A Radiologic Chronology of His Medical Care," *Radiographics* 15, no. 2 (March 1995): 407–18.

137 *Dr. David Rockoff had closely*: Interview with Rockoff.

137 *that it was a .38*: Interviews with Rockoff, Aaron, and Gens. This is an astounding blunder. A Secret Service agent seized Hinckley's weapon at the scene and gave it to the FBI, which kept it in a room at the Hilton while authorities collected other evidence and questioned witnesses. So why was there so much confusion about the type of gun Hinckley used? When the shots rang out, a U.S. Park Police motorcycle officer ran to help tackle Hinckley and dropped his .38-caliber revolver on the ground, right next to Brady's head. He eventually retrieved the revolver but not before the gun was "mistaken for the weapon used" by Hinckley, according to the Treasury report.

137 *Nancy Reagan had been politely*: Interview with Opfer; Nancy Reagan, *My Turn*, p. 6.

137 *The hospital's acting chief of surgery*: Giordano narrative; interview with Theodore Tsangaris.

138 *For one thing, they hadn't completed*: Interview with Giordano; Giordano narrative.

138 *When Mrs. Reagan entered*: Interview with Opfer; Nancy Reagan, *My Turn*, p. 6.

138 *Laxalt, beside her, saw a frightened*: Laxalt, *Nevada's Paul Laxalt: A Memoir*, p. 331.

138 *"Honey," the president said*: Gens diary; Giordano narrative; Lyn Nofziger notes,

Hoover Institution, Stanford University. Nofziger's notes were provided by Supriya Wronkiewicz, an archivist at Hoover who graciously spared me a cross-country flight or the expense of hiring a researcher to obtain them.

138 *"Please, don't try to talk"*: Nancy Reagan, *My Turn*, p. 6.

138 *As he considered his options*: Interview with Aaron.

139 *"Mr. President, there is a lot"*: *The Saving of the President*.

139 *"Whatever you think"*: Interview with Aaron.

139 *Even so, Giordano*: Interviews with Giordano and Gens.

140 *Aaron kept his doubts*: Interview with Aaron.

140 *As Gens prepared*: Interview with Gens; Gens tape-recorded interview with Pekkanen, 1981.

11: Operating Room 2

142 *At 2:57*: Gens's handwritten notes that he prepared for Reagan's discharge summary; the operating room circulating record notes that Reagan arrived in OR 2 at 3:02 p.m. Many other accounts in newspapers and memoirs provide wildly inaccurate information about the time Reagan spent in the ER and the OR. Even doctors who participated in Reagan's care got it wrong when writing about the day. Aaron, who has Reagan's complete medical file in his possession, confirmed the authenticity of the records I obtained from other sources.

142 *A Secret Service agent had already*: Trainor Secret Service report; interviews with Giordano, Gens, and DeAtley about what route the procession took to the OR.

142 *Ben Aaron had informed*: Interview with Aaron; Nancy Reagan, *My Turn*, p. 6; Deaver transcript, which provides the basis for the dialogue between Aaron, Mrs. Reagan, and Deaver. Aaron confirmed it.

143 *clasped his left hand*: Gens diary.

143 *took his place at Reagan's*: Interview with Edelstein; *The Saving of the President*. Edelstein had arrived at home with his wife and their newborn son just an hour or so before his pager went off and he learned the president was in his emergency room. He then raced to the hospital.

143 *"Watch your legs"*: Gens diary.

143 *might be bleeding to death*: Speakes, *Speaking Out*, p. 10.

143 *Reagan spotted*: Interview with Baker; Nofziger notes.

144 *"I love you"*: Nancy Reagan, *My Turn*, p. 6; interview with Gens.

144 *Only a few minutes*: Interview with Kobrine.

144 *"You have to save him"*: Interviews with Kobrine and Sarah Brady.

145 *"God damn it, I told"*: Interview with Kobrine.

145 *Ben Aaron adjusted*: Interview with Aaron; *The Saving of the President*.

146 *"I just put a chest tube"*: Interviews with Dr. Michael A. Manganiello and Giordano.

146 *Parr had put his scrubs*: Interviews with Parr, other Secret Service agents, and various doctors and nurses.

146 *Parr noticed a windowed observation deck*: Timothy Burns Secret Service report.

147 *A nurse squeezed*: *The Saving of the President*.

147 *"We're going to be putting"*: Interview with Lichtman. .

147 *"I hope you are all Republicans"*: Interviews with Giordano, Aaron, and Gens.

147 *An ophthalmologist was summoned*: Interview with Manganiello; Gens notes.

147 *Lichtman began the*: Interview with Lichtman.

148 *just after 3:08 p.m.*: OR circulating record.

148 *An hour earlier, Richard Allen*: Interview with Allen; Allen notes.

148 *The complex had been built*: Interview with Michael K. Bohn, former director of the Situation Room, and author of *Nerve Center: Inside the White House Situation Room*. The Situation Room is technically in the White House basement but has windows that look out on the lawn between the West Wing and the Old Executive Office Building.

149 *no other televisions or even a phone*: Allen had at least one secure telephone installed in the room as the day wore on.

149 *At about 3:15 p.m., Allen*: Allen notes; Allen brought a personal tape recorder into the room and began recording at 3:24 p.m.

149 *the hospital's phone lines*: Interviews of participants and Secret Service reports; Secret Service agent Patrick Miller, a supervisor in the Washington field office, told inspectors that agents encountered "significant problems . . . with telephone and radio communications." The "telephones available at the hospital were overburdened to the extent that they were virtually useless on many occasions," the report said. "He in fact recalls having attempted to use the phone where there was no dial tone. The phones appeared to be dead." As the day wore on, communications improved, especially between the Situation Room and a command post established at the hospital.

149 *had heard from Jim Baker*: According to Allen's notes, Baker called at 3:17 p.m. That was more than fifteen minutes after Reagan was taken to the operating room but still nine minutes before the belly tap began. I suspect that Baker and Meese did not want to alert anyone to Reagan's surgery until it had officially started.

149 *"Remind me to tell you a sensation"*: Allen tapes; Allen notes.

151 *Jim Baker knew that the administration*: Interview with Baker.

151 *"We have this information"*: Television video footage of press briefing.

152 *He had ordered that a heart bypass machine*: Interview with Cheyney.

152 *2.275 liters of blood*: Gens notes; Aaron reflection.

152 *Joe Giordano asked for*: Interview with Giordano.

12: A Question of Authority

154 *At about 3:30*: Interview with Allen; Allen notes and Allen tapes. Caspar Weinberger arrived at about 3:30 p.m. He was late, in part, because he had sent his military driver on an errand for his wife, according to Bobby Inman, a former

navy admiral and deputy director of the CIA. Inman and his driver gave Weinberger a ride to the White House.

154 *Meese reported*: Interview with Allen; Allen notes. At times, Allen put his tape recorder up to the phone's receiver.

154 *He then reminded Weinberger*: Weinberger memo, RRPL. In relaying this conversation in his memo, Weinberger wrote: "He then said to me, 'Under these circumstances, it is my understanding that National Command Authority devolves on you.' I said that I believed the chain started with the Vice President. Ed Meese said the Vice President was on a plane in Texas, which was being diverted back to Washington and that it would take him approximately two hours to get here. I asked about the communication to the plane, and which plane it was, and Ed said that he did not know but he did not think there was secure communication. He mentioned again the chain of leadership under the National Command Authority and I confirmed I was the next in line after the Vice President."

The National Command Authority is distinct from the order of presidential succession. The details of National Command Authority are classified but generally concern procedures that "cover certain delegations from the president to the vice president and the secretary of defense in the event of specific circumstances," according to a memo drafted by White House counsel Fred Fielding the day after the shooting.

155 *Concerned that they might need the*: The football contains the nuclear war plans and attack options; the laminated code card has a series of alphanumeric codes that the president uses to authenticate his identity in the event he wants to launch a nuclear weapon. If the president cannot be reached, the military finds the next person in the chain of command—the vice president and then the secretary of defense, who also have authentication cards. The FBI seized Reagan's card when it collected evidence from the hospital. This set off a fight between FBI agents, who considered the card to be evidence, and military officers, who wanted it back because it was a national security secret. The FBI took the card and put it in a safe. It was eventually returned to the military after Attorney General William French Smith mediated the dispute. The clash became public in December 1981, when the *Washington Post* published a story about the FBI's seizure of the card. FBI Agent James Werth recalled obtaining the card from a pile of Reagan's possessions at the hospital. The agent, aware of the card's importance, said he called a supervisor and told him what he had discovered. Within an hour, he was ordered to hold on to the card and "under no circumstances" was he to turn it over to anyone else. For safekeeping, Werth said, he took off his shoe, put the card in it, placed the shoe back on his foot, and continued collecting evidence at the hospital. That night, he turned the card over to his superiors.

155 *Just as Allen and Weinberger*: Allen tapes.

157 *John Hinckley, leaning*: Interview with Stephen T. Colo.

157 *It was 3:50 p.m.*: Interview with Colo; Colo Secret Service reports.

157 *The agent said nothing*: Testimony of Colo at a pretrial evidence suppression hearing.

158 *Colo tracked down Eddie*: Interview with Colo.

158 *At 5:15 p.m., FBI agents*: FBI reports and time line.

159 *Richard Allen, however*: Interview with Allen.

160 *some of Reagan's closest*: Martin Schram, "White House Revamps Top Policy," WP, March 22, 1981, p. A1.

160 *raising the unlikely prospect*: Interview with Baker. Numerous newspaper and wire service stories detailed Haig's comments about Latin America in the weeks preceding the shooting. Haig even threatened to "go to the source" of arms shipments from Cuba to El Salvadoran guerrillas. White House advisors were upset that Haig "placed public emphasis on El Salvador as the bulwark of the Reagan stand against communism at a time when Reagan was trying to place public emphasis on his economic program," the *Washington Post* reported on March 26, 1981.

160 *he wasn't happy either*: Haig details his displeasure with White House staffers in *Caveat*. Allen showed me extensive notes he took of conversations with Haig in the days and weeks before and after the shooting in which the secretary of state sharply criticized Reagan's top White House aides.

160 *he'd nearly resigned*: Haig, *Caveat*, p. 146.

160 *Afterward, Reagan*: Reagan Diaries, p. 29; Haig, *Caveat*, pp. 147–48.

161 *Haig was concerned*: Interview with Goldberg, who shadowed Haig for most of the day and was one of his closest advisors; Haig, *Caveat*, p. 156.

161 *Haig was shocked*: Interview with Goldberg.

162 *watched saline solution*: Interviews with Gens and Giordano.

162 *He'd never seen*: Interview with Gens.

162 *"Does anybody know"*: Interview with Gens; Gens tape-recorded interview with Pekkanen, 1981.

163 *Gens checked the Pleur-evac*: Gens diary; interview with Gens.

163 *2.6 liters*: Gens diary; Aaron reflection; interviews with Gens and Aaron; anesthesia record.

163 *The office was so cramped*: Gens diary; interviews with Gens and Giordano.

163 *Nancy Reagan found*: Interview with Sarah Brady.

163 *The first lady then followed*: Interview with Opfer; interview with O'Neill, the doctor who suggested the chapel; interview with Marie Miller, an executive coordinator at the GW medical library, who used to work down the hallway from the chapel and described it to me.

164 *"All we can do is pray"*: Interview with Opfer.

164 *A little later, Sarah Brady*: Interviews with Opfer, Sarah Brady, and Baker; Nofziger, *Nofziger*, p. 294.

164 *Baker and Meese left*: Interview with Baker.

165 *Olson, the assistant attorney general*: Interview with Theodore Olson.

165 *There were no precedents*: Interview with Olson. In describing the Twenty-fifth Amendment and its history, I relied on John D. Feerick's *The Twenty-Fifth Amendment*. The first transfer of authority from a president to a vice president under the Twenty-fifth Amendment came when President Nixon resigned in 1974 and Vice President Gerald Ford took over, according to Feerick, the country's leading authority on the amendment. Without the Twenty-fifth Amendment, Ford would never have been in position to become president. Nixon utilized the amendment in 1973 to nominate the Michigan congressman to replace Spiro Agnew, who had resigned. Ford was then confirmed by a majority vote of both houses of Congress, a requirement under the Twenty-fifth Amendment.

Before the Twenty-fifth Amendment was ratified in 1967, the office of the vice president remained vacant until after the next election. Although the Twenty-fifth Amendment was not invoked on March 30, 1981, Reagan became the first president to use it to temporarily transfer power to his vice president. In 1985, while undergoing surgery to remove a cancerous polyp from his colon, he shifted presidential authority to Bush. In his letter to the Speaker of the House and the president pro tempore of the Senate informing them of his decision, Reagan did not specifically invoke the Twenty-fifth Amendment. In fact, he went out of his way to say that he did not believe the amendment was meant to deal with "such brief and temporary periods of incapacity." He added that he did not want to set a precedent for other presidents by invoking the amendment in such a situation. Even so, he followed all of the requirements necessary to transfer power to Bush under the amendment. Feerick said in an interview that "there is no question" that this was the first official transfer of power from a disabled president to a vice president. In his memoirs, Reagan wrote that he had indeed invoked the amendment. When Reagan signed the letter transferring authority to Bush, he told Fielding: "Tell George that Nancy doesn't come with this."

166 *Sitting at the conference table*: Interviews with Fielding and various other former White House officials.

167 *"He's on the operating table"*: There is a distortion on Allen's tapes at this point in the recordings. This is the only time where Allen and I disagree about what was said in the Situation Room. Allen believes that Haig says, "He's *not* on the operating table." And then Gergen responds, "He is on the operating table!"

167 *Fielding turned to his right*: Allen and Fielding recall exchanging glances at this moment.

13: "I Am in Control Here"

169 *At about 4:30 p.m.*: Interviews with Giordano, Gens, and Aaron; Gens notes.

169 *Adelberg boldly asked*: Interview with David Adelberg.

169 *Aaron was determined*: Interview with Aaron.

170 *admired his physique*: Interviews with Aaron, Cheyney, and Adelberg.

170 *he could see the lung*: Interviews with Aaron and Cheyney; Aaron reflection.

170 *he scooped out*: Aaron reflection.

171 *the hole puzzled him*: Interview with Aaron.

171 *"He's right upstairs here!"*: Darman, *Who's in Control?*, p. 51.

171 *"Is the president in surgery?"*: Transcript of briefing, RRPL; video of briefing on various television networks.

171 *growing increasingly frustrated*: Interview with Lesley Stahl.

172 *in "over his head"*: Casey memo, RRPL.

172 *"What's he doing up there?"*: Ursomarso memo, RRPL.

173 *For Haig, this was*: Haig, *Caveat*, p. 159. Haig's recollections of events in *Caveat* are inaccurate at times but provide insights into his thought process before he dashed to the press room.

173 *Gergen and Ursomarso*: Interview with Gergen; Ursomarso memo, RRPL.

175 *Allen was stunned*: Interview with Allen.

175 *The secretary of defense was baffled*: Weinberger memo, RRPL. The exchanges among the various officials in the next few paragraphs are drawn from White House memos, Regan's *For the Record*, Weinberger's *Fighting for Peace*, and Darman's *Who's in Control?*

176 *the nearest sub could*: Weinberger explained this conversation with the general to the other officials in the Situation Room, according to Allen's tapes. Weinberger also wrote about his discussion with the general in *Fighting for Peace*, pp. 87–88.

176 *"Al, are you listening?"*: Allen tapes.

177 *was not the sort to back*: Weinberger, by all accounts, was a fierce bureaucratic infighter, and he rarely lost such battles. A fan of Winston Churchill, the defense secretary hung on his wall a partial quotation from the British prime minister: "Never give in, never give in, never, never, never, never—in nothing, great or small, large or petty." He was also very close to Reagan. The president called him "my Disraeli," a reference to another British prime minister.

177 *At 3:25, the plane had*: Treasury report.

177 *scribbling that it*: Copy of card, GBPL.

177 *he wondered aloud*: Diary entry of Rep. Jim Wright, provided by Wright.

178 *The pilots and Secret Service agents*: Interviews with Orchard and Pollard.

178 *Bush's military aide and a Secret Service agent*: Interview with John Methany, the military aide.

178 *By 4:10 the*: Treasury report.

178 *lobby the vice president*: Interview with Pollard; Bush, *Looking Forward*, pp. 220–22; Untermeyer diary.

178 *Bush then dictated*: Copy of message, which arrived at 4:50 p.m., RRPL.

179 *Aaron eyed a clock on*: Interview with Aaron.

179 *They pumped several other*: Anesthesia record.

179 *an anesthesiologist carefully*: Interview with Lichtman.

179 *Cheyney and Adelberg took*: Interviews with Cheyney and Adelberg.

179 *"I think I might call it quits"*: Interview with Aaron; Aaron reflection.

179 *At one point*: Interview with Cheyney.

180 *"Having a good time, Ben?"*: Interviews with Lichtman and Aaron; *The Saving of the President*.

180 *his anxiety grew*: Interview with Aaron.

180 *ashtrays scattered*: Photos of Situation Room, RRPL.

180 *sipped Coke, coffee, and Sanka*: Allen tapes.

181 *Fielding had obtained the presidential succession*: Interview with Fielding; Allen tapes; Darman, *Who's In Control?*, p. 53; copies of succession letters, RRPL.

181 *In Darman's view*: Darman, *Who's In Control?*, p. 53.

181 *in his view, Fielding*: Interview with Baker.

181 *Don Regan, the*: Regan memo; Regan, *For the Record*, p. 187. Word of Brady's death quickly spread from the Situation Room to Capitol Hill, where reporters learned about it. Within minutes, all three major networks were erroneously reporting that Brady had died. Max Friedersdorf, Reagan's congressional liaison, describes the sequence of events in an oral history with the Miller Center (October 2002).

182 *Kobrine told them*: Dr. Michael Manganiello, an opthalmologist who assisted in the care of Brady and Reagan, vividly recalls this moment. Kobrine, who has a reputation for fiery language, said that he does not dispute Manganiello's version of events.

182 *shaved the press secretary's head*: Interviews with Kobrine, Dr. Ed Engle, and Dr. Roderick Clemente.

183 *"Those fuckers," Kobrine said*: Interviews with Manganiello and Kobrine.

183 *At 5:25 p.m., a radiology technician*: Anesthesia record.

183 *David Gens trailed the technician*: Interview with Gens.

183 *Aaron studied the image*: Interview with Aaron.

183 *Thinking about why*: Interviews with Aaron and Cheyney; Aaron reflection.

183 *a No. 15 blade*: Interview with Aaron.

184 *It was 5:40 p.m.*: In a Secret Service report, an agent reported that Aaron retrieved the bullet at 5:40 p.m. and placed it in a cup. The cup was marked with the words, "Taken from President Reagan 3-30-1981 by Dr. (redacted) at 5:40 p.m." The FBI reported that the bullet was removed "at approximately 5:39 p.m."

14: The Waiting Room

185 *While awaiting further*: Nancy Reagan, *My Turn*, p. 7; interview with Opfer.

185 *Then all three major networks*: I watched news coverage recorded by Bob Parker, a former CNN producer who provided me with a DVD of the broadcasts. There is also a wealth of the day's news coverage on the Internet.

186 *He warned her*: Interview with Opfer; Nancy Reagan, *My Turn*, p. 8.

186 *"That thing is out of control"*: Deaver transcript; interview with Baker. Deaver later wrote in *Behind the Scenes* (pp. 29–30) that Haig's performance "did not exactly inspire confidence" and that the secretary of state looked "like a man about to crack." Deaver added that Haig's assertion that he was in control "at that moment seemed inappropriate."

186 *Nofziger turned back to the podium*: Nofziger, *Nofziger*, p. 294; Nofziger notes. The political aide's notes list all of Reagan's lines and quips from the time he entered the ER until he was operated on. Nofziger died in 2006. In his autobiography, he described the importance of Reagan's jokes and one-liners to the country (p. 295): "These lines assured the nation that the president was going to be all right. They also said that here was a most unusual man, what Americans like to think they're all about, a swashbuckling people who laugh in the face of death and don't shrink from the teeth of danger. . . . Here was a man who for years had talked the good fight to all Americans, but none of them knew how he would react to the blows—until now—and now his courage made all but the most bitter Reagan haters proud to be Americans."

187 *remove the entire lower*: Interview with Aaron.

187 *before six p.m.*: OR circulating record. The precise time was 5:50 p.m.

187 *She and a colleague*: Interview with Lula Gore.

188 *it had been a rough few hours*: Discharge summary; Gens notes; anesthesia record. Reagan did not receive any whole blood during surgery. Blood banks typically break donated blood into its key components—red blood cells, plasma, and platelets. Reagan received about eight units of red blood cells. He received three units of plasma and one pack of platelets. Both of those components promote blood clotting.

188 *Still, the three-hour operation*: The OR circulating record shows that Giordano began the belly tap at 3:26, and Aaron began closing up the chest incision at 5:50, and that surgery was concluded at 6:32 p.m. I derived other times from various medical files (the time of the X-ray in the operating room, for example, is noted in the anesthesia record), Gens notes, and the recollections of other participants. Giordano and Gens believe the belly tap took about thirty minutes, but Gens notes and the anesthesia record indicate the procedure lasted until about 4:30, an hour-long span that may also have included time waiting for lab results and other nonsurgical matters. The anesthesia record, Gens notes, and interviews with Gens and Aaron indicate that chest surgery started at approximately 4:45 p.m.

188 *For several minutes*: Allen tapes.

188 *Richard Allen was only half listening*: Interview with Allen.

189 *Baker appeared no worse*: Allen tapes; interview with Allen; photos of men in Situation Room, RRPL.

190 *At 6:45*: OR circulating record.

190 *made only a brief stop*: Colombani notes. Tim McCarthy's surgery went quickly and smoothly. Colombani, the doctor who initially treated him, and Dr. Neofytos Tsangaris opened up the agent's abdomen, removed collecting blood, and repaired damaged tissue. The bullet had entered just below McCarthy's right pectoral muscle, then ripped through his lung and diaphragm, pierced the liver, and lodged in his right flank. After stitching up the damaged tissue and cauterized bleeding vessels, Colombani was about to sew up the hole in the diaphragm when he announced that the surgery was nearly over.

"What?" said a Secret Service agent standing behind him. "We need the bullet."

"Why do you need the bullet?" Colombani asked.

"We need it for ballistics."

"But you have the guy who shot them."

The agent explained that Brady's bullet had fragmented and that Reagan's appeared to be distorted. Colombani shrugged, probed McCarthy's flank muscles, retrieved the bullet, and dropped it with a clink into a metal specimen pan.

190 *before being transferred*: Tim McCarthy spent the night in the intensive care unit. When McCarthy came out of anesthesia, his friend Trainor, the agent who won the coin flip contest and thus avoided duty at the Hilton, was at his bedside.

"That's the last time I'll ever flip with you again," McCarthy said.

"Yeah, Timmy," Trainor said, "but you're a hero."

190 *Reagan was parked feetfirst*: Interview with Denise Sullivan.

190 *At about 7:15, as he began*: Interview with Sullivan; progress notes from the recovery room.

190 *"Mr. Reagan," she said*: Interview with Cathy Edmondson.

191 *As Reagan slowly began*: Interview with Edmondson and Sullivan.

191 *decided to treat Reagan*: Interview with Sullivan.

191 *"I'm going to ask you"*: Interview with Sullivan.

191 *He and his wife were eating*: Interview with Ron Reagan; "President's Son May Perform," AP, March 31, 1981.

192 *"I'm so frightened," she said*: Nancy Reagan, *My Turn*, p. 9.

192 *"Don't worry, Mom"*: Interview with Ron Reagan.

192 *slipped between the portable screens*: Dr. Jack Zimmerman reflection.

192 *"I love you," she said*: Nancy Reagan, *My Turn*, p. 9.

192 *"I can't breathe . . . at all"*: Interview with Parr. Jerry Parr put this note in the

pocket of his surgical scrubs and found it years later in his attic. He mailed the note to the Ronald Reagan Presidential Foundation, but it does not appear to have the note. Nancy Reagan also described the note in *My Turn* (p. 9).

192 *"He can't breathe!"*: Nancy Reagan, *My Turn*, p. 8.

192 *Ron tried to reassure*: Interview with Ron Reagan.

193 *"photography of Soviet"*: CIA memorandum, March 30, 1981.

194 *The FBI agents leading*: Government psychiatric report; interviews with Colo and George Chmiel. FBI agent Henry Ragle told government psychiatrists that Hinckley was "probably the politest fellow I have ever arrested," according to the government psychiatric report. Colo and Chmiel agreed with that assessment. Descriptions of Chmiel and Ragle came from former agents in the Washington field office, including Richard Qulia, who also spent time with Hinckley that day. Ragle died in 2003.

194 *The first agent*: Interview with Chmiel. Chmiel did not put this exchange in any report. Agents were so worried about accomplices that they succeeded in getting his court-appointed attorney, Stuart Johnson, to ask Hinckley if he really was a loner. Johnson was appointed by a federal judge to represent Hinckley and finally made it to the FBI's Washington field office at 7:30. He received a briefing from top law enforcement officials about what Hinckley had told agents, and they then asked Johnson for permission to keep questioning his client. Johnson refused. However, he did grant one request. "Can you do us a favor?" an agent asked Johnson and his cocounsel, Edgar Wilhite. "It's a big favor. Can you find out if there is anyone else out there wanting to hurt the president?"

Inside a small interview room, the attorneys spoke with Hinckley for about an hour. After the lawyers had finished, Johnson found the agent. "You have nothing to worry about," the attorney said—in a way that he felt did not violate attorney-client privilege.

195 *it was Agent Henry Ragle's turn*: Interview with Colo; Ragle testimony at pretrial evidence suppression hearing.

195 *string of terse queries*: Interview with Colo; Colo was impressed with Ragle's open-mindedness, saying it was a sign that the FBI agent was a good investigator.

196 *brought a fast-food hamburger*: Ragle FBI report; FBI arrest log.

196 *Colo used a personal history*: In re-creating the interview of Hinckley, I relied on interviews with Colo and Chmiel, a memo authored by Colo detailing the session with Hinckley, and a transcript of tape-recorded notes that Colo made shortly after the interrogation. I also utilized FBI reports filed by Chmiel and Ragle, and testimony elicited during a pretrial suppression hearing from Colo and Ragle.

198 *He ran to find Ragle*: Despite their success in getting Hinckley to open up, the suspect's statements were blocked from trial by a federal judge. U.S. District

Judge Barrington D. Parker ruled that the federal agents had violated the suspect's rights by questioning him after he had asked to see an attorney while in
custody at D.C. police headquarters. Shortly after FBI agents took custody of
Hinckley, Myers, the homicide detective, told them that the suspect had asked to
see an attorney before saying anything. That should have ended questioning
until the attorney arrived. But the FBI agents read him his rights again and
pressed ahead with the interrogation, violating Hinckley's constitutional protection against self-incrimination, according to Parker's ruling, which was upheld
on appeal. The suppression of those statements likely did not affect the outcome
of the trial—the information Hinckley provided the agents was introduced
through other witnesses anyway. Most outside observers agree that the verdict
largely hinged on testimony from psychiatrists. For those interested in the trial, I
recommend Lincoln Caplan's *The Insanity Defense and the Trial of John
W. Hinckley, Jr.*

15: "What Does the Future Hold?"

199 *When the president seemed uncomfortable*: Interviews with Edmondson and Sullivan; anesthesia record; Zimmerman reflection.

199 *doctors increased his pain*: Anesthesia record.

199 *Doctors who had examined*: Zimmerman reflection; interview with Aaron.

199 *Ben Aaron, who was keeping*: Interview with Aaron.

200 *assistants sterilized the bronchoscope*: Zimmerman reflection.

200 *Aaron lubricated the*: Interviews with Aaron, Zimmerman, Edmondson, and Sullivan; Zimmerman reflection; anesthesia record.

200 *more conservative procedure*: Interview with Zimmerman; Zimmerman reflection.

200 *"Don't pull at it now"*: *The Saving of the President*; interview with Edmondson.

201 *blood tests steadily improved*: Zimmerman reflection.

201 *"All in all, I'd rather be in Phil."*: Copy of notes provided by Joanne Drake, chief
of staff of the Ronald Reagan Presidential Foundation. Secret Service agents
confiscated the notes as they were passed to nurses by the president. Eventually,
they were given to Mrs. Reagan. Agents jotted times on some of the notes but not
on all of them. I was able to triangulate the sequence of notes by using those
times and by interviewing nurses and doctors.

201 *Sullivan thought hard*: Interview with Sullivan.

201 *After Lyn Nofziger's*: Nofziger, *Nofziger*, p. 294; interview with Dr. Dennis
O'Leary.

202 *O'Leary sketched out his opening*: Interview with O'Leary.

203 *"The president is"*: Transcript of press conference, RRPL; network news coverage
of press conference.

203 *If Jerry Parr hadn't*: If Parr had gone to the White House, Reagan would have most likely died, according to Gens, Giordano, and Aaron. Nancy Reagan also credited Parr with saving the president's life. In a 1998 interview with CNN's Larry King, the former first lady said: "If Jerry hadn't made the change from driving to the White House to the hospital, I wouldn't have a husband."

203 *in O'Leary's defense*: Interview with O'Leary; doctors—including Aaron and Giordano—felt that O'Leary did a good job at the press conference.

203 *understated the amount of blood*: O'Leary said Reagan received five units of blood in the emergency room, and none in the operating room. In fact, Reagan received three units of packed red blood cells in the emergency room and just over five units in the operating room.

204 *"This guy is good"*: Allen tapes.

204 *adjourned at eight p.m.*: Allen tapes and notes.

204 *Baker, Meese, and the others*: Photographs, GBPL.

204 *Frazzled, he couldn't*: Interview with Khachigian.

204 *"I am deeply"*: Transcript of statement, RRPL.

204 *Before heading home*: Interview with Giordano.

205 *sat down next to Reagan*: Interview with Gens; Gens diary.

205 *But Reagan had long*: Reagan, *Where's the Rest of Me?*, pp. 194–95.

206 *"Don't fight it"*: Interviews with Edmondson and Sullivan.

206 *Jerry Parr left the hospital*: Interview with Parr.

207 *George Opfer sat*: Interview with Opfer.

207 *Nancy Reagan was curled*: Noonan, *When Character Was King*, p. 185.

207 *GW's doctors gave Jim*: Interview with Kobrine.

208 *stayed at her husband's side*: Interview with Sarah Brady.

208 *Allen, whose wife*: Interview with Allen.

208 *While Bell monitored*: Interviews with Joanne Bell and Marisa Mize.

208 *"I'm going to hold"*: Interview with Mize.

209 *Aaron told Zimmerman*: Zimmerman essay.

209 *Oscar-winning film*: The 1945 film starred his first wife, Jayne Wyman. Reagan and Wyman's divorce was finalized four years later.

210 *"You are in the GW recovery"*: Interview with Mize; Mize notes.

210 *"How long in the hospital?"*: Interview with Mize. Just after asking that question, Reagan was reminded of his allergies. "I left something out. I do have something of an allergy to tape and moleskin," he wrote. In the 1940s, Reagan broke his leg in six places during a charity softball game. His leg was wrapped in adhesive tape and moleskin. A day later, he learned he was allergic to moleskin and tape when his eyes were swelled shut and he began itching all over.

211 *As the hour passed four a.m.*: Interviews with Bell, Mize, Price, Pett, and Zimmerman; Zimmerman reflection; *The Saving of the President*.

Epilogue

213 *After a fitful*: Interviews with numerous doctors and nurses.

213 *stood at attention*: Interview with Bell.

213 *conducted a basic*: Interviews with Maureen McCann and Carolyn Ramos.

214 *"slapping a side of beef"*: Nancy Reagan, *My Turn*, p. 11.

214 *ice chips*: Interview with McCann.

214 *"I should have known"*: Tom Matthews, "Reagan's Close Call," *Newsweek*, April 13, 1981.

215 *"I had hoped it was"*: Interview with McCann.

215 *"Oh, damn"*: Transcript of Baker press conference, March 31, 1981, RRPL.

215 *The first several*: Interviews with doctors; review of doctors' notes; Aaron reflection.

215 *Not until April 6*: DDPRR; Max Friedersdorf, oral history at Miller Center (October 2002).

215 *temporary setback*: Interviews with doctors and nurses; Aaron reflection; discharge summary.

216 *returned to the Oval Office*: DDPRR, April 24, 1981.

216 *On April 28*: Text of speech, RRPL; multiple news accounts of speech, as well as a video of address downloaded from the Ronald Reagan Presidential Foundation and Library website; "Reagan Returns to Public with Plea on the Economy," AP, April 28, 1981.

217 *On April 11, 1981*: *Reagan Diaries*, pp. 30–31.

217 *the president prayed*: *Reagan Diaries*, p. 30; Ronald Reagan, *An American Life*, p. 261.

218 *Soon after his discharge*: Ronald Reagan, *Reagan: A Life in Letters*, pp. 737–41; Ronald Reagan, *An American Life*, pp. 269–73.

218 *"He was a performer"*: Interview with Ron Reagan.

219 *"Somebody ought to entertain"*: Interview of President Reagan by author Mollie Dickenson in May 1985 that was tape-recorded by WHCA, RRPL.

219 *in mid-March to 73 percent*: Barry Sussman, "Shooting Gives Reagan Boost in Popularity," WP, April 2, 1981, p. A1; "Public Approves of President Far More Than of His Policies," WP, June 4, 1981, p. A12.

220 *"what happened to Reagan"*: David Broder, "End of a Dream," WP, April 1, 1981, p. A21.

220 *"politically untouchable"*: Interview with David Broder.

220 *"cemented a bond"*: Interview with Lou Cannon.

221 *By the time he left office*: "Final Job Approval Rating for Recent Presidents," Gallup website, www.gallup.com.

222 *"When life gives you lemons"*: Sue Anne Pressley, "When History, Destiny Converged," WP, March 30, 2006, p. B1.

223 *Before leaving GW*: Interview with Tim McCarthy.

224 *In 1985, after twenty-three years*: Interview with Parr.

225 *The Secret Service tried to deflect blame*: Testimony of Secret Service director H. Stuart Knight before the Senate Appropriations Subcommittee on Treasury, Postal Service, and General Government, April 2, 1981. "What would we have done about it if notified? At a minimum, interview the gentleman," Knight testified. Whether that would have stopped Hinckley is unclear. Colo, an experienced investigator, said that Hinckley would not have caused him much concern if he had interviewed him before the attack.

    The Secret Service also repeatedly pointed out that the area behind the rope line had not been designated a press area by the White House. Such a decision would have required an agent to check identification of reporters and limit that area to cameramen and journalists, and Hinckley would never have been permitted to get so close. There is often a tug-of-war between the White House and the Secret Service over presidential security and access to the president.

225 *the Secret Service did change*: After the shooting, the service rarely let a president enter or exit a limousine in public view. Instead, agents pulled the president's limousine into garages or into tents, preventing potential assassins from getting a shot at the president during such vulnerable moments. The Washington Hilton also changed—it constructed a concrete bunker–like garage outside of the VIP entrance to shield presidents and other dignitaries during their arrivals and departures.

226 *In 2010, it had 3,500*: Information provided by the Secret Service; Secret Service budget for salaries and expenses, Department of Homeland Security.

226 *A few days later*: Interview with Sullivan; copy of the letter Reagan sent to Sullivan.

226 *occasional notes from Reagan*: Interview with Giordano; copy of the note provided by Giordano.

227 *Dr. Benjamin Aaron, Dr. David Gens*: *The Saving of the President*; White House photo of meeting, RRPL.

227 *$96 million*: Monte Reel, "90 Feet and a World Away," WP, August 21, 2002, p. B1.

227 *In 1981, there were*: Testimony before the House Subcommittee on Health and the Environment, Committee on Energy and Commerce, April 7, 1981.

227 *Today, there are more*: Interview with Harry Teter.

228 *Though his boyish looks*: Author observation of Hinckley during 2008 court hearings.

228 *One of his first acts*: Interview with Ryan.

BIBLIOGRAPHY

Books

Abrams, Herbert L. *"The President Has Been Shot": Confusion, Disability, and the 25th Amendment in the Aftermath of the Attempted Assassination of Ronald Reagan.* New York: W. W. Norton, 1992.

Allen, Richard V. *Peace or Peaceful Coexistence?* Chicago: American Bar Association, 1966.

Anderson, Martin. *Revolution.* Orlando, Fla.: Harcourt Brace Jovanovich, 1988.

Baker, James A., III, with Steve Fiffer. *"Work Hard, Study . . . and Keep Out of Politics!": Adventures and Lessons from an Unexpected Public Life.* New York: G. P. Putnam's Sons, 2006.

Barletta, John R., with Rochelle Schweizer. *Riding with Reagan: From the White House to the Ranch.* New York: Citadel Press, 2006.

Barrett, Laurence I. *Gambling with History.* New York: Penguin Books, 1984.

Bohn, Michael K. *Nerve Center: Inside the White House Situation Room.* Washington, D.C.: Brassey's, 2003.

Bremer, Arthur H. *An Assassin's Diary.* New York: Harper's Magazine Press, 1973.

Brown, Mary Beth. *Hand of Providence: The Strong and Quiet Faith of Ronald Reagan.* Nashville, Tenn.: WND Books, 2004.

Bugliosi, Vincent. *Four Days in November: The Assassination of President John F. Kennedy.* New York: W. W. Norton, 2007.

Bugliosi, Vincent. *Reclaiming History: The Assassination of John F. Kennedy*. New York: W. W. Norton, 2007 (Kindle edition).

Bumgarner, John R. *The Health of the Presidents: The 41 United States Presidents Through 1993 from a Physician's Point of View*. Jefferson, N.C.: McFarland & Company, 1994.

Bunch, Will. *Tear Down This Myth: How the Reagan Legacy Has Distorted Our Politics and Haunts Our Future*. New York: Free Press, 2009 (Kindle edition).

Bush, George. *All the Best, George Bush: My Life in Letters and Other Writings*. New York: Touchstone, 2000.

Byrne, Malcolm, and Andrzej Paczkowski, eds. *From Solidarity to Martial Law: The Polish Crisis of 1980–1981: A Documentary History*. Budapest, Hungary: Central European University Press, 2007.

Cannon, Lou. *President Reagan: The Role of a Lifetime*. New York: PublicAffairs, 2000.

Cannon, Lou. *Reagan*. New York: G. P. Putnam's Sons, 1982.

Caplan, Lincoln. *The Insanity Defense and the Trial of John W. Hinckley, Jr.* Boston: David R. Godine, 1984.

Darman, Richard. *Who's in Control?: Polar Politics and the Sensible Center*. New York: Simon & Schuster, 1996.

Davis, Patti. *The Long Goodbye*. New York: Alfred A. Knopf, 2004.

Davis, Patti. *The Way I See It: An Autobiography*. New York: G. P. Putnam's Sons, 1992.

Deaver, Michael K. *A Different Drummer: My Thirty Years with Ronald Reagan*. New York: HarperCollins, 2001.

Deaver, Michael K. *Nancy: A Portrait of My Years with Nancy Reagan*. New York: William Morrow, 2004.

Deaver, Michael K., with Mickey Herskowitz. *Behind the Scenes*. New York: William Morrow, 1988.

Dickenson, Mollie. *Thumbs Up: The Life and Courageous Comeback of White House Press Secretary Jim Brady*. New York: William Morrow, 1987.

Diggins, John Patrick. *Ronald Reagan: Fate, Freedom, and the Making of History*. New York: W. W. Norton, 2007.

Elman, Richard. *Taxi Driver*. New York: Bantam Books, 1976.

Excerpts from the History of the United States Secret Service, 1865–1975. Washington, D.C.: Government Printing Office, 1978.

Farrell, John A. *Tip O'Neill and the Democratic Century*. New York: Back Bay Press, 2002.

Feerick, John D. *The Twenty-fifth Amendment: Its Complete History and Applications*. New York: Fordham University Press, 1992.

Franklin, Jon, and Alan Doelp. *Shocktrauma*. New York: St. Martin's Press, 1980.

Gergen, David. *Eyewitness to Power: The Essence of Leadership: Nixon to Clinton*. New York: Simon & Schuster, 2000.

Gillon, Steven M. *The Kennedy Assassination—24 Hours After.* New York: Basic Books, 2009.

Haig, Alexander M., Jr. *Caveat: Realism, Reagan, and Foreign Policy.* New York: Macmillan, 1984.

Hannaford, Peter D. *The Reagans: A Political Portrait.* New York: Coward-McCann, 1983.

Hinckley, Jack, and Jo Ann Hinckley, with Elizabeth Sherrill. *Breaking Points.* New York: Berkley, 1986.

Kengor, Paul. *God and Ronald Reagan: A Spiritual Life.* New York: ReganBooks, HarperCollins, 2004.

Kessler, Ronald. *In the President's Secret Service: Behind the Scenes with Agents in the Line of Fire and the Presidents They Protect.* New York: Crown, 2009.

Kuhn, Jim. *Ronald Reagan in Private: A Memoir of My Years in the White House.* New York: Sentinel, 2004.

Laxalt, Paul. *Nevada's Paul Laxalt: A Memoir.* Reno, Nev.: Jack Bacon & Co., 2000.

MacEachin, Douglas J. *U.S. Intelligence and the Confrontation in Poland, 1980–1981.* University Park: Pennsylvania State University Press, 2002.

Manchester, William. *The Death of a President.* New York: Harper & Row, 1967.

Mann, James. *The Rebellion of Ronald Reagan: A History of the End of the Cold War.* New York: Viking Penguin, 2009.

Mayer, Jane, and Doyle McManus. *Landslide: The Unmaking of the President, 1984–1988.* Boston: Houghton Mifflin, 1989.

McCarthy, Dennis V. N., with Philip W. Smith. *Protecting the President: The Inside Story of a Secret Service Agent.* New York: Dell, 1987.

McGrath, Jim, ed. *Heartbeat: George Bush in His Own Words.* New York: Scribner, 2001.

Meese, Edwin III. *With Reagan: The Inside Story.* Washington, D.C.: Regnery Gateway, 1992.

Melanson, Phillip H. *The Secret Service: The Hidden History of an Enigmatic Agency.* New York: Carroll & Graf, 2005.

Nofziger, Lyn. *Nofziger.* Washington, D.C.: Regnery Gateway, 1992.

Noonan, Peggy. *When Character Was King: A Story of Ronald Reagan.* New York: Penguin Books, 2002.

O'Neill, Thomas P., Jr., with William Novak. *Man of the House: The Life and Political Memoirs of Speaker Tip O'Neill.* New York: Random House, 1987.

Petro, Joseph, with Jeffrey Robinson. *Standing Next to History: An Agent's Life Inside the Secret Service.* New York: Thomas Dunne Books, 2005.

Platzgraff, Robert L., and Jacquelyn K. Davis. *National Security Decisions: The Participants Speak.* Lexington, Mass.: Lexington Books, 1990.

Randall, Bob. *The Fan.* New York: Random House, 1977.

Ratnesar, Romesh. *Tear Down This Wall: A City, a President, and the Speech That Ended the Cold War.* New York: Simon & Schuster, 2009.

Reagan, Michael, with Joe Hyams. *Michael Reagan: On the Outside Looking In*. New York: Zebra Books, 1988.

Reagan, Nancy. *I Love You, Ronnie: The Letters of Ronald Reagan to Nancy Reagan*. New York: Random House, 2000.

Reagan, Nancy, with William Novak. *My Turn: The Memoirs of Nancy Reagan*. New York: Random House, 1989.

Reagan, Ronald. *An American Life*. New York: Simon & Schuster, 1990.

Reagan, Ronald. *Speaking My Mind: Selected Speeches*. New York: Simon & Schuster, 1989.

Reagan, Ronald, with Douglas Brinkley, ed. *The Reagan Diaries, January 1981–October 1985*. Volume 1. *The Reagan Diaries, November 1985–January 1989*. Volume 2. New York: Harper, 2009.

Reagan, Ronald, with Jim Denney. *The Common Sense of an Uncommon Man: The Wit, Wisdom, and Eternal Optimism of Ronald Reagan*. Compiled by Michael Reagan. Nashville, Tenn.: Thomas Nelson, 1998.

Reagan, Ronald, with Richard G. Hubler. *Where's the Rest of Me?* New York: Karz Publishers, 1981.

Reagan, Ronald, with Kiron K. Skinner, Annelise Anderson, and Martin Anderson, eds. *Reagan: A Life in Letters*. New York: Free Press, 2004.

Reagan, Ronald, with Kiron K. Skinner, Annelise Anderson, and Martin Anderson, eds. *Reagan, in His Own Hand: The Writings of Ronald Reagan That Reveal His Revolutionary Vision for America*. New York: Free Press, 2001.

Regan, Donald T. *For the Record*. New York: St. Martin's Press, 1989.

Robinson, Peter. *How Ronald Reagan Changed My Life*. New York: ReganBooks, 2004.

Schrader, Paul. *Taxi Driver*. London: Faber and Faber, 1990.

Schweizer, Peter. *Reagan's War: The Epic Story of His Forty-Year Struggle and Final Triumph over Communism*. New York: Doubleday, 2002.

Shirley, Craig. *Rendezvous with Destiny: Ronald Reagan and the Campaign That Changed America*. Wilmington, Del.: ISI Books, 2009.

Smith, I. C. *Inside: A Top G-Man Exposes Spies, Lies, and Bureaucratic Bungling Inside the FBI*. Nashville, Tenn.: Nelson Current, 2004.

Speakes, Larry, with Robert Pack. *Speaking Out: The Reagan Presidency from Inside the White House*. New York: Avon Books, 1988.

Stockman, David A. *The Triumph of Politics*. New York: Avon Books, 1987.

Thomas, Tony. *The Films of Ronald Reagan*. Secaucus, N.J.: Citadel Press, 1980.

Von Damm, Helene. *At Reagan's Side*. New York: Doubleday, 1989.

Walker, Martin. *The Cold War: A History*. New York: Holt Paperbacks, 1993.

Weinberger, Caspar W. *Fighting for Peace: Seven Critical Years in the Pentagon*. New York: Warner Books, 1990.

Wilentz, Sean. *The Age of Reagan: A History, 1974–2008*. New York: Harper Perennial, 2009.

Wills, Garry. *Reagan's America*. New York: Penguin Books, 2000.

Wirthlin, Dick, with Wynton C. Hall. *The Greatest Communicator: What Ronald Reagan Taught Me About Politics, Leadership, and Life*. Hoboken, N.J.: John Wiley & Sons, 2004.

Journal Articles, General Articles, and Chapters in Books

Aaron, Benjamin L., and S. David Rockoff. "The Attempted Assassination of President Reagan: Medical Implications and Historical Perspective." *Journal of the American Medical Association* 272, no. 21 (December 7, 1994): 1689–93.

Aaron, Benjamin L., and S. David Rockoff. "The Shooting of President Reagan: A Radiologic Chronology of His Medical Care." *Radiographics* 15, no. 2 (March 1995): 407–18.

Beahrs, Oliver H. "The Medical History of President Ronald Reagan." *Journal of the American College of Surgeons* 178, no. 1 (January 1994): 86–96.

Blatt, Alan J., Charles C. Branas, Marie C. Flanigan, Ellen J. MacKenzie, Charles S. ReVelle, C. William Schwab, Harry M. Teter, and Justin C. Williams. "Access to Trauma Centers in the United States." *Journal of the American Medical Association* 293, no. 21 (June 1, 2005): 2626–33.

Bloom, Mark. "All the President's Doctors." *Medical World News* (April 27, 1981): 9–10, 13, 17–18, 20.

Boyd, D. R. "Trauma—A Controllable Disease in the 1980s (Fourth Annual Stone Lecture, American Trauma Society)." *Journal of Trauma* 20, no. 1 (January 1980): 14–24.

Boyd, David R. "Chapter 1. The History of Emergency Medical Services (EMS) Systems in the United States of America." *Systems Approach to Emergency Medical Care* (June 1983): 1–40.

Boyd, David R., Richard Crampton, Richard F. Edlich, Carl Jelenko III, Ronald L. Krome, and Frank Poliafico. "Emergency Medical Support Plan for the President of the United States and VIPs." *Journal of the American College of Emergency Physicians* 6, no. 10 (October 1977): 462–64.

Donahoe, Jeffrey. "Head for George Washington." *GW Medicine* (Spring 1991): 8–14.

Farjah, Farhood, and Donald Trunkey. "Medical and Surgical Care of Our Four Assassinated Presidents." *Journal of the American College of Surgeons* 201, no. 6 (December 2005): 976–89.

Frangou, Christina. "The American Trauma System: Gaps Riddle a Strong Structure." *General Surgery News* 36, no. 11 (November 2009): 1, 24.

"GWU Nurses Who Cared for President Say It Was (Almost) in a Day's Work." *American Journal of Nursing* 81, no. 6 (June 1981): 1090, 1108, 1129–30.

Marsh, Fran. "12 Days at GW Hospital." *GW Times* 10, no. 4 (July–August 1981): 1–3.

Pekkanen, John. "The Saving of the President." *Washingtonian*, August 1981.

Trunkey, Donald D. "The Development of Trauma Systems." In Juan A. Asensio and

Donald D. Trunkey, eds., *Current Therapy of Trauma and Surgical Clinical Care*, pp. 1–13. Philadelphia, Pa.: Mosby Elsevier, 2008.

Trunkey, Donald D. "The Emerging Crisis in Trauma Care: A History and Definition of the Problem." *Clinical Neurosurgery* 54 (2007): 200–205.

Government Reports, Records, and Transcripts

"Accidental Death and Disability: The Neglected Disease of Modern Society." National Academy of Sciences (September 1966).

Chase Untermeyer interview of Vice President George H. W. Bush aboard Air Force Two, March 30, 1981. Handwritten notes of Vice President Bush. Both records retrieved by Untermeyer from George Bush Presidential Library.

FBI reports obtained under Freedom of Information Act, 2010. These include newly released bureau interviews of President Reagan, Dr. Benjamin Aaron, Dr. Daniel Ruge, Thomas K. Delahanty, and paramedics.

Memos and notes written by administration officials describing their actions on March 30, 1981, RRPL. These include memos from Defense Secretary Caspar Weinberger, Treasury Secretary Don Regan, and handwritten notes of Ken Khachigian, among others.

"Michael Deaver Testimony," March 31, 1981, transcript of interview of Michael Deaver by Richard Darman, provided by Amanda Deaver and Jeff Surrell.

Secret Service reports (387 pages obtained through the Freedom of Information Act, 2010).

Transcripts of trial of Arthur H. Bremmer, 1972.

Transcripts of trial of John W. Hinckley Jr., 1982.

Ronald Reagan Medical Records

Anesthesia Record

Operating Room Circulating Record

Hospital Physical Examination Form

Discharge Summary of Ronald Reagan, April 11, 1981

Miscellaneous Records, Notes, First-Person Accounts, and Unpublished Records

Notes: Kathy Paul, Marisa Mize, Maureen McCann, Dr. Paul Colombani, and Dr. David Gens.

Dr. Benjamin Aaron, sixteen-page personal reflection, 1981.

Dr. David Gens, "Diary of Presidential Stay at G.W.U.H.," ten pages, 1981.

Dr. David Gens, tape-recorded personal narrative, 1981.

Dr. Joseph Giordano, six-page narrative of Reagan's care, 1981.

Jerry Parr, "A Spiritual Autobiography."

Dr. Jack Zimmerman, twenty-eight-page personal reflection, 1981.

Interviews, Other Than by the Author

Dr. David Gens: Tape-recorded interview by reporter John Pekkanen in 1981. Tape provided by Gens.

Ronald Reagan: Interview by Laurence Barrett on December 29, 1981, and taped by WHCA, RRPL.

Ronald Reagan: Interview by Helen Thomas and Jim Gerstenzang, wire service reporters, on April 22, 1981, and taped by WHCA, RRPL.

Ronald Reagan: Interview by Mollie Dickenson on May 23, 1984, and taped by WHCA, RRPL.

First-Person Published Accounts

Giordano, Joseph. "Doctor's Story: A Delay Could Have Been Fatal." *Los Angeles Times*, April 4, 1981, p. 1.

Parr, Jerry. "One Moment in Time." *Guideposts*, March 1992.

Price, G. Wesley. "An Eyewitness Account by the First Doctor to Get to the President." *Washingtonian*, August 1981.

Sermon

Harper, John C. "The Son of the Man." Sermon delivered at St. John's Church, Lafayette Square, Washington, D.C., March 29, 1981. Provided by St. John's Church.

Collections

The papers of James A. Baker III at Seeley G. Mudd Manuscript Library at Princeton University.

Ronald Reagan Presidential Library. Various files, including those containing papers on the assassination attempt, speech writing, schedules, the National Security Council, and a number of former White House staffers.

Miller Center of Public Affairs, University of Virginia. Oral history transcripts of Richard Allen, Lyn Nofziger, Martin Anderson, Michael Deaver, and Max Friedersdorf.

The papers of Lyn Nofziger at the Hoover Institution Archives, Stanford University.

Periodicals and Wire Services

Associated Press
Baltimore Sun
Boston Globe
Chicago Tribune
Copley News Service
Des Moines Register
Kansas City Star
Kansas City Times

Los Angeles Times
Miami Herald
Newsweek
New York Times
Peoria Journal Star
Philadelphia Inquirer
Quad-City Times (Davenport, Iowa)
Southtown Star (Chicago)
State Journal-Register (Springfield, Illinois)
Time
United Press International
U.S. News & World Report
Washingtonian
Washington Post

Selected Interviews

I have grouped interviews by general topic area. Subjects are listed in alphabetical order with their relevant titles in March 1981. I have identified people here and in the text of the book by the names they used in 1981. However, if a person has a different surname today (such as a woman who has since married), I have noted that in parenthesis.

MEDICAL CARE

Dr. Benjamin Aaron, GW chief of cardiovascular and thoracic surgery.

Dr. David Adelberg, GW surgical intern.

Joanne Bell, GW recovery room nurse.

Dr. Bradley Bennett, GW surgical resident.

Dr. Howard Champion, chief of trauma services and director of critical care services at Washington Hospital Center.

Dr. Kathleen Cheyney, GW thoracic surgical fellow.

Dr. May Chin, GW anesthesiology resident.

Dr. Roderick Clemente, GW neurosurgical resident.

Dr. Paul Colombani, GW chief surgical resident.

Craig DeAtley, GW physician's assistant.

Dr. Michael W. Dennis, WHC neurosurgeon.

Dr. Sol Edelstein, GW director of division of emergency medicine.

Cathy Edmondson, GW recovery room nurse.

Dr. Ed Engle, GW neurosurgical resident.

Dr. David Gens, GW chief surgical resident.

Dr. Joseph Giordano, GW head of trauma teams.

Lula Gore (Bauer), GW operating room nurse.

Robert Hernandez, D.C. paramedic.

Cyndi Hines, GW emergency room technician.

Dr. Jeff Jacobson, GW neurosurgical resident.

Dr. Judith Johnson, GW anesthesiology resident.

Dr. Arthur Kobrine, GW neurosurgeon.

Wendy Koenig, GW emergency room nurse.

Dr. Manfred Lichtman, GW anesthesiologist.

Dr. Michael Manganiello, GW ophthalmology resident.

Maureen McCann (O'Bryan), GW nurse in intensive care unit.

Dr. Joyce Mitchell, GW emergency room physician.

Marisa Mize, GW nurse in recovery room.

Dr. Dennis O'Leary, dean of clinical affairs for the George Washington University
    Medical Center.

Dr. William O'Neill, GW surgical intern.

Kathy Paul (Stevens), GW nurse in emergency room.

Dr. Stephen Pett, GW thoracic surgical resident.

Dr. G. Wesley Price, GW surgical resident.

Carolyn Ramos (Francis), GW nurse in intensive care unit.

Dr. David Rockoff, GW chief of radiology.

Dr. Drew Scheele, GW surgical intern.

Denise Sullivan, GW nurse in recovery room.

Dr. Theodore Tsangaris, son of Dr. Neofytos Tsangaris (deceased), GW's acting chief
    of surgery.

Judith Whinerey (Goss), GW assistant nurse in charge of the emergency room.

Dr. Jack Zimmerman, GW director of intensive care unit.

REAGAN WHITE HOUSE, U.S. GOVERNMENT, AND MILITARY

Rick Ahearn, advance representative.

Richard V. Allen, national security advisor.

Martin Anderson, domestic policy advisor.

James A. Baker III, chief of staff.

Darryl Borgquist, researcher in White House speech-writing office.

James Brady, press secretary.

Sarah Brady, wife of press secretary.

Kenneth Cribb, assistant to the president for domestic affairs.

Catherine Donovan, wife of Labor Secretary Raymond Donovan.

Raymond Donovan, labor secretary.

Fred Fielding, White House counsel.

David Fischer, presidential assistant.

David Gergen, White House staff director.

Woody Goldberg, executive assistant to secretary of state.

Peter Hannaford, 1980 Reagan campaign advisor.

Bobby Inman, deputy director of CIA.

Richard Kerr, director of CIA office of current operations.

Ken Khachigian, chief White House speechwriter.

Mari Maseng (Will), White House speechwriter.

John Matheny, major, U.S. Air Force, military aide to Vice President Bush.

Peter McCoy, chief of staff to Nancy Reagan.

Edwin Meese III, counselor to the president.

Jose Muratti, lieutenant colonel, U.S. Army, military aide to the president.

Theodore Olson, assistant attorney general for the office of legal counsel.

Stetson Orchard, major, U.S. Air Force, pilot of Air Force Two.

Sheila Patton (Tate), spokeswoman for Nancy Reagan.

Pete Peterson, master sergeant, U.S. Army, WHCA.

David Prosperi, assistant press secretary.

Michael Reagan, son of Ronald Reagan.

Ron Reagan, son of Ronald Reagan.

Tom Ruge, son of Dr. Daniel Ruge, White House physician.

Frederick Ryan, chief of staff for President Reagan in retirement.

Kenneth W. Starr, counselor to Attorney General William French Smith.

Margaret Tutwiler, assistant to Chief of Staff James Baker.

Chase Untermeyer, executive assistant to Vice President Bush.

Frank Ursomarso, director of the White House office of communications.

Danny Villanueva, friend of Ronald Reagan.

Gary Walters, assistant White House usher.

Richard Williamson, assistant to the president for intergovernmental affairs.

Jim Wright, congressman, House majority leader.

SECRET SERVICE, LAW ENFORCEMENT, HOTEL SECURITY, AND HINCKLEY

George Chmiel, FBI agent.

Stephen T. Colo, Secret Service agent.

Robert DeProspero, Secret Service agent, deputy special agent in charge of presidential protective detail.

Larry Dominguez, Secret Service agent.

Dennis Fabel, Secret Service agent.

Alexander Fury, Washington Hilton hotel chief of security.

Ted Gardner, FBI agent, head of Washington field office.

Mary Ann Gordon, Secret Service agent.

Herbert Granger, D.C. police sergeant.

Bill Green, Secret Service agent.

Johnny Guy, Secret Service agent, assistant special agent in charge of presidential protective detail.

Richard Hardesty, D.C. police officer.

Stuart Johnson, first court-appointed defense attorney for John W. Hinckley.

Paul Kelly, Secret Service agent.

Ernest Kun, Secret Service agent.

James Le Gette, Secret Service agent.

John Magaw, Secret Service agent.

Timothy McCarthy, Secret Service agent.

Russell Miller, Secret Service agent.

Eddie Myers, D.C. police homicide detective.

George Opfer, Secret Service agent.

Jerry Parr, Secret Service agent, special agent in charge of the presidential protective detail.

Ed Pollard, Secret Service agent.

Robert Powis, special agent in charge of the Washington field office of the Secret Service.

Richard Qulia, FBI agent.

Ray Shaddick, Secret Service agent, a shift leader on the presidential protective detail.

John Simpson, Secret Service agent, assistant director for protective operations.

Danny Spriggs, Secret Service agent.

Joe Trainor, Secret Service agent.

Drew Unrue, Secret Service agent.

Fran Uteg, Secret Service agent.

Jim Varey, Secret Service agent.

Frederick White, assistant director of administration, Secret Service.

MEDIA

Sam Donaldson, White House correspondent, ABC News.

Ron Edmonds, White House photographer, AP (winner of the Pulitzer Prize for photos he took of Reagan being pushed into the car. One is on this book's front jacket).

Bill Plante, CBS News.

Dan Rather, anchor, CBS News.

Lesley Stahl, White House correspondent, CBS News.

EXPERTS

Michael Bohn, former director of the Situation Room.

Dr. David Boyd, former director of Emergency Medical Services Systems, a division of the Department of Health, Education and Welfare.

John D. Feerick, professor of law, Fordham University Law School.

John Finor, president of the Association of Firearm and Tool Mark Examiners.

Harry Teter, executive director of the American Trauma Society.

Dr. Donald Trunkey, professor of surgery, Oregon Health & Science University.

ACKNOWLEDGMENTS

CAME TO THIS BOOK QUITE UNEXPECTEDLY. ONE DAY IN JULY 2008, I attended a hearing at which doctors and lawyers for John W. Hinckley Jr. were urging a federal judge to grant the would-be assassin more freedom from St. Elizabeths Hospital. I had just started covering the D.C. federal court beat for my newspaper, the *Washington Post*, and when I took a seat in the front row of courtroom 29A, I didn't know much about Hinckley or his attempt to kill President Ronald Reagan in March 1981. About all I remembered was that Hinckley had wounded Reagan and three other men, including press secretary Jim Brady, outside of the "Hinckley Hilton," the moniker given to the sprawling hotel by many Washingtonians, and that later Hinckley had been found not guilty by reason of insanity. But there I was—just fifteen feet from a man who nearly assassinated a president—as his lawyers and the court's prosecutors argued over the scope of potential privileges, and Hinckley's siblings testified about his life in recent years.

As the hearing wore on, I found myself closely studying the psychiatric patient sitting at the defense table. Dressed in a dark blazer and gray slacks, Hinckley spent much of the hearing resting his chin on his hand while wearing a blank expression on his face. He neither frowned nor smiled, even when testimony delved into his sex life and the meaning of his music. It was as if a costume maker had cast an impression from Hinckley's face while he was sleeping, and he was now wearing that emotionless mask for the world to see.

When that long day of testimony ended—the hearings would stretch over four more days—I went back to my office and filed a rather perfunctory story that described how Hinckley's brother and sister did not view him as a danger to the community and thought he would benefit from getting a driver's license and having more unsupervised time at their mother's home. After finishing the article, I gave Hinckley no further thought.

A few days later, however, I was summoned to the FBI's Washington field office by its top agent, Joseph Persichini Jr., who wanted to discuss an undercover investigation that he knew I had recently stumbled upon. A press aide joined us, and while we were sitting at the large conference table in Persichini's office, Persichini abruptly stood up, walked over to his desk, and opened a drawer. A moment later, he slapped something heavy into my hand. I looked down: it was a revolver. "That's Hinckley's gun," Persichini said, smiling.

I was stunned. Why was the gun that had nearly killed a president of the United States being stored in an FBI agent's desk drawer instead of a museum?

Intrigued by these two chance encounters with a dramatic day in American history, I soon paid a visit to the D.C. public library, looking for books about the assassination attempt and its aftermath. I found exactly two—one that focused on the Twenty-fifth Amendment and another about Hinckley's trial and the insanity defense. This greatly surprised me, especially since numerous books had been written about our fortieth president; later, I decided that most scholars were probably not interested in the events of that day because Reagan had survived his wound, gone on to serve two terms, and ultimately become one of the most significant presidents of the twentieth century. By now, though, I was curious to learn more about what happened that day and I began reading everything I could find about the assassination attempt—in newspaper and magazine archives, in government publi-cations, and in medical journals. Then I began calling former federal agents, former White House aides, and a number of doctors who had treated Reagan after he was shot, all of whom provided me with their recollections.

Looking back, I now realize it was those interviews that opened my eyes to the possibility of writing a book about the shooting and its after-math, and for that I owe a great debt to those who took the time to talk with someone who at that early stage had a limited understanding of how to research and write a book. First, I must thank former Secret Service agent Jerry Parr, who spent countless hours answering my questions (even while on vacation in Europe), helping me track down other agents and then answering even more questions. Other Secret Service and FBI agents were also extremely helpful, and without their assistance I could never have told the full story of the assassination attempt. In particular, I thank John Simpson, Ray Shaddick, Mary Ann Gordon, Drew Unrue, Bill Green, Russell Miller, Stephen T. Colo, and George Chmiel. I was also aided by former Secret Service agents Ernest Kun, Paul Kelly, and Larry Dominguez, who do not appear by name in the narrative of this book but without whom I could not have achieved a comprehensive understanding of the history of the Secret Service.

This endeavor also owes much to the many doctors and nurses who took so much time to explain Reagan's care, describe his medical procedures, and translate emergency and operating room jargon into English. For this, I must first thank several former nurses at George Washington University Hospital who spent a great deal of time with me and are too often not given sufficient credit for their extraordinary work that day. They include Kathy Paul (Stevens), Judith Whinerey (Goss), Wendy Koenig, Marisa Mize, Denise Sullivan, Cathy Edmond-son, and Joanne Bell. I am also grateful to a number of GW's doctors: David Gens, Benjamin Aaron, Joseph Giordano, and Jack Zimmerman, among many others, spoke to me for hours in person and by telephone.

I must also thank Assistant U.S. Attorney Thomas Zeno and Mar-garet McCabe, a paralegal, in the District of Columbia's U.S. Attorney's

Office. At my request and while juggling the demands of a busy job, McCabe dug through dusty and poorly labeled files and boxes in search of records, transcripts, and trial exhibits. She almost always returned with a trove of useful documents. Without McCabe's help, I would not have been able to tell Hinckley's story in such detail. I also must thank the clerks of the U.S. District Court for the District of Columbia—and Bryant Johnson, in particular—for tracking down Hinckley's long-missing trial transcript, even after I had sadly concluded that it had been misplaced and lost to history.

I could not possibly have written about President Reagan and his experience of the assassination attempt without interviewing those who served him. I am enormously grateful to former national security advisor Richard V. Allen for always taking my calls, answering my questions, and letting me read his extensive notes from his time in the White House (he is one of the most fastidious note takers I have ever met). He also graciously granted me access to more than four hours of audiotape recordings he made in the Situation Room on the afternoon of the assassination attempt. The tapes provide a remarkable record—not only of what transpired in one of the government's most sensitive rooms but also of what was happening around the world. I also must thank James A. Baker III, Edwin Meese III, Richard Williamson, Mari Maseng (Will), Ken Khachigian, Margaret Tutwiler, and David Gergen, among others, all of whom offered vivid recollections of March 30, 1981, and who helped me better understand Reagan and his presidency.

At the Ronald Reagan Presidential Library, Ray Wilson, Michael Pinckney, and Steve Branch deserve special recognition for pointing me to documents, photographs, and audio recordings that would have taken me weeks of sleuthing to find on my own. I would also like to thank Joanne Drake, the chief of staff for the Ronald Reagan Presidential Foundation, for allowing me to inspect the handwritten notes passed to GW's doctors and nurses by the president after the shooting. It is difficult to describe the extraordinary experience of holding one of these notes and tracing Reagan's scribbles across the page with a finger.

This book could never have been written without those who taught me to report and write: Don Cheeseman, the late Richard Drozd, Stephen Ochs, John Kupetz, Tom McGinty, Joel Bewley, Peter Callas, John Fairhall, Bill Ordine, Michael James, Michael Gray, Tony Barbieri, Bill Marimow, Bill Miller, Gabe Escobar, Andy Mosher, Steven Levingston, Gene Fynes, the late Marcia Greene, Lynn Medford, Carol Morello, Mike Semel, and Kevin Merida. At the *Washington Post*, my professional home for the last six years, I received constant support and encouragement from the best newspapering staff in the world. Marcus Brauchli and Emilio Garcia-Ruiz did not hesitate to grant me an extended leave to write this book; James McLaughlin, the *Post's* associate general counsel, was instrumental in helping me obtain records from the normally tightfisted Secret Service; and Eddy Palanzo, a researcher, helped me find many of the wonderful photographs that appear in the book. And like every *Post* reporter who has come before me and written a book, I owe heartfelt thanks to the company's chairman, Donald E. Graham—a tireless advocate for aggressive local news coverage and a close reader of crime stories—for providing an amazing place for reporters to practice their craft.

To say that writing a book is a team effort is an understatement. My own squad of able researchers and transcriptionists—James de Haan, Matt Castello, Julie Tate, and Marian Sullivan—were instrumental in ensuring that this project was completed on time. My agent, Rafe Sagalyn, taught me how to write a book proposal and got me to think like an author, not a newspaper reporter. My publisher, Henry Holt and Company, showed a surprising degree of confidence in a first-time author, and for that I must thank its president, Stephen Rubin. Others at Holt, including Maggie Richards, Maggie Sivon, Emi Ikkanda, Meryl Levavi, and Chris O'Connell, put in long hours to streamline, package, and market the book; meanwhile, copy editor Jolanta Benal gave the manuscript a thorough and much-appreciated scrubbing. Finally, I owe an unquantifiable debt to my editor, John Sterling, who taught me how to write a narrative history and was always levelheaded, optimistic, and understanding—especially when I was not. The readers of this book have benefited greatly from his keen eye and deft pen.

The most important tributes belong to those who have supported me throughout this two-year odyssey, especially my mother and father, Kay and Del Wilber Jr.; my sister, Lindsay Guthrie, and her husband, Phillip Guthrie; my uncle, Rick Wilber; and my good friends Diane Sullivan and Zachary Coile. My two young boys, Quentin and Ryan, always made me smile when I walked in the front door, no matter how frustrating the day. But one person more than any other deserves thanks for helping me complete this project: my wife, Laura Sullivan. She never failed to offer candid advice, critical assessments, and unflagging encouragement. She was the first to bet on me, and I can confidently say that without her there would be no *Rawhide Down*.

INDEX

Page numbers in *italics* refer to illustrations.